The Arena Riggers' Handbook
Second Edition

Delbert L. Hall, Ph.D.

and

Brian Sickels

Spring Knoll Press
Johnson City, Tennessee 37601

Table of Contents

Acknowledgements

We want to thank all the people who served as technical advisors and proofreaders in making this book possible, especially David Carmack of Columbus-McKinnon for his help on the chapter on Hoists, Ben Kilmer, lead rigger at the Prudential Center, for his suggestions on the chapter on Work Methods, Matt Lewandowski for his proof-reading of the chapter on Electricity, and Simon "Captain" Howdy for his comments on the Knots chapter. Additional thanks go out to Noga Eilion-Bahar of Eilion Engineering for her assistance on the chapter on Dynamic Forces, Klaus Becker and Shane Martin. We also want to thank Joseph Washburn of IA Local 699 for his assistance.

For the use of photos, Sapsis Rigging, IATSE, local 8, IATSE local 77, IATSE local 470, Mick Alderson, Ben Kilmer, Columbus-McKinnnon, Mountain Productions, Jonathan Deull, James Thomas Engineering, TomCat Truss, Tyler Truss, Eilion Engineering, Lex Products, Guardian Metal Products, Miller-Honeywell, and Petzl. Without support from these people and organizations this book would not be possible.

Preface

Arena rigging had its origins with the Ice Capades of the early 1960s. Back then, the ceiling beams of arena venues were designed to support just that- the weight of the roof plus snow loads, and not much else. Hanging tons upon tons of truss, speaker arrays, cable and chain hoist was unheard of. Equipment suspended was limited to pipes, PAR cans and cable- nothing like what we experience today. Riggers suspended loads from I-beams and ceiling-truss using chain falls or block and tackles with little concern for fall protection or safety.

With the establishment of workman's compensation laws, the Occupational Safety and Health Administration (OSHA) was established in the early 1970s as a means of regulating safety in all industries. While ANSI, the American National Standards Institute has been around since 1918, the arena rigging industry was too new to draw much attention. While The United States Institute for Theatre Technology (USITT) had been around since the early 1960s, its focus at the time was oriented more towards theatre education. In short, there was no organization that formally addressed rigging and safety training in the arena and outdoor concert venues.

Photo from the mid 1980's. Note the "lid-less" riggers are wearing positioning belts with leashes and their tools are unsecured. OSHA would not pass laws regarding fall protection for another 10 years.

At the same time, production designers began pushing the envelop with greater and greater production demands as newer technologies became available. Truss, slings, and electric chain hoists were adopted from other industries to help handle these ever-increasing loads. Tragically, with these increased demands, there would be an increase in rigging accidents and failures. Most of these would result in serious injuries, costly litigation, and even deaths. This fledgling industry was growing very fast. By the 1980s, people were beginning to realize that if this industry didn't start regulating itself, the government would!

By in large, the entertainment industry today is self-regulating. In 1987, the Entertainment Services and Technology Association (ESTA) was established to fulfill a need for creating standards specific to entertainment. Its members represented a wide spectrum of entertainment markets; theatre, theme parks, churches, schools, nightclubs, etc. Not surprisingly, a similar British organization known as the Professional Lighting and Sound Association (PLASA), worked to fulfill a similar purpose. In 2010,

ESTA merged with PLASA, and today PLASA has the most comprehensive standards program available worldwide to the entertainment industry. In addition to PLASA, there are many other respected associations whose aim is to advance standards in the industry. The United States Institute for Theatre Technology (USITT) and The Canadian Institute for Theatre Technology (CITT) also endeavor to further this goal. Many admirable, industry professionals have dedicated themselves to countless hours serving on committees' intent to create industry standards. As a result of their efforts, OSHA now recognizes that entertainment rigging is just as hazardous as any other occupation in the general construction industry.

PLASA has spearheaded the ANSI accredited Technical Standards Program (created by ESTA), which has been instrumental in creating *"standards and recommended practices that facilitate the use of new and existing equipment and promote safe working conditions in the industry."* In addition, a similar structure exists in Europe where PLASA works closely with the British Standards Institution (BSI) in the UK, The European Committee for Electrotechnical Standardization (CENELEC) and International Organization for Standardization (ISO) in Europe. In 2005, ESTA created the Entertainment Technician Certification Program (ETCP) thereby offering a means by which entertainment technicians could attain certification in their respective areas. ETCP Certification and training is available for all technicians in the areas of electrics, arena rigging, and theatre rigging, and today, ETCP Certification is the most recognized technical certification in the industry. In addition, many IATSE locals and rigging companies offer free training for their members and employees to aid in certification.

A class in Fall Rescue trains riggers in quick recovery methods and emergency response.

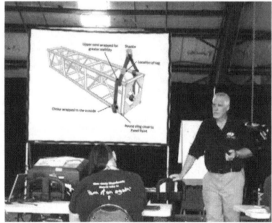

A class in rigging truss offers training on everything from load calculations to hanging points.

IATSE Local 8 is one of many unions that offer free training courses for their members. Columbus McKinnon offered the class shown here for their chain hoist certification.

Entertainment rigging is still a very dangerous profession. But because of the efforts of many organizations and individuals, it is now becoming safer than it has been in previous years. Entertainment professionals are becoming more skilled and competent in safe rigging practice. In addition to the ANSI accredited Technical Standards Program, OSHA, and classes and seminars offered by PLASA, USITT, CITT and IATSE, books on entertainment rigging and electrics are becoming more and more available to aid in that dissemination of practice. As universities and colleges vie for students, courses in the physics and practice of arena and theatre rigging are becoming more prevalent. The Arena Rigging Handbook offers a dissemination of much of the material and practice available today.

From all of this, the most important lesson for any rigger is "know your limitations and seek out proper advice when necessary." This is still an industry where experience is gained from apprenticeship and where experience comes from working in the industry. Books and classes are helpful, but there is no substitute for experience.

Rig Safe,

Brian and Delbert

About this Edition

In 2015, when Brian and I created the first edition of this book, we did not feel that there was a good, affordable book for entertainment technicians who wanted to learn about arena rigging (especially anyone wanting to become an ETCP certified rigger), so we wrote the first edition of this book. Since that time, we have continued to grow as riggers, learn new techniques, and hopefully improve as writers.

By 2023, while working on a new edition of *Rigging Math Made Simple* (the ninth edition), I felt that it was time to create a new edition of this book, too. Joseph Washburn, a fellow member of IATSE Local 699, and I had recently been working on an online training course for new arena riggers, and I had a lot of ideas about how this book could be improved.

This book is not an exhaustive book on arena rigging – there are lots of things that arena riggers need to know that are beyond the scope of this book. *Rigging Math Made Simple*, Ninth Edition, is highly recommended for anyone wanted to learn more about rigging math. Also, Harry Donovan's Entertainment *Rigging - A Practical Guide for Riggers and Managers* is a must read for any good arena rigger.

Like many other topics, to really learn how to be an arena rigger, you must get experience at it. Most arena riggers that I know are happy to help young (and not so young) people learn to be a rigger – whether it is a down-rigger or an up-rigger. The most important factor in being a good rigger is having the right attitude – being willing to learn and being conscious of safety. Always remember that rigging is a team activity.

I hope you enjoy this book, and it helps you become a better arena rigger.

-Delbert L. Hall

Part I:

Introduction to Arena Rigging

Chapter 1:
Arena Rigging Basics

Introduction

In this chapter we will look at what is expected of the riggers on a typical "rigging call" for a show in an arena. Rigging in an arena is typically be divided into two sessions: the Load-in and the Load-out. In each of these sessions, the up-riggers and down riggers will have specific tasks to do.

The person from the production who is responsible for the rigging might go by the title "Production Head Rigger", "Production Lead Rigger", "Production Coordinator" or a similar title. The venue will also have a head rigger, often called the "House Head Rigger" or "Local Head Rigger." In this book, we will use the titles "Production Lead Rigger" and "House Head Rigger" when refering to these positions.

Pre-Planning

Before the Load-in starts there is usually a meeting between the Venue Operator, House Head Rigger, House Manager, Production Head Rigger, and if necessary, a qualified engineer. The show-rigging plot is laid over the venue floor plan so that the placement of the stage and rigging points can be determined well in advance. House Management is going to be concerned with maximizing the sale of tickets and how much floor seating is going to be available for sale. The House Head Rigger is going to be looking at the best placement of the concert stage and rigging points over the house steel. He will also be looking for positions where the rigging points will fall *directly* over the venue's beams (called "Dead-hangs") and rigging points that require bridles. Collaboration and pre-planning are the keys to making the load-in as fast and easy as possible. The illustration below shows a partial rigging plot that has been laid out over the venue steel. Note that the rigging points are shown in relationship to the truss. The approximate load for each point is indicated next to the point, which includes 25% of the static load to account for dynamic loading.

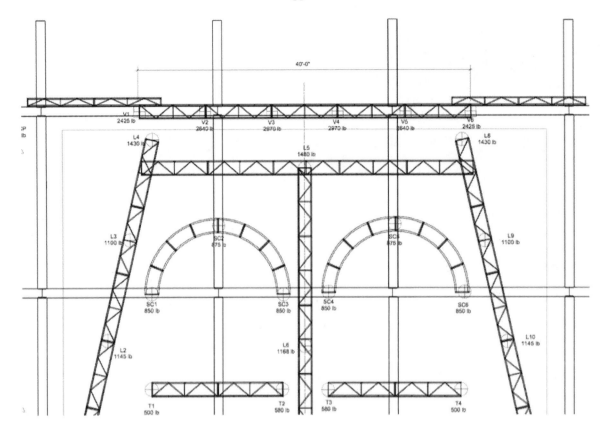

Upstage portion of a rigging plot over-laid over house steel. The 0-0 reference point is not always shown on the rigging plot, but it needs to be determined.

Letters and numbers above the loads are assigned to correspond to the rigging plot spreadsheet. The spreadsheet sample below is only for the video wall (V) points from the above plot. Normally, all points will be shown.

SAMPLE RIGGING PLOT SPREAD SHEET

Dimentions are from Centerline and DS edge of stage.

All measurements in feet. Weight in pounds.

POINT	POSITION from DS	POSITION SR/SL	WEIGHT in LBS	NOTES
V1	52 US	20 SR	2425	V points are video
V2	52 US	12 SR	2640	Trim= 42 ft from floor
V3	52 US	4 SR	2970	
L4	52 US	4 SL	2670	
V5	52 US	12 L	2540	
V6	52 US	20 SL	2425	

A sample rigging spread sheet. Note the measurements for the video truss are taken from the DS edge of the stage. This will help to determine 0-0 reference.

Laying out the Floor

Once the management staff and production riggers agree on the floor plan and seating arrangement, the next stage in the production process will begin with laying out the floor. This is sometimes called a "walk and chalk." The House Head Rigger begins by establishing the 0-0 reference point. There is no agreement on this, but it is often *either* the downstage or upstage edge of the stage and centerline. Regardless, 0-0 *does* need to be determined before any of the floor layout begins. For this reason, 0-0 is *not* always shown on the rigging plot. The centerline of the arena is measured out starting with a tape measure from the 0-0 reference point. Horizontal references are measured off the centerline both SR and SL to the side dasher. These two additional measuring tapes running 40' to 50' off the centerline tape. Five-point lasers can be extremely useful in the layout, making sure that the SL and SR tapes run perpendicular to the center tape. Next, the Production Head Rigger will come along and mark out the location of each rigging point in wet-chalk, sometimes with reference to whether the point is for video, audio, projection, rigging or cable pick. Other show specific markings such as hoist capacity may be indicated at this time. The House Head Rigger then follows along, marking out the bridle and basket information next to the rigging point.

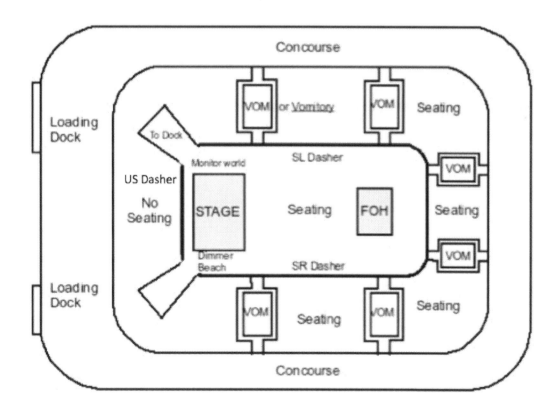

Arena Floor Layout.

photo courtesy of IATSE local 470

Floor Markings and Rigging Points

The following illustrations show some the most commonly used rigging point markings. The actual rigging "point" is the intersection of the horizontal and vertical chalk markings. It should be noted that not every Production Rigger use these particular markings.

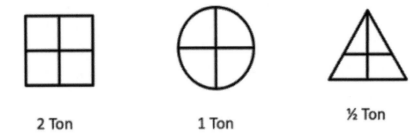

2 Ton   1 Ton   ½ Ton

Most Production Head Riggers will include the capacity of the chain hoist along with the symbol, just so that there is no confusion.

In addition to the markings that indicate the location of each point and the capacity of the chain hoist, there are also markings that indicate how the basket is made (if it is a standard basket or a split basket, a dead-hang point or a bridle, and the lengths of steel needed to make up the point). Now, let's look at some typical floor marks and discuss their meaning.

Dead-Hang Markings

Dead-hangs are points where the chain hoist hangs directly below a steel beam. The floor marks below are for Dead-hung points. Both marks indicate a point made with a 5' basket, but the one on the right includes a 10-foot stinger (a piece of steel that attaches to a basket or apex shackle of a bridle and used to lower the height of the chain hook).

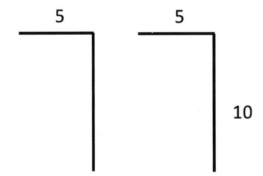

We know that these are "dead-hung" points because there is only one basket indicated. There does not need to be a shackle on the end of the stinger, or on a choked point. The basket marking is placed directly next to its point chalk mark. Below is an illustration of how a standard basket is made on the ground by the down-rigger.

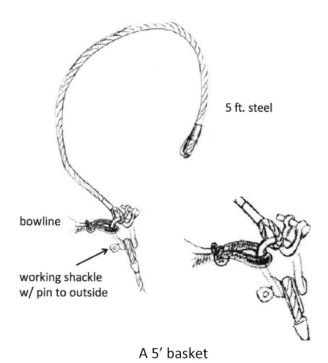

5 ft. steel

bowline

working shackle
w/ pin to outside

A 5' basket

photo courtesy of Mick Alderson and IATSE Local 470

The down-riggers MUST know how to correctly make the basket and where the to tie the up-rigger's rope to the basket. A good phrase that will help you remember the order of components attached to the rope to the working shackle is "Please Rig Super Safe."

Please Rig Super Safe

P – R – S – S

Pin – Rope – Steel – Shackle

Pin (of the working shackle) – (rigging) **Rope** (tied in a bowline) – **Steel** (for the basket) – (connecting) **Shackle**

Getting this order correct is VERY important. If it is not correct, it will make it difficult for the up-rigger to attach the basket around the beam and could make the up-rigger's job more dangerous. The size of loop in the bowline tied to the working shackle could vary, depending on the length of the rigger's arms, the size and shape of the beam, and other factors. A three-foot loop is typically a good starting point but asking the up-rigger for his/her preference on the size of the loop is a good idea.

In addition to the standard basket shown above, there is a second type of basket, called a Split Basket. A Split Basket is made with two pieces of steel, one longer than the other (for example, a 15' Split Basket would be made of a 5' and a 10' steel). These pieces of steel are joined together around the beam by the up-rigger. Split Baskets are indicated by the initials "SP" followed by the total length of the basket steel. A 15' split basket would be marked "SP 15." Later you will see an example of this floor marking.

Tying a split basket to an up-rigger's rigging rope is a little different than a standard basket. Below is a drawing of a 15' Split Basket ready to be pulled up.

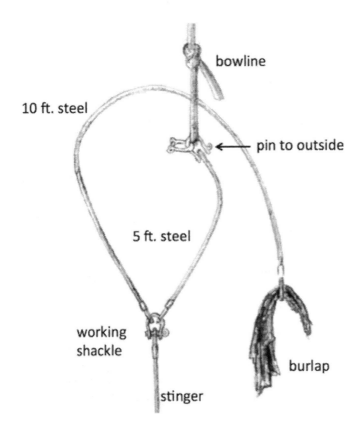

Steel that is 1.5-foot, 2-foot and 2.5-foot lengths are called "dog bones". Other common steel lengths include 5-foot, 10-foot, 20-foot, 30-foot, 50-foot, and 100' lengths. Color-coding of the steel is usually NO COLOR for dog bones, RED for 5' lengths, WHITE for 10' lengths, and BLUE for 20'lengths. However, some rental houses may color their steel to identify it as theirs in order to keep it separate from other companies. *Usually (but not always)*, 30-foot steel is GREEN and 50-foot steel is YELLOW. Again, there is no standardization in the industry for any of this. In addition, steel comes in 3/8" and ½" diameters, with 3/8" diameter steel for 1-Ton hoists and ½" diameter steel for 2-Ton hoists. Below is an example of a 5' piece of steel.

Bridle Markings

Bridles are used when the there is no beam directly above the desired location of the chain hoist. A bridle has two or more legs, but two-legged bridle are far the more common than other bridles. Bridle Markings provide the riggers with the information on how to make up the bridle and basket for each rigging point. Like the marking for dead-hung points, these are drawn next to the rigging point chalk marks.

The Bridle Marking below shows two split 15 baskets (SP 15), two 20-foot bridles, and a 5-foot stinger. Since both legs are identical, this is sometimes called an "even-bridle." Note: Stingers will be discussed in more detail in Chapter 6.

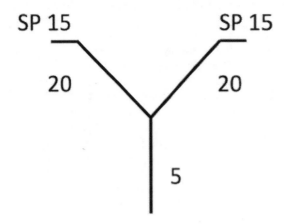

Not every Bridle Marking will show the basket. For example, if the arena venue uses the same basket for every point (which is not unusual) then the basket may not be shown. However, many House Head Riggers include the basket on every chalk mark, just so that there is no confusion.

Often, the bridle leg is made from multiple pieces of steel. For example, a 17-foot leg would be made from a 10' steel, a 5' steel, and a 2' steel. The pieces of steel are joined with screw-pin anchor shackles, and a shackle is used for the apex, where the two legs come together. The most common shackle sizes are 5/8" and 3/4". Sometimes shackles are joined in a group of five shackles, called a "Knuckle."

The orientation of the Bridle Marking tells the up-rigger which beams to make the bridles on. Generally, bridles either run SR to SL or US to DS to avoid tangling bridles.

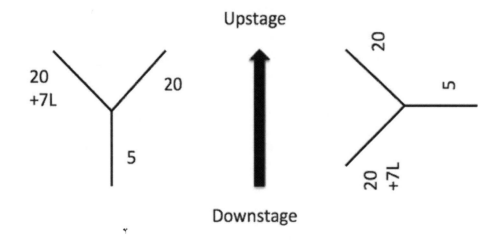

Bridle Legs are made to the SR and SL I-Beams

Bridle Legs are made to the US and DS I-Beams

When the down-rigger makes up the steel, the steel for a stinger or bridle leg is arranged so that the longest piece of steel is on the bottom and the pieces of steel gets shorter as you approach the basket. The connecting shackles are positioned in a bail up/pin down orientation.

Indicating STAC Chain

"STAC" chain stands for Special Theatrical Alloy Chain and is used to adjust the length of a bridle leg so that the bridle point or apex will fall at the rigging point chalk mark below on the floor. These chains have links with and inside dimension of 3.73". Adjusting the number of chain links helps make the leg the correct length (or as close as possible. Below is a photo of a STAC chain.

STAC chain is sometimes referred to as "Deck Chain."

The number of STAC chain links needed for the leg should be indicated on the Bridle Markings, and tell the down-rigger how many chain links to add to the long leg of the bridle being sent up to the up-rigger. The number of links is preceded by the plus sign ("+") and followed by the letter "L".

This chain only goes on the long leg – the short leg does not get any STAC chain. This chain is attached between the leg and the basket. The illustration below shows two 20-foot bridle legs with one of the legs having 7-links of STAC chain.

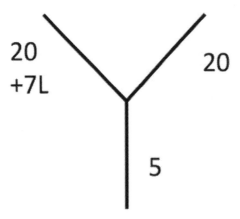

Venue Specific Chalk Markings

Some venues use "venue specific" floor markings. It is very important for riggers new to the venue to quickly learn these markings.

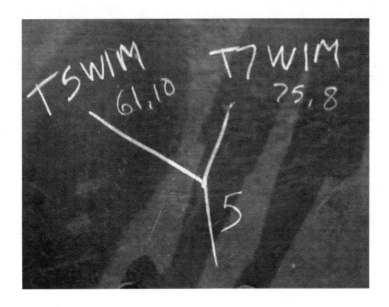

The "basket notations" T5W1M and T7W1M are location references. The first notation is Truss 5, Window 1, Mississippi. "Mississippi" refers to one of the streets running outside the building. Rather than referring to SR or SL, the riggers there use the street names for easy reference; Mississippi for SR and Georgia for SL. T5 and T7 refer to Ceiling Beams called "Trusses" that are numbered starting upstage to downstage. The "Trusses" all have windows. Starting at the centerline moving toward the Mississippi side, the windows count 1,2,3,4,5, and so on. From the centerline moving toward the Georgia side, the windows again start 1,2,3,4,5, and so on.

So, T5W1M tells both the up and down-rigger that the bridle point needs to be sent/ pulled up to Truss 5, Window 1, on the Mississippi side. The other bridle point will be sent/ pulled up to Truss 7, Window 1, Mississippi.

The baskets are all pre-hung in the windows, so all that needs to be sent up are the bridle legs. The numbers 61.10 and 75.8 refer to the lengths of the bridle legs that need to be made up by the down-rigger. The number 5 indicates the length of the stinger.

Calculating Bridles

A good House Head Rigger will be able to accurately lay out the floor in as short a time as possible. Wasting time trying to work bridle angles out at the last moment takes time and is frustrating for everyone. Obviously, a House Head Rigger will have a good working knowledge of the venue, the spacing distance between the beams, and beam size so that he can quickly write the bridle markings on the floor and determine the size basket in as little time as possible. So, how does the House Head Rigger know the length of each bridle leg and the number of links of STAC to write down?

It is best to work out as much of the bridle information based on beam bay sizes ahead of time. Some House Head Riggers use spreadsheets for this purpose. Creating bridle *"cheat sheets"* are another means that House Head Riggers can plan their work in advance. Or the House Head Rigger might use a bridle app on his/her phone to do the calculations. These aids help the House Head Rigger know exactly what steel is needed to make the bridles. This subject will be discussed in more detail later in Chapter 6.

Typically, this pre-planning session will begin about an hour before the load-in, so all stage markings may not be completed before the load-in start.

General Information about the Load-in

No matter your job or the type of call, there are a few rules that both up-riggers and down-riggers rigger should follow:

1) Arrive at least 15 minutes early for the call. Check-in with the job steward and then with the House Head Rigger. The House Head Rigger may ask you about your experience, if he/she is not familiar with you. This is also a good time to ask the House Head Rigger questions about the show and/or the venue. Then use the rest of the time to go to the restroom, check your equipment and get to know the other riggers on the call. Remember, you are a team, so knowing the other riggers can be very useful.
2) Be sure to have all required tools and safety equipment.
3) Be in good physical and mental condition to do your job. Showing up hung-over or on drugs will not be tolerated.
4) Work will start promptly on time, so be ready.

Most load-ins begin with a short safety meeting. You are usually reminded to be safe and to look out for everyone else on the call.

When the load-in begins, all riggers typically start as down-riggers. This means that they help get the rigging boxes and motor boxes into the venue and start making up the steel needed for all of the points that have been marked on the floor. If all of the points have not been marked, the House Head Rigger will continue marking them as the other riggers make up the steel.

Motor boxes are rolled into place near point marking on the floor. These marking indicate the size/capacity of the motor/hoist needed for each point. If the steel for a point has not been made yet, often the hook for that motor is often placed on the point marking on the floor. This way, the down-riggers can attach the hook to the apex shackle as soon as the steel is made. The hook is then placed back on the chalk mark so that everyone knows that this steel is for this particular point.

The Up-riggers
When the House Head Rigger feels that enough steel has been made-up on the floor, he/she will send the up-riggers up the beams. When the up-riggers go "up," EVERYONE on the floor will be instructed to put on their hardhats, if they have not already done so. Hardhats help protect anyone on the floor from possible falling objects that might be accidentally dropped by an up-rigger. ALL down-riggers MUST have a hardhat.

Up-riggers ready to haul up the bridles. Note most up-riggers often work in pairs.

photo courtesy of Ben Kilmer

Since the role of the down-rigger is to assemble the bridle legs/ baskets according to the floor markings and tie on the up-rigger's rope, it is very important that the down-rigger maintains good communication with the up-rigger during the entire process. *Everything should be in support of making the up-rigger's job as easy as possible.* Walkie-talkies are used if available to aid in communication, while lasers are used to help spot the rigging points where they fall in the ceiling.

Once the leg has been assembled, the up-rigger has the task of hauling up the bridle steel and chain to the beams. This is no small task especially if the beams are 100 - 150 feet in the air! If the chain is double reeved, as seen in some 2-ton chain hoists, the up-rigger must haul up twice the amount of chain. In both cases, the load that needs to be lifted can be very heavy. A pulley can aid in hauling up of bridle legs as necessary. In many cases when a pulley is used, the up-rigger will need a rope that is twice as long as the distance from the floor to the beams, the down-riggers are used to help lift the basket, steel, chain, etc. up to the up-rigger.

When the up-rigger pulls the steel up, the down-riggers need to carefully watch the steel as it goes up to ensure that the shackles and steel do not become twisted. Catching and fixing problems, such as a side-loaded shackle, at this point can save a lot of time, as well as ensure that the rig is safe.

"Making the pin" is a term that is sometimes used to refer to the up-rigger placing the pin in the connecting shackle and forming a basket around a beam. Burlap that has been folded three or four times is placed between the beam and the basket steel. The burlap pads the beam and protects the steel from chaffing. Once "made" the basket can be slide into position.

An up-rigger "making the pin." Note his foot is holding the rope while the pin is made.

photo courtesy of IATSE Local 8

The photo above shows an up-rigger positioned on an I-beam with the basket and bridle leg hauled up to the beam. Note the bowline that was previously tied by the down-rigger is now being used as a stirrup to hold tension on the leg. This leaves the basket free to be positioned around the beam. The burlap that was sent up with the basket is temporarily laid aside. Once the basket is in position, the burlap will be wrapped around the corners of the beam to protect the basket. Let's look at illustrations of different types of baskets.

Below is an illustration of a dead-hung point made to a beam. Burlap protects the steel from the sharp corners of the I-beam. Be sure to cover all corners that the steel will touch.

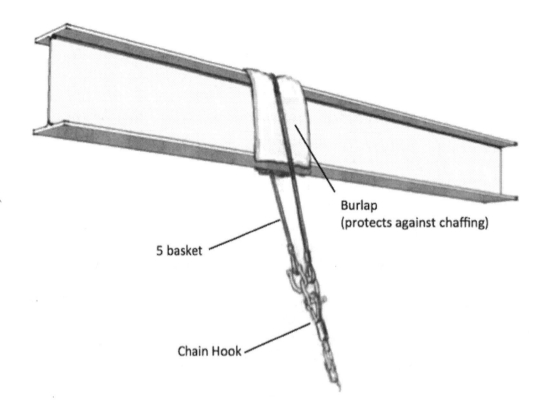

Burlap
(protects against chaffing)

5 basket

Chain Hook

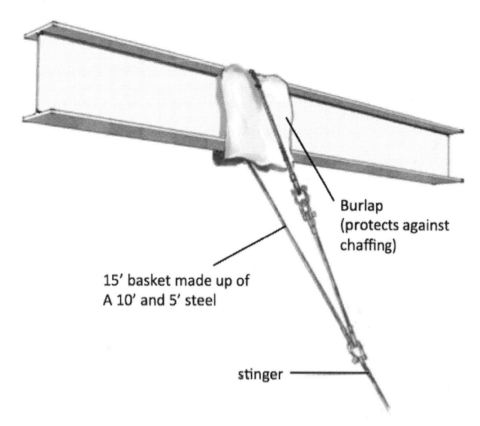

Burlap
(protects against
chaffing)

15' basket made up of
A 10' and 5' steel

stinger

I-Beam showing a split basket. Fold the burlap at least three times.

The choker basket is often used when headroom is at a premium. In some venues the choker basket is rigged from an aerial lift rather than from above, as access to the shackle can be difficult. In this instance, the bell end of the shackle is used as a collector for the steel. Do not use the pin end of the shackle as a collector. If the shackle were reversed, any movement in the steel could cause the pin to rotate.

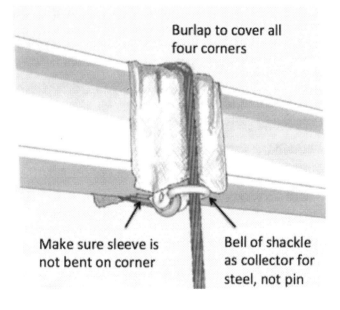

Burlap to cover all
four corners

Make sure sleeve is
not bent on corner

Bell of shackle
as collector for
steel, not pin

This arrangement is not used too often, as it makes the shackle difficult to reach if the up-rigger is on the beam. Note the bell end of the shackle is used as collector, not the pin end. Again, fold the burlap at least three times in order to protect the steel from the sharp edges of the beam. Be sure to cover all exposed corners. Use additional burlap if necessary.

Wrapping roof truss is more commonly done in convention centers or positions in semi-outdoor music centers. This is similar to wrapping a truss at a panel point except the basket will be secured to the top chord and not the lower. The illustration below shows a dead hang attached to the upper chord. A bridled leg would need to be attached to a panel point at the lower chord or positioned such that the basket runs between the chords.

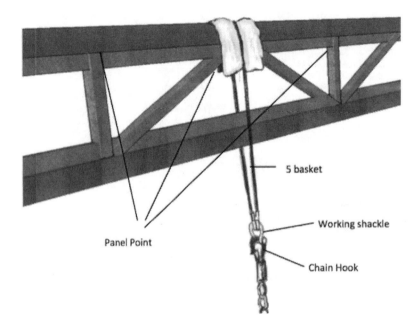

Steel Roof Truss wrapped with a dead hang. Note the basket is positioned at the panel point of the roof truss. A bridle would be positioned at the panel point of the lower chord or run between the chords.

Sometimes a rigging point needs to be attached to a counterweight grid. Most grids are made up of steel channel that spans the I-beams. In this case, a closed basket is sent up to the grid and a steel piece of Schedule 40 is inserted in the loop of the basket. The up-rigger drops his line down between the spaces of the channel to the rigging chalk mark on the floor. A laser placed on the chalk mark and aimed straight up can be very useful in helping the up-rigger find the point. The down-rigger makes up a *closed* basket and ties the drop line onto the basket with a bowline. The basket is pulled up through the steel channel and a piece of Schedule 40 pipe is inserted through the loop. Because there are no hard edges on the pipe, burlap is not necessary.

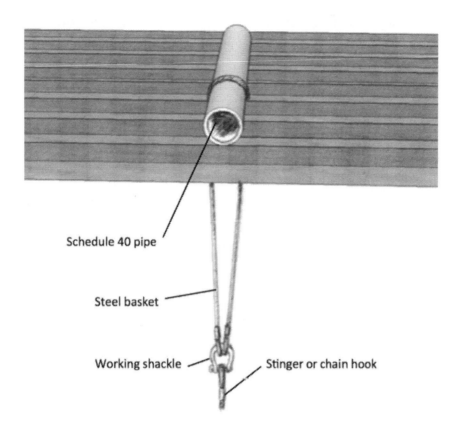

Schedule 40 pipe

Steel basket

Working shackle   Stinger or chain hook

A closed 5' basket. Burlap is not necessary as there are no sharp corners in the pipe. If the basket is run through an I-Beam, then burlap would be required.

There are some venues that use small sections of aluminum I-beams to slip through the basket loop. In this case, burlap is necessary to wrap the I-beam and protect the steel basket.

The Arena's Beams

In must arenas, the up-riggers rig to truss that supports roof of the building. The steel that comprises these roof truss come in many different sizes and shapes. "I" and "T" (and invert "T"s) are probably the most common shapes of the steel used in these truss.

Trusses have a tope chord and a bottom chord. The term "Low Steel" usually refers to the bottom chord of the truss, while "High Steel" refers to the top chord. Typically, most points are rigged to the low steel, because it is a lot easier to rig from. However, depending on the number of points needed, the desired height of the apexes, and the load needing to be suspended (and other factors) points are sometimes rigged from both the low and high steel.

In many venues the up-rigger must be suspended from the high steel as he/she attaches the basket around the beam. This is one of the reasons why rigging to the high steel is more difficult than rigging to the low steel.

Rigging Speaker Arrays

Speaker arrays can be very heavy and often use 2-Ton chain hoists. Two or more hoists are often used so that the tilt of the speakers can be adjusted. Also, sound engineers are often very particular about the direction that the speakers are pointed and often want baskets moved on the beam (sometimes multiple times) before the speakers are pointed in the desired direction. Tie-line can also be used to help control the direction the speakers are pointed.

Wind

Even when rigging indoors, wind can be a factor. Doors left open can create drafts that can blow the rigging around. Speaker arrays, video walls, and curtains can act as sails, catching the wind and putting a great deal of lateral force on the rigging. The force of the wind on the rigging can be tremendous and has been known to cause accidents. Extra caution should be taken any time there is a wind blowing on the rigging.

At the End of the Load-in

When all of the points are hung, the House Head Rigger will dismiss most of the riggers. Several riggers will remain on call until everything is in the air, just in case a problem occurs, and riggers are needed.

The Load-out (aka "the Out")

When the show ends, the first thing that the riggers will do will be to find all of the rigging and motor boxes, from wherever they have been stored during the show, and bring them to the arena floor – near the stage. Organizing these boxes now can same time later. This can be done while the stagehands clear the stage and the audience leaves the arena floor. It is not unusual for the House Head Rigger to keep some of the up-riggers form the load-in on the floor for the Out. This is because there is more to do on the floor during the Out.

The Production Head Rigger may handout pickles to some of the down-riggers when the Load-out begins. Pickles are controllers for individual chain hoists and the down-rigger will use them to run the chain out of the chain bags one the chain motors have been landed. Below is a photo of a typical pickle for controlling a chain hoist.

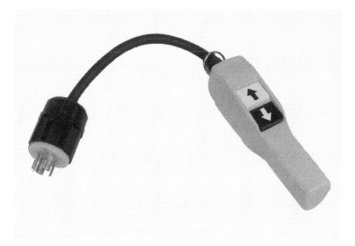

Once the stage is clear, motor boxes for the chain hoists that are over the stage are rolled on the stage. Motor boxes are also rolled near other points that may be coming in early on the Out.

Motor boxes should be clearly marked with the size of hoists that they are designed to hold. Also, typically, each motor box will hold two chain hoists.

When a truss or speaker is brought in, the down-riggers roll motor boxes near each motor. When the hoist is disconnected from the truss or speaker, a down-rigger pulls the hoist over a motor box and it is lowered into the box. The down-rigger can now roll the motor box out the way while the stagehands disassembler the truss or do whatever they need to do. As this is happening, the down-rigger will use a pickle to run all of the chain out of the bag and into the motor box. DO NOT stop on the limit – back it off a few inches. Stopping on the limit switches can damage them. Next, the down rigger removes the chain bag from the motor and usually temporarily hooks it to the lid of the motor box.

When the area is clear, the down-rigger rolls the motor box directly under the apex, or as close as possible. When the up-riggers lower the point, the down-rigger guides the chain so that it land in the motor box directly next to the hoist. When the apex gets to working height, the down-rigger disconnects the chain hook, and attaches it to the inside of the box (if there is a place for it), or lays it on top of the chain. When the bowlines get to working height, the down-riggers untie the bowline from the baskets. As the up-riggers pull their ropes up, a down-rigger holds onto the end of the rope, raising it above his/her head. This is done so that the end of the rope does not whip around and hit someone as it is being pulled up. All of the steel, is now pulled off to the side, and the down-rigger puts the chain bag into the box and moves to the next point coming in.

It is important that the down-rigger be very observant and be ready to untie steel from the ropes as soon as it gets to working height. Efficiency is the goal – the down-riggers should not keep the up-riggers waiting. This often means that some down-riggers will just deal with motors, while other down-riggers untie the steel as it comes in.

Some down-riggers are usually assigned to task of disassembling the steel that has come in and putting everything back into the rigging boxes. Since there is a lot of steel coming to the floor, in a relatively short time, this is a big job.

When a motor box has two motors in it, the lid is closed, and it is moved off to the side. This helps the riggers know what motors boxes full and which boxes have space for a motor. Some House Head Riggers might put a piece of bright colored tape on the lid of a full motor box, to indicate that it is full.

When all of the points are down, the up-riggers come to the arena floor. If there is still steel that needs to be disassembled and put away, all riggers help finish this task. When all the rigging work is finished, all riggers are dismissed at the same time.

Summary

Working in any arena or convention center venue always presents its own set of realities. The methods discussed in this chapter examined standard methods for attaching a truss from the truss to suspension points. In every case, it is important to remember that no rigging situation *is* ever going to be the same.

Lastly, rig safe! No one is as perfect a rigger as they wish they could be. Collaboration and team effort are paramount to a successful and safe rig. If you are in doubt, *ask*. If you see something rigged wrong, *say* something. Everyone deserves to go home in one piece.

Chapter 2:
Tools for Riggers

All riggers need personal tools to help them do their jobs. In this chapter we will look at some of those tools. Let's start with a few general lists.

Tools for Down Riggers
Hardhat/Helmet
Gloves
Self-leveling Laser Level
Small wrench
Pocket Pickle (optional)

Additional Tools for the House Head Rigger
Five-beam Self-leveling Laser Level
Laser pointer
Wet Chalk
Tape Measures
Work belt with pouch

Tools for Up-Riggers
Fall Arrest Harness
Lanyards
Carabiners
Climbing Runners
Pulleys
Grillions
Goggles
Rigging Rope

Now that we have a list of some of the tools needed by riggers, let's go through it and discus what these items are and why they are needed.

Hardhats/Helmets

Recreational climbing helmets are another piece of climbing gear that have found its way into the arena rigging industry. They are strong, lightweight, and secure under the rigger's chin. They also offer better protection against side impact, which can occur, should a climber swing up against the tower a little too hard. They also allow for much better visibility when looking up. Petzl manufactures a line of climbing helmet that is intended for industrial and rescue use. This line of helmets also complies with ANSI standard Z-89.1 – 2009 and OSHA 1926.135(b). In fact, Petzl offers visors and face shields meeting the ANSI Z-87.1 standard for eye protection.

A climbing helmet is strong and lightweight securing under the chin.

photo courtesy of Sapsis Rigging

Gloves

Groves are used by most down-riggers to both protect their hands, and to help them get a better grip on the slick chains in the chain hoists. Gorilla Grip gloves is one brand of inexpensive glove that provides excellent grip, even on oily chains. They are available from many big box stores.

Self-Leveling Laser Level

To indicate where a point needs to be made on a beam, the down-rigger places a Self-Leveling Laser Level on the floor and it projects a small dot (either GREEN or RED) on the ceiling, directly above the device. GREEN lasers are brighter than RED lasers, so they are preferred. Some laser levels project beams in three directions, while others project beams in five directions (a five-beam laser lever is shown below).

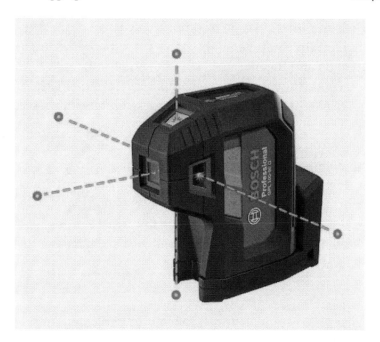

Small Adjustable Wrench

When trying to disassemble the steel during the Out, a down-rigger may come across a shackle pin that cannot be unscrewed by hand. A small adjustable wrench can be very useful for helping loosen these pins.

Laser Pointers

A small laser pointer can be useful to the House Head Rigger when pointing-out points in an arena.

Wet Chalk

Sidewalk chalk, often called wet chalk, is used by the House Head Rigger to mark points and bridles on the arena stage and floor.

Tape Measures

A retractable tape measure, usually around 30' long, is a commonly used tool for the House Head Rigger.

Work Belt with Pouches

The House Head Rigger may want a work belt with pouches to make carrying his/her tools more convenient.

Personal Fall Arrest System (PFAS)/Harnesses

For many decades, rocking climbing (seat) harnesses were commonly worn by arena riggers, even though they did not meet ANSI standards for personal fall arrest harnesses. Why? Because climbing harnesses were much more comfortable than traditional fall arrest harnesses. Fortunately, over the past decade, there has been many improvements to fall arrest harnesses, riggers are much better educated about fall protection and the industry as a whole has embraced ANSI standards and OSHA regulations. In fact, several entertainment rigging companies have been involved in designing fall arrest harnesses for entertainment riggers. As a result, rock climbing harnesses in arena rigging are now "a thing of the past."

Technically, OSHA says that employers must provide Personal a Fall Arrest System (PPE), including fall arrest harnesses, for its employees working at heights; and, if an employee provides their own harness, the employer must approve the use of the harness, in writing. However, in the real world, arena (union) riggers are expected to provide their own fall arrest harness and lanyards. The only piece of safety equipment that I have seen unions provide is hardhats; and these are primarily used by over hire workers who work as loaders or stagehands.

Lanyards
Lanyards are part of a fall arrest system. Lanyards fall into to two categories: Single Leg Lanyards and Twin Leg Lanyards. Twin Leg Lanyards have the advantage of allowing the rigger to clip into one point before unclipping from another point, ensuring that the rigger is never unprotected.

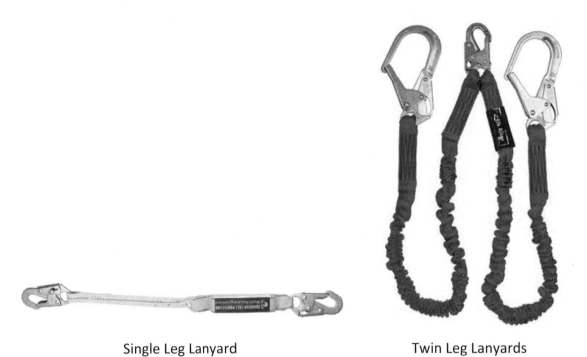

Single Leg Lanyard   Twin Leg Lanyards

Lanyards are typically available in 3', 4', and 6' lengths. Many lanyards have built-in shock absorbers that can reduce the force of a fall to under 900 pounds. Lanyards are available with either standard snap hooks or larger rebar snap hooks that can be connected to handrails, ladder rungs, or other larger items. Lanyards should comply with OSHA 1926.502, ANSI Z359.13, and ANSI A10.32.

Carabineers

While the preferred piece of hardware for connecting slings to other slings and hardware is a screw pin anchor shackle, carabineers, which are light-weight and quick and easy to connect/disconnect are still used for some rigging applications. Here is what you should know about carabineers.

First, unlike shackles which are stamped with a WLL (in tons), carabineers are marked with their breaking strength (in kiloNewtons). One kiloNewton (kN) is equal to 224.8 pounds. So, if a carabineer is marked "23 kN," then its breaking strength is 5,170 pounds. But its WLL, assuming you apply a Design Factor of 5, is only 1,034 pounds.

An auto-locking carabineer-3-stage model that meets the needs of industrial and rescue users.
photo courtesy of Sapsis Rigging

Unlike shackles, where the pin is in double shear, the gate of a carabineer is under tension. In fact, it is the gate of the carabineer that is its weakest point, so it must be carefully inspected before each use.

Lastly, while shackles can be used as collectors, with multiple lines connecting to the bail of the shackle, carabineers should only have two points connected to the carabineer, and the load should be on the carabineer's center axis. Some carabineers are marked with their BS when the carabineer is "side loaded" (the load is on the gate in shear rather than in tension. However, this load is a small fraction of its BS when the load is aligned with the center axis. A tri-loading a shackle puts shear force on the gate (the weakest part of a carabineer) and will result in a significantly lower breaking strength.

There are many different types of carabineers. When purchasing carabineers, make sure the gate is auto-locking. This is mandatory in all arena venues. Non-locking carabineers are only acceptable to clip your keys onto your belt. They are not acceptable for rigging.

Climbing Runners

These versatile, nylon "mini slings" wrap around beams and pipe to secure an anchor point to attach carabineers and wheels. They are rated at 22 kN and come in a variety of widths, lengths and colors.

A nylon climbing runner

Daisy Chains

Daisy chains are a type of adjustable runner that has crept into the rigger's tool bag because they allow for the quick connection of carabineers and pulleys around anchor points. Daisy chains are to be used for climbing only and with **two** carabineers. They are NOT to be used as part of your personal fall arrest system! Should the daisy chain experience a shock load, the pocket stitching could be ripped out leaving you clipped into nothing! The same could happen if this type of chain is used to haul up points. The daisy chain shown below is banned from most arena venues for this reason. DO NOT USE THIS TYPE OF DAISY CHAIN! Black Diamond puts out an excellent video on the dangers of daisy chains. See: https://vimeo.com/14679471

This single stitched daisy chain is extremely dangerous and is banned from most arena venues.

The Metolius chain shown below is acceptable because each loop is stitched individually.

The Metoluis chain with each looped stitched.

Pulleys

Another piece of recreational hardware that Is extremely useful is the pulley. Often called "wheels" by riggers, these are used to aid in the hauling up of rigging lines. The up-rigger will run his line through the pulley, attaching the pulley to a carabineer to a climbing runner to a secure position in the ceiling. This will allow other riggers to help when hauling up the point.

Petzl Pulley. The Pulley is attached to a
carabineer and then to a climbing runner.
photo courtesy of Petzl

Petzl Pro Traxion Locking Pulley.
Photo courtesy of Petzl

Grillions

Grillions are used as positioning devices. They can be obtained with either a snap hook or rebar hook for securing to an anchor point. An ascender clips to the harness and allows the rigger to adjust his position.

photo courtesy of Sapsis Rigging

Goggles

Some venues have a flame retardant sprayed over the steel beams. When these beams are over the head of the up-rigger, this retardant can come off and get into the up-rigger's eyes. Goggles can be very helpful in these situations.

Rigging Rope

There are several important factors in choosing a good rigging rope. First is the "feel" of the rope. You do not want a rope that is too soft, too stiff or too slick. ½" and 5/8" diameter ropes are the most popular with most up-riggers. Many riggers like a 5/8" diameter solid-braid multi-filament polypropylene Derby rope as their rigging rope. The 5/8" diameter gives it a better grip than many smaller diameter ropes. It is also available in most big box stores.

Also important is the length of the rigging rope. Many riggers have ropes of different lengths, for different venues. For most venues, the rope needs to be at least 10 feet longer than the distance from the beams to the floor. If a pulley is going to the used, and the down-riggers used to help lift the load, then the rope may need to be at least twice the distance from the floor to the beams.

5/8 in. Diameter Solid Braid Multi-Filament
Polypropylene Derby Rope

Pocket Pickle

Some down-riggers prefer to purchase and use this "mini" version of the larger motor control pickle discussed in Chapter 1, because it fits conveniently in a pocket or clipped to a belt loop.

Chapter 3:

Knots and Rope Handling

Understanding the basic knots and how to tie them correctly is essential to rigging. A good internet resource for learning knots is Animated Knots by Grog: http://www.animatedknots.com.

Parts of rope

A rope is technically called a line and is divided into parts.

- *The working end* or *tail* is the end of the rope that is used to actually tie the knot. The working end can also be referred to as the tag or tail.
- *A bight* is formed by making a U-shape section to the rope. Most knots begin by forming a bight.

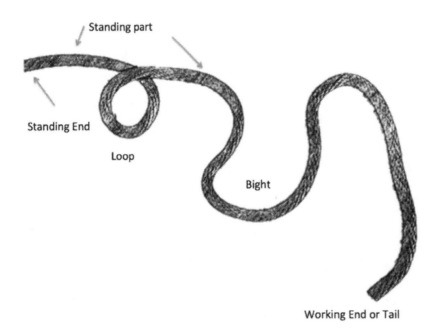

Parts of a rope

- *The loop* is formed by putting a twist in the bight. This twist will form either an overhand loop or an underhand loop. An overhand loop is when the working end of the rope lies over the top of the *standing part*.
- *The standing part* is the length of rope that lies between the *working end* and the *standing end*.
- *The standing end* (or bitter end) is the opposite of the working end or tail of the rope.

Knot Efficiency

No knot is 100% efficient (will hold 100% of the breaking strength of the rope). The bending of the rope creates friction that reduces the strength of rope. The tighter the bends, the more the efficiency is reduced. The least efficient knot is an overhand knot, which is is only 50% efficient. Most knots are between 60% and 75% efficient. Since there is really so little difference in the efficiency of most knots, it is not something that I think technicians should be overly concerned with.

There are literally thousands of different knots, but most falling into the one of the follows three types:

Hitch *is u*sed to attach a rope to something like a pipe batten, cleat, belaying pin and cable bundle. Types of knots include the *clove hitch, cleat hitch, Prusik* and the *trucker's hitch*

Loops consist of any type of knot that creates a closed loop for attachment. Types of knots include the *bowline, alpine butterfly loop, hangman's noose, figure 8.*

Bend: Joins two ropes together. Examples include the *sheet bend, alpine butterfly bend, Carrick bend, figure 8 bend, sheet bend* and *square knot*

Every knot has its strengths and weaknesses, which is why it is important to know more than one knot of each type. One of our favorite knot books is *The Book of Knots (how to tie 200 practical knots)* by Geoffrey Budworth and Jason Dalton. This book not only shows you how to tie knots, but it also rates each knot as to strength, security, ease of tying and ease of untying. These ratings, along with other information about each knot, can help you chose the best knot for particular needs.

An important note about *The Book of Knots*: Some books sellers may tell you that this book is "Out of Print." It is not. This book is published by Barnes and Noble and they can print copies when they need them.

Most Important Knots to Know

We will start with the most crucial knots to arena rigging; the *Bowline, Clove Hitch, Half Hitch, Figure Eight, Figure Eight Loop, Alpine Butterfly* and *Choker*. These are knots that every arena rigger should know and be able to tie. We will then move on to some others.

The Bowline

The *Bowline* is the most basic knot to the rigger. The down-rigger must be able to tie a *Bowline* in order to send up the steel baskets to the up-rigger and, at the end of the show, the up-rigger must be able to tie a *Bowline* to send the baskets back down.

To tie a *Bowline*, make an overhand loop in your left hand making sure that the standing part of the rope is under the loop. Grab the tail with the right hand, come up under and though the loop. Next, take the tail around the back of the standing part, come around and go back through the loop. To tighten, pull both the standing part and the tail. In arena rigging situations, the up-rigger will most likely ask for a specific length to the loop. Depending on the size I-beam in the venue, the up-rigger will pull up the rope, laying the bowline knot over the beam and stepping on the knot. This will give easy access to the shackles.

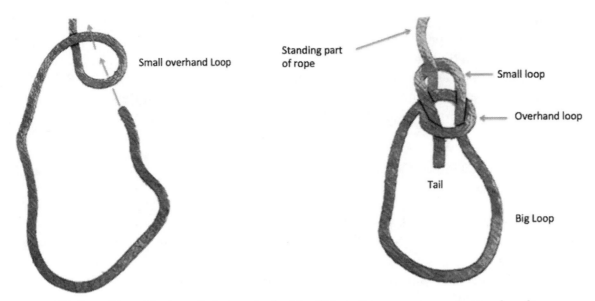

The bowline with the tail tied to the inside. This is the correct way to tie a bowline.

The tail should be tied to the inside of the loop. If the tail is tied to the outside, the knot can capsize by rolling over a beam suddenly releasing the load. The illustration below shows the bowline with the tail to the outside.

The Bowline tied with the tail to the outside. This should be avoided as the knot can capsize and come undone if rolled over an I-beam.

Clove Hitch and Half Hitch

The *Clove Hitch* is another essential hitch. It is a knot that is able to tighten itself around pipes and cable bundles. A simple all-purpose hitch, the "clove", as it customarily called, is easy to tie and untie. It is a good binding knot, but as any hitch knot, it should be used with caution because it can slip or come undone if constant pressure is not maintained on the line. That is why two half hitches are often tied when finishing a *Clove Hitch* as it keeps the hitch from loosening when there is no pressure.

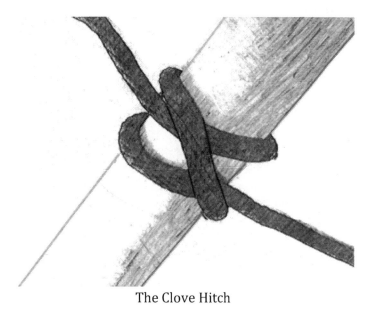

The Clove Hitch

Take the tail of the rope and wrap it around the pipe once making an X. Wrap the rope again, this time insert the tail under the X.

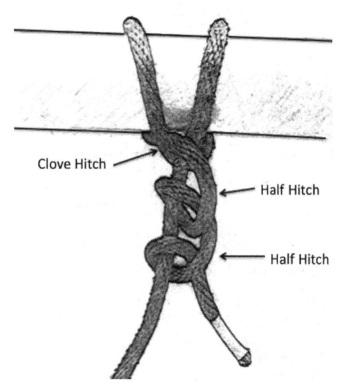

The clove hitch with two half hitches

Lastly, take the tail and insert it around and thru the standing part of the rope for the *Half Hitch*. Two half hitches secure and complete the knot.

The Figure 8

The *Figure Eight* knot is tied at the end of a rope that is running through a pulley (block). Its purpose is to keep the rope from accidently running through the sheave and un-reeving itself. An easy knot to learn, the *Figure Eight* takes the shape of the number 8.

Figure 8

The Figure Eight (or Flemish) Loop

The *Figure Eight Loop* is a loop formed on a bight. It allows for a loop to be tied to a ring, a carabineer, or your harness. It is reasonably easy to remember, tie, and check as it takes the form of the figure eight that we tied above. It is also an extremely secure loop knot.

Start by making a bight in the standing part of the rope

Next. run the bight under the standing part of the rope

The bight is run through the loop at the base making the number 8

The completed Figure Eight loop

Alpine Butterfly

The *Alpine Butterfly Loop* is also known as the *Lineman's Knot*. It is an excellent, mid-line rigging knot as it forms a fixed loop in the middle of the rope without needing to have access to the ends. This is made on the bight. The mid-line loop makes it convenient for multi-directional loading, attaching carabineers and anchorages.

Step 1: Wrap rope around hand

Step 2: Cross the tail end across palm

Step 3: Take top loop and pull below crossed tail

Step 4: Pull loop under wraps and pull through

The finished *Alpine Butterfly Loop*

The Choker Hitch

The *Choker Hitch* is a self-tightening knot that is formed on a bight. It is used in wrapping round slings around truss and securing rope around battens.

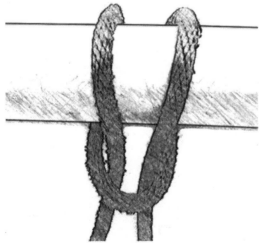

The choker hitch

Additional Knots to Know

The next series of knots are not as important to the arena rigger as the first seven, but they are certainly useful to have in your repertoire.

The Trucker's Hitch

The *Trucker's Hitch* is considered a "lashing or tie down" knot. It is very useful to "temporarily" lash down equipment when ratchet straps are not immediately available. This is not to say that the *Trucker's Hitch* should take the place of ratchet straps. It should not. The knot is limited to the breaking strength of the rope and D:d ratios on the loops. It should only be used to "temporarily" lash down equipment in a pinch. As you will see, the knot forms a very crude block and tackle with a 3:1 ratio. Tying a *Trucker's Hitch* is can be done in several steps. Lets assume we are securing a load to a palette cart.

The standing end of the rope is secured to the opposite end of the cart with a bowline. The working end of the rope is thrown over to the opposite side of the load.

Step 1: Mid way up this opposite side, make a *slip knot* in the rope (shown left). (The *Alpine Butterfly Loop* can be used too).

Step 2. Run the Tail through an attachment point at the bottom of the palette and thread the tail through the loop formed midway in the rope.

Step 1: The slip knot is the loop formed midway in the rope.

Step 3. Pulling on the working end of the rope will tighten the line with a 3:1 ratio.
Step 4: Once tension on the load is complete, secure the *Trucker's Hitch* with two *Half Hitches.*

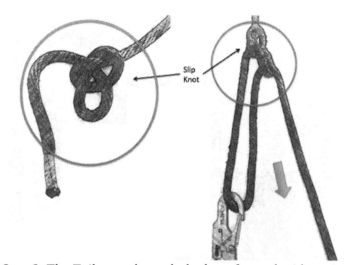

Step 2: The Tail runs through the loop formed midway in the rope.
Step 3: Pulling on the working end of the rope will tighten down the load with a 3:1 ratio.

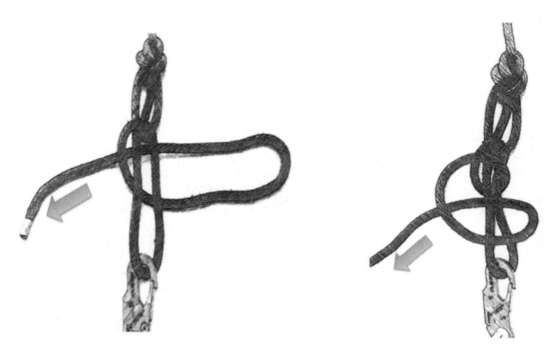

Step 4: Once tension on the load is complete, secure the *Trucker's Hitch* with two *Half Hitches*.

The finished Trucker's Hitch

Carrick Bend

The Carrick Bend is used for joining two larger diameter lines that cannot be easily tied with other knots. While it is easy to tie, it is not always easy to remember. Unlike many bends, it is easy to untie and it will not jam closed after taking on heavy loads.

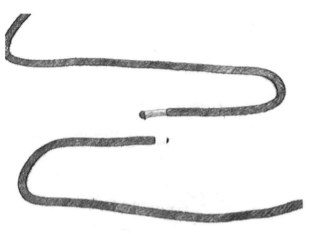

Step 1: Form the two lines in a bight; an upper rope and a lower rope

Step 2: Next, form a loop in the lower line as shown. The tail should be laying under the standing part

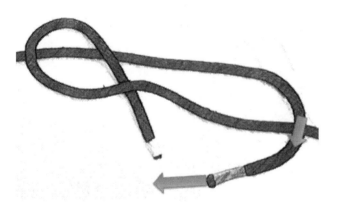

Step 3: The tail of the upper line will run over the standing part of the lower line

Step 4: Next, the tail of the upper line will run under the tail of the lower line and over the loop

Step 6: The tail of the upper line will run under the standing part of the lower line and back up over the loop. The end result will look like a pretzel with both ends pointing away from you.

Step 7: Next, tighten the knot a bit - being sure to still leave a good amount of tail. Pull the two standing ends to cause the knot to "turn on itself" and tighten.

Note: Some people tie this knot with the tails opposite each other (as shown here) while other tie it with the tails (next to each other). Because this knot is symmetrical, the knot holds equally no matter which way the tails point.

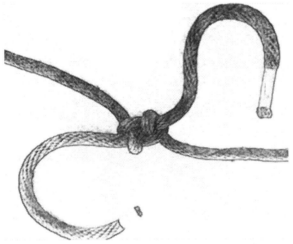

The finished Carrack Bend

The Overhand Knot

The *Overhand Knot* is a very secure, permanent knot that is often hard to untie. It is often tied at the end of a rope to keep the ends from unraveling until they can be properly whipped or lashed at a later time.

The Overhand Knot

The Double Sheet bend

The sheet bend is another knot that joins two ropes together. This knot is effective in binding two ropes together when each rope is of a different diameter.

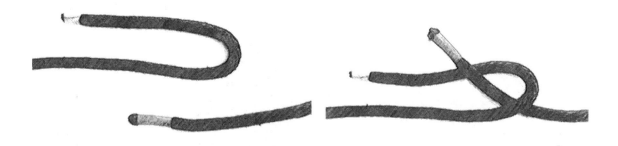

Step1: Shape the upper line into a bight

Step 2: The tail of the second line runs under and through the bight

Step 3: The tail will run up and under the standing part and tail of the first line

Step 4: Pull the tail through leaving enough tail to finish the knot

Step 5: The tail will pull through the loop forming a half hitch. If you stop here, you have a *single sheet bend*.

Step 6: Next, pass the tail back under the standing parts and thread under and through the half hitch

The finished double sheet bend

The Prussik

Prussik was an Austrian Climber who introduced this wrap/hitch back in the 1930's. It is a great friction knot that allows one rope to be secured to another so that it will not slide. If it is choked around another rope or multi-cable, it is extremely secure; if it is loosen, it will slide up or down the rope it is fastened to. In theatre applications, the *prussik* is often used as a "sunday" to tie off the purchase line of a counterweight system or to choke a cable bundle for strain relief.

The *Prussik* is a good all around friction knot

The Bowline on a Bight

The Bowline on a Bight makes two loops in the middle of the standing part of a rope. You do not need to thread the tail like we did in the *Bowline*. This knot also makes a convenient seat when a bo'sun's chair is unavailable.

Step 1: Form the standing part of the line into a bight

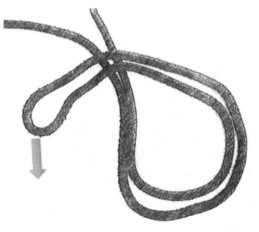

Step 2: Make an overhand loop with the bight

Step 3: The tail end of the bight will cross towards the loop

Step 4: The tail end of the bight will enter the loop from the underside

Step 5: Divide the tail of the bight so that it will cross under the loop of the bowline

Step 6: Pull the loop of the bight up and over the standing part of the rope

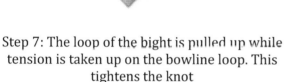

Step 7: The loop of the bight is pulled up while tension is taken up on the bowline loop. This tightens the knot

The completed bowline on a bight

The Rigger's Rope
Rope Type
The question most often asked by beginning riggers is, "what type of rope is best to purchase?" Most riggers use a 5/8" dia. solid braid multifilament polypropylene or polyester line. You want a rope that is extremely flexible and easy to handle. A 5/8" diameter rope is easy to pull and hold onto. What you DO NOT want to use is a rope from the recreational climbing industry. Its application is for just that: ascending or descending. It is too stiff and its 3/8" diameter is too small to handle when hauling up points.

Recommendations are:
1. *5/8" Spectrum ShowBraid.* This is a double-braided rope constructed of a core of filament polyester with a filament polyester sleeve. It offers low stretch and very good wear characteristics.
2. *5/8" solid braid multifilament polypropylene.* This solid braid polypropylene is more economical than polyester. It uses much smaller fibers compared to other polypropylene ropes, which give it a softer feel. The fibers do tend to pick if they catch on small abrasions.

Spectrum Show Braid   *Solid Braid Multifilament Polypropylene*

Coiling a rope

Learning how to coil a rope properly will help keep twists and knots out of the rigging line and allow it to play back out evenly when needed. Riggers will NEVER coil a rope around their elbow, as this does not allow the rope to lie evenly in the coils. Nothing can be more frustrating, or a demonstration of amateur status, than to lower down a rigging line only to have knots and twists show up in your line. When a rope is coiled, it must spin one turn in order for it to lie evenly. Coiling around the arm does not allow the rope to twist. The result is a rope that develops twists that form a figure 8 in the coil that remain when rope is uncoiled.

Never coil a rope around your arm. It puts twists in the line that remain.

Proper coiling will keep the line free of kinks and twists. Start by holding the tail end of the rope in one hand and pulling the standing end of the rope out a comfortable distance with the other. Form a loop allowing the coil to form naturally while twisting the rope one turn with your fingers. The rope must make one turn for every loop in the coil. The coil formed will be around two feet in diameter with no twists. If the rope is extremely long or heavy, use the same technique by laying the rope out on the floor (Note: the same method is used to coil lighting or audio cable). If there is an extreme amount of kinks and twists, you may need to stretch the rope out on the floor its entire length before coiling. Coiling the line when working on an I-beam is called *flaking*. While sitting on the beam, the up-rigger can make the coils by laying the coils over the beam or around his neck, forming the loops as described above.

Hold the tail end in one hand while forming a loop with the other

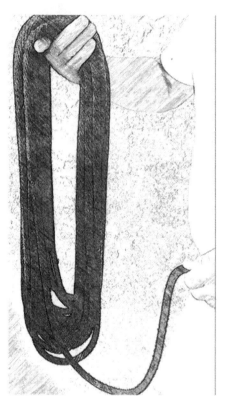

Form a loop allowing the coil to form naturally while twisting the rope one turn with your fingers

Finishing and Stowing

Finishing the coil is done so that the loops formed will not become tangled while the rope is being stored or transported. There are basically two methods for finishing the coil.

- *Gasket Coil (Butterfly Coil)*: The first method is preferred when the rope is to be stored (stowed) for a period of time. It secures the coils firmly by wrapping the entire line with a perpendicular wrap. Once the coil is made, leave around four feet of line for the wrap. While still holding the coil in one hand, wrap the entire coil with the excess three feet. Forming a loop with the last sixteen inches, pull the loop through and over the entire coil.

Wrap the entire coil with the extra three feet of tail. Forming a loop with the last sixteen inches, pull the loop through the inside of the coil and over the top

The finished line ready to be stowed

- *Rigger's Method (The Alpine Coil)*: The rigger's method, *or alpine coil* (as it is better known), allows for the coil to be carried over the shoulder, leaving the hands free for climbing. Start by coiling the rope as described above. Again leave about four feet of tail for the wrap. Next, form a bight in the in the tail end close to the coils. Wrap the remaining rope around the bight working the wrap forward. Tuck the tail into the bight and pull the bight closed.

Form a bight in the in the working end close to the coils. Wrap the remaining rope around the bight working the wrap forward. Tuck the tail into the bight and pull the bight closed.

The finished *Riggers Coil*

Rope maintenance

Polyester and polypropylene rope are very resilient to use (and misuse) and will last for many years. Still, proper care should be taken to avoid contact with chemicals, UV radiation and sharp corners and edges. After use, coil the rope, as described above, being careful to remove all kinks, knots and twists in the line. Check the rope before each use for abrasion and wear. The ends should be checked for unraveling. Basically, your rigging line should be stowed so that it is ready for use when needed.

Throwing the Rope

Before throwing a rope, it must be properly coiled or flaked to prevent tangling when it is deployed. If using a coiled or flaked rope, it can remain at your feet or on the I-beam. If the rope is lying across beams, make sure that there will be enough slack in the line to throw. From the coil or slack, make several small coils in the throwing hand based on the throwing distance. Hold the excess rope in the other hand. The rope maybe thrown overhand or underhand, but the throw should be as smooth as possible keeping the throwing arm as straight as possible. Look slightly above your target. Aim for that spot. Throw the rope up and out making sure the throw is as smooth as possible. Just before the rope is released, yell out the warning "rope" to make sure other riggers are aware of the action.

Chapter 4:

Fall Protection

Falls can occur in any occupational setting. They can occur with such simple acts as walking up or down stairs, to walking out on I-beams in an arena, to focusing lights from an A-frame ladder. In 2013, the Bureau of Labor Statistics reported that 828 fatalities occurred in in the construction industry. Of these, 302 resulted from falls making this the leading cause of death in the industry. Sadly, these statistics have remained fairly constant over the last several years, fluctuating only by a few percentage points.

In this chapter, we will discuss fall prevention, the ability to recognize fall hazards, the requirements of fall protection, and differences between fall restraint and fall arrest. In addition, we will examine PFAS (or Personal Fall Arrest System) equipment, rescue plans, and the process for creating a safe working environment. It will be important to remember as we go through this chapter, that no, one, single, fall scenario or situation is ever the same. Every fall situation is going to be different and will require its own Fall Protection Plan. Let us first begin by examining what happens during a fall.

The Anatomy of a Fall

A fall begins usually with a loss of balance is followed by a misplaced center of gravity. Loss of balance begins when there is an interruption to otherwise steady and controlled movement. Misplaced center of gravity happens when there is an internal loss of bearings. As soon as we experience a loss in balance, our brain tries to compensate by redirecting the body's center of gravity. If the brain is successful, then normal activity resumes. If it is not, then the brain goes into immediate "damage control" by assessing the situation to minimalize the impending damage to follow. Most people think that they can react to the initial stages of falling by immediately reacting as soon as a "loss of balance" is experienced.

Guess Again!

It takes a person about $1/3^{rd}$ of a second for a person to become aware that they are falling and another $1/3^{rd}$ of a second to react to the fall. In that $1/3^{rd}$ of a second, the body has already free fallen 18 inches. In $2/3^{rd}$ of a second approximately 7 feet of free fall has occurred. In $8/10^{th}$ of a second, the brain is now able to respond to the fall, but the body has now travelled approximately 10 feet.

Forces

A 215-pound worker falling 6 feet can generate a fall force of as much as 2,795 pounds on the body. At 10 feet, these forces can be as high as 4,515 pounds. Without a proper deceleration harness, these forces can cause serious injury and even death. With proper fall protection, these forces at 10 feet are reduced to 829 pounds[1]. This why OSHA limits the forces on the body to no more than 1,800 pounds with an arresting harness and a free fall distance to no more than 6 feet. The diagram below illustrates the distances that would be experience during and after a fall.

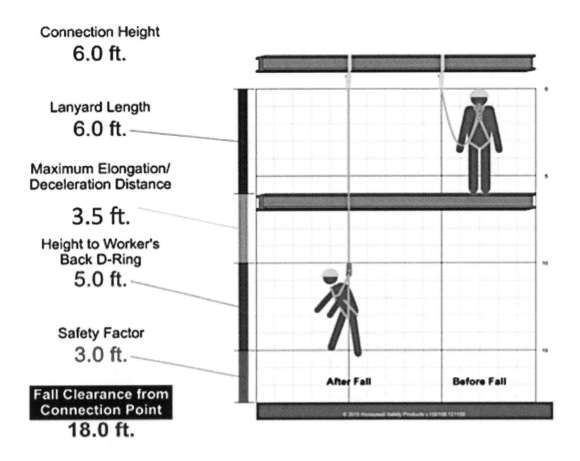

Connection Height
6.0 ft.

Lanyard Length
6.0 ft.

Maximum Elongation/
Deceleration Distance
3.5 ft.

Height to Worker's
Back D-Ring
5.0 ft.

Safety Factor
3.0 ft.

Fall Clearance from Connection Point
18.0 ft.

After Fall Before Fall

Note that the anchor point is 6 feet above the worker. The length of the lanyard is 6 feet. OSHA allows for only 6 feet of free fall, so it is best to keep the anchor point as high as possible[2]. If a worker were to fall, then he/she would only fall the length of the arresting lanyard and an additional 3.5 feet, which is the maximum deployment of the shock absorber. Add in the average height of the worker 6 feet and a 3 feet safety factor that accounts for any elongation of the system, then the distance from anchor point that accounts for any elongation of the system, then the distance from anchor point can be as much as 18 feet. This is why it is very important to make sure of your distance from the anchor point to the ground as well as any obstructions in between. A fall arresting system is useless if you hit the ground or any obstruction somewhere within that 18 feet. Suspension trauma and fall arrest solutions to this problem will be explored later in this chapter.

---

[1] The formula for shock loads is Force=((Free Fall Dist. / Stopping Dist.)+1)
[2] In the entertainment industry, this anchor point may be only waist high, as we will see with Horizontal Life Lines.

Fall Protection (fall arrest and fall restraint) begins with Fall Prevention

Fall Protection begins with Fall Prevention. The working environment cannot be deemed safe unless fall protection is incorporated into every aspect of the workplace. Prevention begins with planning and planning begins with an analysis of all the potential fall hazards that can place workers at risk. Once these hazards have been identified, then a Fall Prevention Plan can be put into effect.

The important thing to remember is, don't feel overwhelmed about creating a Fall Prevention Plan. There are plenty of resources available to assist and on-line templates are available. OSHA (The Occupational Safety and Health Administration) and CCOHA (Canadian Centre for Occupational Health and Safety) are two such resources. ANSI (American National Standards Institute) publishes standards relating directly to the entertainment industry. In addition, Fall Prevention classes can also be found through such organizations as PLASA and USITT. They can be contacted directly for additional information and class schedules. Information is also available at the end of this chapter.

A plan should include but is not limited to:
- The identification of potential fall hazards
- What type of fall protection is required for the specific job
  - Hand railings or guard rails
  - Fall Restraint
  - Fall Arrest
  - others
- The training of employees on recognition of safety hazards associated with the working environment
- The training of employees on the safe use of fall protection equipment
- What to do in the case of an emergency. The Emergency Action Plan

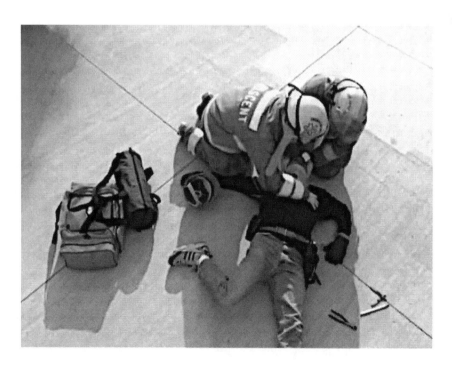

An Emergency Action Plan is an important part of Fall Prevention

photo courtesy of Miller-Honeywell

Fall Protection is the end result of Fall Prevention

Essentially, *Fall Protection* is a system that will prevent a person from falling to a lower level. It is a series of steps taken to control or eliminate the possibility of an accidental fall. It can be as simple as placing a handrail along stairs, or a railing along the edge of a platform. At times, however, hand railings or guardrails are not enough, and workers need to access areas that are extremely close to fall areas. In these cases, more protective equipment is required. A "leash" or tether worn with a Body Belt is one means of providing protection. It allows a worker to approach a fall area but will not allow the worker to fall to a lower level. This is known as *Work Positioning* or *Fall Restraint*. *Fall Arrest*, on the other hand, is a system that will "arrest" a person in mid-fall and prevents them from serious injury or death. A full Body Harness worn with a shock-absorbing lanyard is one such method; another is Body Harness worn with the Self-Retracting Lifeline (or SRL). In any case, *Fall Restraint* and *Fall Arrest* are the end products of a comprehensive Fall Prevention Plan.

The Requirements for Fall Protection – Understanding the Regulations

The Entertainment Industry is considered to be part of "general industry" and is covered under OSHA regulations 29 CRF, 1910 and 1926. OSHA regulations are not specific to the entertainment industry like ANSI recommendations. You may have noted the use of the word "regulation" vs. "recommendation." The differences between ANSI and OSHA are that ANSI recommendations are created by specific industries (such as the Entertainment Industry) and are considered to be "self-regulatory". ANSI recommendations are simply that - recommendations. OSHA regulations on the other hand are "law" and enforceable. Whereas ANSI recommendations may not be enforceable like OSHA's, failure to abide by ANSI recommendations have resulted is stiff penalties and fines in court.

Paraphrasing the regulations

Here are some key points that are paraphrased for convenience. Please consult the OSHA website listed in the back of this chapter for the exact phrasing.

1. *Fall Protection* must be provided when workers are at:
   - 4 feet – general industry
   - 6 feet – construction
2. *The Fall Arrest* system must -
   - limit the maximum force on a person to 1,800 (8 kN) pounds when used with a body harness.
   - be rigged so that an employee cannot free fall more than 6 feet.
   - bring an employee to a complete stop and limit the employee's maximum deceleration distance to 3.5 feet.
   - utilize an *Anchorage Point* for attachment of a *Personal Fall Arrest System* (PFAS). The Anchorage Point must be capable of supporting at least 5,000 pounds (22.2 kN) per person attached. It also must be independent of supporting any other structure or equipment.
3. The *Fall Restraint* system
   - must limit the maximum force on a person to 900 pounds (4 kN) when used with a Body Belt.
   - allows for the use of Body Belts as part of a Fall Restraint system. They are not acceptable for use as a Fall Arrest system.
4. Training
   - Before fall equipment is used, employees must be trained in the safe use of the equipment and the PFAS.

5. Workplace safety
   - The Employer is responsible for safety in the workplace. They are also responsible for providing the necessary equipment and training to keep employees safe.
6. Competent Person
   - An OSHA "competent person" is defined as "one who is capable of identifying existing and predictable hazards in the surroundings or working conditions which are unsanitary, hazardous, or dangerous to employees, and who has authorization to take prompt corrective measures to eliminate them".
7. Qualified Person
   - A qualified person is one who, by possession of a recognized degree, certificate, or professional standing, or who by extensive knowledge, training, and experience, has successfully demonstrated his ability to solve or resolve problems relating to the subject matter, the work, or the project.

Knowing the ABCs of fall protection

Knowing your ABCs is an easy way to remember the parts of a fall arrest system. These consist of:

- The Anchor Point
- The Body Harness
- The Connecting Device

A - Anchor Point

There are many different types of anchorage points- all vary on the needs of that industry. The types of anchorage points discussed in this chapter will relate specifically to the entertainment industry. Essentially, **an anchorage point is a means of** attachment for a *Personal Fall Arrest System*- specifically, the connecting device. The Fall Arrest Anchorage Point must be capable of supporting at least 5,000 pounds (22.2 kN) per attached worker. If two workers are to be connected, then the load capacity of the anchorage point must be doubled. The anchorage point must also be independent of supporting any other structure or equipment. The **Fall Restraint Anchor point must support at least 1000 lb. per employee attached.**

Permanent Anchorages

The first type of permanent anchorage points is Horizontal Lifelines or HLL often found rigged on arena I-beams. Riggers working at height on the I-Beams will be attached to permanently installed HLL. This type of lifeline allows the worker to easily move horizontally across the beams.

Riggers attach a steel basket around an I-beam. Note their shock-absorbing lanyard is connected to a horizontal lifeline overhead similar to the one shown below.

photo courtesy of Ben Kilmer

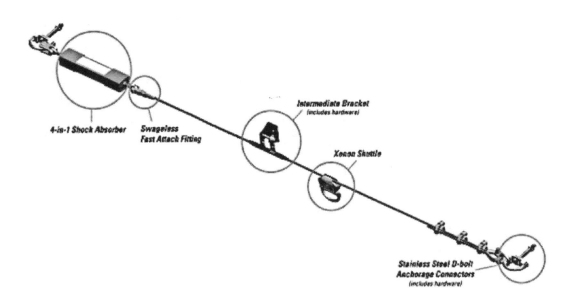

4-in-1 Shock Absorber   Swageless Fast Attach Fitting

Intermediate Bracket
(includes hardware)

Xenon Shuttle

Stainless Steel D-bolt
Anchorage Connectors
(includes hardware)

This illustration shows an HLL that in intended for permanent installation.

photo courtesy of Miller-Honeywell

Other permanent anchorage points are fixed such as the one shown to the below left. However, as you can see, it does not allow the worker as much horizontal mobility as does the permanent HLL. The anchorage point to the right allows for greater flexibility of movement.

This photo shows a permanently mounted D-ring attachment bolted to the bottom flange of an I-beam.
photo courtesy of Miller-Honeywell

The beam trolley allows for an anchorage point to be made where more flexibility of movement is required.
photo courtesy of Sapsis Rigging Inc.

Temporary Anchorages

Other types of anchorage points are those that are temporary. Beam clamps allow for an attachment point to be made directly to an I-beam. They are flexible enough to allow an anchorage point to be made wherever one is needed. Unfortunately, they also do not allow for a great deal of horizontal movement.

A Beam Clamp attachment point. Note the worker's connecting device runs from the dorsal ring of his harness to the anchorage point.
photo courtesy of Miller-Honeywell

The Double Ring Tie-off Strap is a simple strap that can be choked around an I-beam providing a similar anchorage point.
photo courtesy of Miller-Honeywell

The Guardian Beamer 2000 and 3000 are lightweight and adjustable anchor points that can move along with the rigger. Many riggers use these as anchor point while installing permanent anchorages and lifelines as they are quick to attach to the flange of the beam.

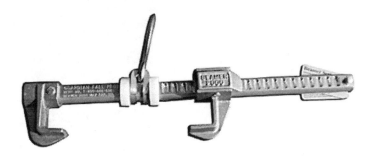

The Beamer 2000, a lightweight, adjustable, and portable anchor point.

photo courtesy of Guardian

At times riggers will need to access truss while it is trimmed to its final height.
Follow spot operators too will need to climb into their follow spot chairs from wire rope ladders suspended from the truss to the floor. Once up, they must walk along the truss cords to their spot positions. Horizontal Lifelines provide the necessary anchorage points. Similar to the permanent Horizontal Lifeline, portable HLLs run along the truss from end to end. Pear rings at the chain hoist hook support the lifeline as it runs down to connect at a strap at the truss ends.[3] They are rated for one or two persons. Please note that all horizontal lifeline connectors must have a legible tag stating that the product meets ANSI Z359.1-2007 standards for Personal Fall Protection Systems. If the tag is missing or illegible, don't use it!

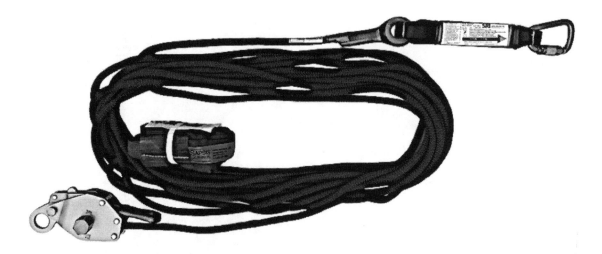

The ProPlus Temporary Horizontal Lifeline system is ideal for touring shows and venues where the truss location changes from show to show. It is designed to be used by 1 or 2 technicians at a time.

photo courtesy of Sapsis Rigging, Inc.

---

[3] See the new ANSI E1.39 – 2015 standard regarding the Selection and Use of Personal Fall Arrest Systems on

Portable Structures Used in the Entertainment Industry

photo courtesy of Sapsis Rigging, Inc.

The *Self Retractable Lifeline* or SRL is viable alternative to the shock-absorbing lanyard. It is generally used when working on ladders, truss, truss towers or when the fall distance is less than 18 feet. The worker connects his harness directly to the lifeline. Any sudden vertical fall force will activate the SRL mechanism within 6" and decelerate the worker to within 2 feet, locking- similar to that of a seat belt engaging. While a 6-foot shock-absorbing lanyard will allow for six feet of free-fall clearance, the SRL limits free falls to 2 feet. With this shorter distance, the *Self-Retracting Lifeline* can be used with a much shorter distance to the ground. A word of caution! Always know the equipment you are working with. Always read the accompanying manuals. The big danger with SRLs is the possibility of "swing falls", that is, walking horizontally out on a beam or truss, falling , then swinging horizontally into an obstruction. In addition, the WLL of most SRLs is 310 pounds, (this includes all clothing, tools and gear). Check the label for WLL information. Again, just like Horizontal Lifelines, all Self Retracting Life Lines MUST have a tag or legible label stating that the product meets ANSI Z359.1-2007 standards for Personal Fall Protection Systems. If it doesn't have a legible tag, don't use it!

Fall protection is required for vertical ladders without cages over 24 ft. The Climbing Safety Sleeve is designed to be use in this situation. The worker can ascend or descend the ladder while the sleeve simply slides along the pre-rigged rope. If a slip or fall occurs, a locking mechanism engages limiting the fall to a few inches and reducing the possibility of serious injury. Whereas, no fall protection is necessary for portable ladders, the worker must maintain three points of contact with the ladder at all times.

photo courtesy of Sapsis Rigging, Inc.

B - Body Harness and Body Belt

Both the Body Harness and the Body Belt are acceptable means of fall protection, but remember, the two are NOT interchangeable. The *Body Harness* is worn as part of a *Fall Arrest System*, whereas the *Body Belt* is only worn for *Fall Restraint* or positioning. According to OSHA, the maximum forces on a person wearing a Body Harness are limited to 1,800 (8 kN) pounds. The maximum forces on a person wearing a Body Belt are 900 pounds (4 kN).

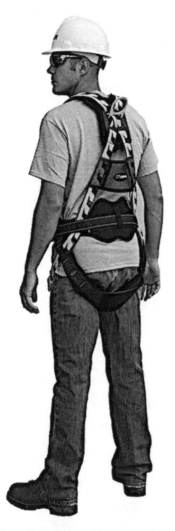

The full Body Harness. Note the Dorsal Ring at the top of the back.
photo courtesy of Miller-Honeywell

The Full Body Harness consist of shoulder straps, straps that wrap between the legs and a Dorsal Ring attachment point. It is usually secured at the chest or waist by interlocking buckles. The Dorsal Ring attachment point should rest squarely between the shoulder blades. Harnesses must be sized for the worker and be snug, not tight to the body. In addition, workers wearing a Full Body Harness must weigh more than 130 pounds. and less than 300 pounds (310 is the limit with tools). Inspection needs to be performed before each use and annually by a competent person. They should never be modified. In the event of a fall, they should be taken out of service immediately and destroyed. When inspecting a harness before use, begin with the belts and the rings. Bend the straps in a U shape, checking for worn or frayed edges, pulled or broken stitching, cuts and chemical damage to the webbing. Check the Dorsal Ring for any distortion or wear to the metal. Check the padding for wear or break through from sharp objects. Examine carefully the buckles and rivets for any distortion and wear. Remember, this is your life you are protecting. Don't take chances. If you find any wear or suspected damage to the harness, don't wear it. Take it to a competent person for further examination and inspection.

Body belts come in single or double D-ring and are used for Fall Restraint and Positioning only. They basically, put the worker on a short leash allowing freedom of the hands for work. If a person can fall over the edge, then a PFAS must be used. Body Belts are not to be used as a Fall Arrest Harness. A person who uses a body belt as a personal fall arrest system is exposing himself to such hazards such as falling out of the belt and serious internal injuries. Inspection and maintenance of the body belt is the same as noted for the Fall Arrest Harness- inspection before each use and yearly inspection by a competent person.

photo courtesy of Miller-Honeywell

C - Connecting Devise

A connecting devise is a lanyard or leash usually made up of rope, wire rope, or strap that connects the harnessed worker to a deceleration device, lifeline, or anchor point. In the case of Body Belts, this can be as simple as a rope or adjustable strap. With a Personal Fall Arrest System a deceleration device will be needed. The most common type of deceleration device used in the entertainment industry is the "rip-stitch" lanyard and the Self Retracting Lifeline. Both serve to dissipate the tremendous energy of a fall arrest and limit the energy imposed on a worker during a fall arrest.

Visual inspection should be performed before each use. Examine the lanyard from one end to the other, slowly rotating the lanyard while inspecting for chaffing, worn or frayed edges. Special attention needs to be at the splice or stitched ends and the shock-absorbing pack. Do not open the pack- simply inspect for wearing or tears. Examine the area where the pack is sewn to the D-Ring. Hardware should be checked for bent or twisted jaws. Have a competent person inspect the lanyard once a year.

Suspension Trauma

Suspension trauma or orthostatic hypotension (shock) is an effect, which occurs when the human body is held in vertical suspension due to the force of gravity and a lack of movement. The effects can begin in as little as 2 or 3 minutes. Venous pooling occurs in the legs due to gravity and can quickly lead to unconsciousness and even death. It is crucial that a rescue begin immediately! No one should ever use a PFAS without an Emergency Action Plan in place. If you do not have a plan, do not put yourself at risk.

The Emergency Action Plan

The Emergency Action Plan is exactly what it says it is; a plan that can be acted on when a person has fallen from height. OSHA requires that employers provide the "prompt rescue of employees in the event of a fall or shall assure that employees are able to rescue themselves." The following are considerations are necessary to any EAP:

- Ensure that workers are able to rescue themselves or, if not, have available the equipment necessary to rescue suspended workers immediately.
- Train workers in the effects of suspension trauma. If they have fallen, they should be taught to pump their legs to avoid the effects of venous pooling
- Realized that suspended workers are in danger of the effects of suspension trauma within minutes and that these effects are life threatening
- Have immediate access to rescue equipment in the vicinity of the job site so that the EAP can be put into effect
- Train all workers in the use of fall rescue equipment

The first reaction to any fall is to call 911 and, in the case of a fall, it is important to do so. However, the EMS does not have the equipment necessary to rescue workers at height. Their response would be to call the fire department. It may take as long as 20 or 30 minutes for the EMS and a fire department squad to arrive on site, and an additional 10 minutes for them to get the necessary equipment in place to begin the rescue- by then, the fallen worker maybe dead. In addition, workers in the entertainment industry are at heights that maybe beyond the limits of fire department rescue equipment, so a rescue from the ground maybe next to impossible. This is why it is so important for a rescue plan to be in place so that rescue can begin immediately.

Once the worker is rescued, it is important to maintain the ABCs - Airway, Breathing, and Circulation and lay the person in a reclined position. However, there is growing controversy over a condition known as "reflow syndrome" in suspension trauma victims. According to the Journal of Emergency Medical Services[4], placing a victim in a supine position allows venous blood to rush to the heart and cause "reflow syndrome." "Venous blood that has pooled in the legs suddenly reaches the heart with immediate ventricular fibrillation, rupture and infarct of the heart, and lethal damage to the liver, kidneys and brain." They maintain that the injured worker needs to be kept in a semi-reclining position (usually a 30 degree recline) and monitored for the effects of suspension trauma. Do not loosen the harness around the legs as this may aggravate the "reflow" condition. If the worker is unconscious, then be sure to keep air passages open. Lastly, make sure the worker is fully evaluated by an Emergency Medical Professional.

---

[4] The Journal of Emergency Medical Services http://www.jems.com/articles/print/volume-34/issue-8/patient-care/dangerous-suspension-understan.html

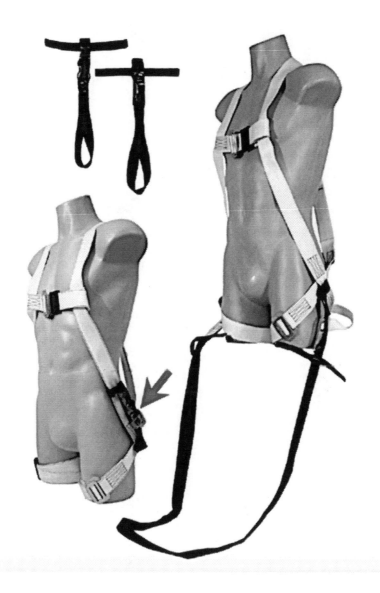

Suspension straps help to reestablish and keep the flow of blood in the legs while suspended. In the event of a fall, the worker can release the straps and step into a loop thus relieving constriction on the legs.

photo courtesy of Sapsis Rigging, Inc.

The Pro-Plus Rescue System.
photo courtesy of Sapsis Rigging, Inc.

Aerial Work Platforms

In addition to climbing I-beams and scaffold, arena workers also must access rigging points from otherwise inaccessible positions. This is where the Scissor Lift and the Articulating Aerial Boom Lift come in handy. A personal fall arrest system (PFAS) is required whenever you are working in an Articulating and/or telescoping boom and bucket truck. They are not required for scissor lifts as the bucket is enclosed and only moves in a vertical position. When operating any aerial work platform, consult the operator's manual for any and all safety requirements. As of January 1, 1998, OSHA's fall protection rule requires the use of a full body harness for fall arrest in place of a body belt when working from an aerial work platform. Manufacturers also require that operators must wear a full body harness and lanyard that is attached to the designated anchorage point when using an articulating boom or bucket.

Some OSHA highlights regarding aerial lifts are:

- Tying off to an adjacent pole, structure, or equipment while working from an aerial lift shall **not** be permitted.
- Employees shall always stand firmly on the floor of the basket and shall not sit or climb on the edge of the basket or use planks, ladders, or other devices for a work position.
- A full body harness shall be worn, and a lanyard attached to an anchor point on the boom or in the basket when working from an aerial lift.
- The brakes shall be set and when outriggers are used, they shall be positioned on pads or a solid surface. Wheel chocks shall be installed before using an aerial lift on an incline, provided they can be safely installed.
- An aerial lift truck shall not be moved when the boom is elevated in a working position with men in the basket, except for equipment, which is specifically designed for this type of operation.

The important thing to remember in all of this is: OSHA requires the use of full body harnesses as fall protection on all aerial and articulating booms. Even though the basket of an articulating boom is enclosed, the arm is subject to extreme fluctuations of movement when moving over regular and irregular surfaces. The potential exists to catapult the worker from the basket, flailing him to and fro. Wearing a Fall Arrest Harness with a 6-foot Arresting Lanyard could be disastrous should the worker be ejected from the basket. For the same reason, moving an articulating boom truck while the arm is articulated is against OSHA regulations and manufactures guidelines. Always be alert to potential fall hazards when operating an aerial lift.

Summary

Remember these important key points:

- Fall Protection begins with Fall Prevention. The working environment cannot be deemed safe unless fall protection is incorporated into every aspect of the workplace. Prevention begins with planning and planning begins with an analysis of all the potential fall hazards that can place workers at risk. Once these hazards have been identified, then a Fall Prevention Plan can be put into effect.
- A plan should include but is not limited to:
    - The identification of potential fall hazards
    - What type of fall protection is required for the specific job
    - Hand railings or guard rails
    - Fall Restraint
    - Fall Arrest
    - The training of employees on recognition of safety hazards associated with the working environment
    - The training of employees on the safe use of fall protection equipment
    - What to do in the case of an emergency
    - The Emergency Action Plan

Resources:

- PLASA (Professional Lighting and Sound Association https://www.plasa.org/
- USITT (United States Institute for Theatre Technology) http://www.usitt.org/
- OSHA (The Occupational Safety and Health Administration) https://www.osha.gov/
- CCOHA (Canadian Centre for Occupational Health and Safety) http://www.ccohs.ca/
- ANSI (American National Standards Institute) http://tsp.plasa.org/tsp/documents/published_docs.php

Part II:

Bridles

Chapter 5:

Basic Bridle Math

Bridling is necessary when a rigging point falls between two or more I-beams, or ceiling truss. They are used to create a new anchor point between existing hanging points. A bridle can be made up of two or more legs of specified length that span between the beams with the apex falling directly over the rigging point. In Chapter 1 we learned that STAC chain allows for adjustments to be made to the apex and where it falls in relationship to the rigging point. The illustration on the following page shows a typical two-leg bridle along with additional considerations. Let's begin by examine the terms:

Vertical and horizontal distance
It is important to know the *Horizontal Distances* between the beams in any arena venue. Accurate measurements can be found on the architectural and/or structural plans of the venue space. Be sure and check the architectural drawings against the structural drawings. Sometimes these can vary. This can also be verified with an actual survey of the space. The *Vertical Distance* will be determined by where the bridle point or *Apex* falls based on the needed headroom and trim height of the truss. Remember it is important to avoid bridle angles that exceed 120 degrees.

Beam Height to floor and Bridle Height Junction
Beam Height to Floor is easy to determine by an actual survey; simply shoot a laser tape measure to from the floor to the bottom flange of the beams. If the distance to too great for a laser tape measure, then the structural plans may need to be consulted. Heights may vary from beam to beam as well. The *Bridle Height Junction* distance is the distance between the bridle apex and the arena floor. This will vary based on the production.

Trim, Drop, and Headroom
Trim refers to the height of the truss measured from the lower chords (or equipment hung) to the floor of the stage or floor of the venue. *Drop* is the distance from the bridle apex to the chain hoist hook in its final trim position. In some venues, the height of the *Beam to Floor* may be so great, that it is not possible for the chain hook to connect directly to the bridle *Apex*. In this case, a stinger may need to be added to make up the additional distance. The stinger essentially makes up the *Drop* if the distance is too great. *Headroom* is the distance from the *Drop* to the final *Trim Height* of the truss including lighting equipment. *Cable Slack* occurs when tension is placed on the bridle legs as the load is lifted. Generally, *Cable Slack* is usually only a few inches but needs to be considered when *Headroom* is at a premium.

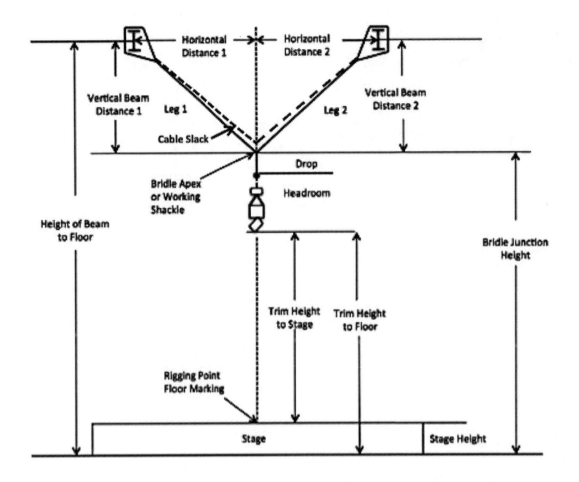

All this may seem a lot to consider when loading in equipment into a space, but it is not as difficult as it may seem. Drafting a similar sectional as the one shown above is a good way to begin. Start with the known basics; the *Height of Beams to Floor* and the *Horizontal Distance between the Beams*. Perusal of the production plans and requirements will help you determine if the production can fit into your space. *Trim* and *Stage Height* are a going to have basic minimal requirements. Determining *Headroom* will be an important consideration if a bridle angle over 120 degrees is to be avoided. Again, it may be necessary to consult with a qualified engineer, as there **will** be additional vertical, horizontal and diagonal forces placed on the venue's roof structure that structural drawings may not show. *"Bringing down the house"* is literally not an option.

As stated earlier, bridles are typically hung in pairs and converge to create a new anchor point (apex) somewhere between two existing anchor points. While bridles can have more than two "legs," this chapter will only deal with the two and three-legged variety. Each leg of a bridle can hang from different heights, be different lengths, and be at different angles. Since we will be computing the lengths of bridle legs, we will call one Leg 1 (L1) and the other one Leg 2 (L2). When we move on to three-legged bridles, we will add Leg 3 (L3).

Two-Legged Bridle Lengths

Let's begin with two-legged bridles. In order to compute the length of each leg, we will need to know a) how low the bridle point is below the anchor point for that leg of the bridle (vertical distance), and b) how far the bridle point is away from the anchor point for that leg of the bridle in a horizontal distance. See drawing below.

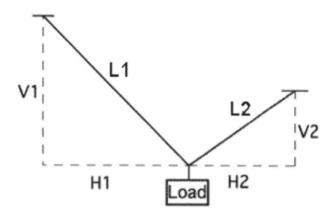

By knowing the V and H lengths, we can compute the length of L (the hypotenuse of the right triangle) by using the Pythagorean Theorem $A^2 + B^2 = C^2$, only we will use $V^2 + H^2 = L^2$, converted into the equation $L = \sqrt{H^2 + V^2}$

Example: Calculate the lengths of L1 and L2 where, V1 = 10', H1 = 4', V2 = 6, and H2 = 3'.

L1 = 10 [X^2] [+] 4 [X^2] [=][$\sqrt{x}$]

L1 = 10.77 feet

L2 = 6 [X^2] [+] 3 [X^2] [=][$\sqrt{x}$]

L2 = 6.7 feet

When working with any type of bridle problem, I like to draw a diagram, similar to the one above, and label the known distances. I find it much easier to solve most rigging problems when I can "see" what it looks like graphically. Try it and see if it helps you.

But what is the angle of the bridle?

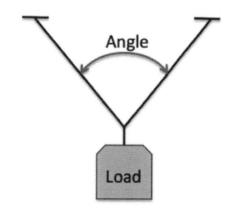

For those of you who are really interested in this question, here is the equation:

$$Angle = \left(Arctangent\left(\tfrac{H1}{V1}\right)\right) + \left(Arctangent\left(\tfrac{H2}{V2}\right)\right)$$

So, to find the angle of the bridles above, using a TI-30XA calculator, we do the following:

Angle = [ON/C] 4 [÷] 10 [=] [2nd] [TAN]   Note: Write the result down (21.8)

[ON/C] 3 [÷] 6 [=] [2nd] [TAN]   Note: Write the result down (26.56)

Angle = 21.8 [+] 26.56

Angle = 48.36 degrees

So, why is it important to know the bridle angle? There are at least two reasons. First, it is a good practice to keep the angle of pull on a shackle to 90 degrees or less, unless headroom is an issue. Secondly, bridle angles greater than 120 degrees (called a "flat bridle") will put a greater force on the support point/structure than the weight load being supported. In fact, a flat bridle can easily create huge (unsafe) forces. It is a lot easier to see/estimate a 90-degree angle than a 120-degree angle. Checking bridle angles is easy and you don't even need a protractor to do so. The illustrations below show how you can check a bridle angle in the field without the use of anything but your hand. The angles shown are close. If you try it with a protractor, you will see how close they really are.

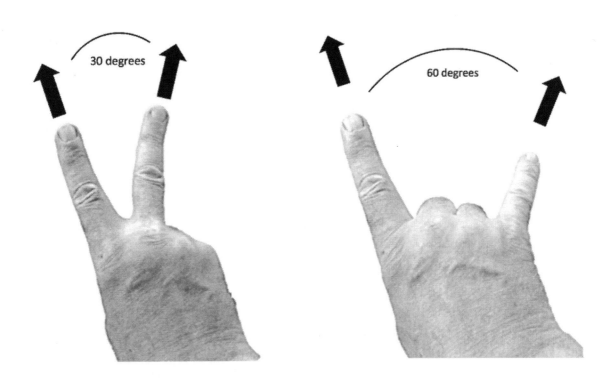

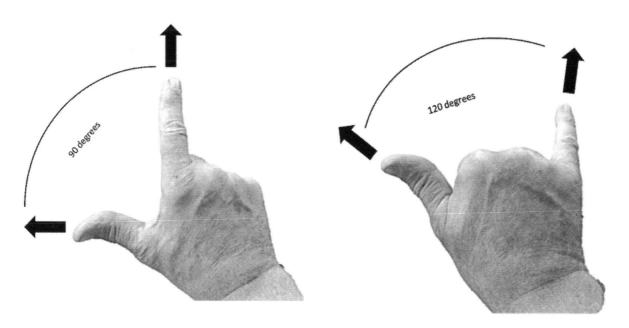

Tension on Two Legged Bridles

Now that you know how to compute the lengths of the bridle legs, you can compute the load on each leg. But before we do that, let's discuss the angle between the two legs. We said in the introduction to this unit that bridles are used to create a new anchor point between two existing hanging points, and this is true. It is also true that the two bridle legs share the load being lifted (but not always equally), and bridles can be used to reduce the load on anchor points. You should realize that it is possible to use different combinations of bridle lengths to get the bridle point at the same horizontal position, relative to the existing hanging points, but at different vertical relations to the existing anchor points. In many cases, it is desirable to have the bridle point as high as possible so that it is not seen. But, the higher you place this point, the wider the bridle angle (angle between the two bridle legs) and the greater the forces on the bridle legs. As a general rule, the bridle angle should not exceed 120 degrees. Remember, if the bridle angle is greater than 120 degrees, then the load on at least one of the legs will be greater than the load being lifted. Bridles with very wide angles (flat bridles) can put tremendous loads on their hanging points. Also, some beams are designed to hold force in a particular direction (usually a vertical direction) and may not tolerate horizontal or resultant forces.

To compute the tension on the two bridles, we use the equations:

$$Tension\ on\ L1 = Load\ \times \frac{L1\ \times\ H2}{(V1\ \times\ H2) + (V2\ \times\ H1)}$$

$$Tension\ on\ L2 = Load\ \times \frac{L2\ \times\ H1}{(V1\ \times\ H2) + (V2\ \times\ H1)}$$

Before you start screaming, "I can't remember all of that!" relax and take a deep breath. I will soon teach you a trick that will make it fairly easy to remember. But before we get to that, draw a diagram like the one below.

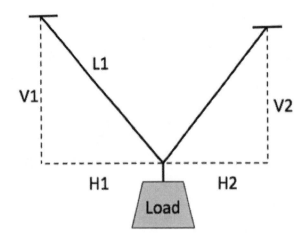

Now, add the following values to your diagram:

L1 = 5'   L2 = 6.7'
V1 = 4'   V2 = 3'
H1 = 3'   H2 = 6'
Load = 500 lb

This will help you to be able to quickly find the values that you need.

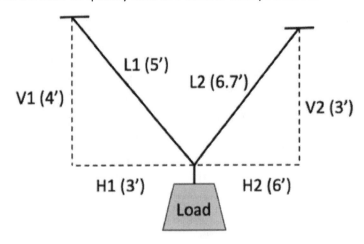

Below is the equation for finding the tension on Leg 1, but I have made the first part of the equation **BOLD**, and I have added an arrow to the diagram so that you can visualize which two numbers are multiplied.

$$\text{Tension on L1} = \text{Load} \times \frac{\mathbf{L1 \times H2}}{(V1 \times H2) + (V2 \times H1)}$$

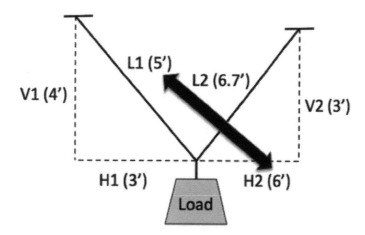

Since you want to find the tension on L1, the "trick" is to begin by multiplying L1 (high) by the "low" side of Leg 2 (which is H2). If you wanted to find the tension on L2, you would multiply L2 (high) by the "low" side of the L1 triangle, which would be H1. Got it? So plugging in these variables in our equation we get:

$$\text{Tension on L1} = \text{Load} \times \frac{5 \times 6}{(V1 \times H2) + (V2 \times H1)}$$

$$\text{Tension on L1} = \text{Load} \times \frac{30}{(V1 \times H2) + (V2 \times H1)}$$

Next, we want to figure out what we divide this number by. This is actually very easy to remember. We just need to remember that we multiply V on one side by H on the other, and add the two numbers together. You can also remember that you always multiply one "high" side and one "low" side, if that helps you. So, let's look at the first pair of numbers for this section of the equation:

$$\text{Tension on L1} = \text{Load} \times \frac{30}{(4 \times 6) + (V2 \times H1)}$$

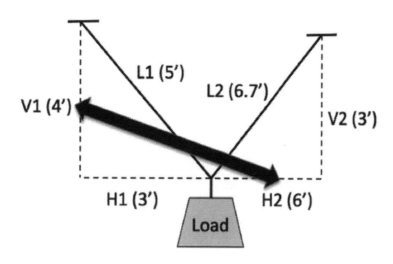

And now the second pair of numbers:

$$\text{Tension on L1} = \text{Load} \times \frac{30}{(4 \times 6) + (3 \times 3)}$$

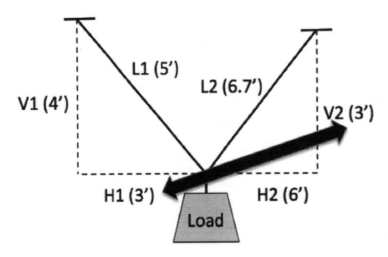

Again, one "high" side and one "low" side. So, now finish solving the equations.

$$\text{Tension on L1} = \text{Load} \times \frac{30}{(4 \times 6) + (3 \times 3)}$$

$$\text{Tension on L1} = \text{Load} \times \frac{30}{24 + 9}$$

$$\text{Tension on L1} = \text{Load} \times \frac{30}{33}$$

$$\text{Tension on L1} = \text{Load} \times .909$$

Finally, we just plug in the Load and multiply.

$$\text{Tension on L1} = \mathbf{500} \times .909$$

$$\mathbf{Tension\ on\ L1 = 454.5\ lb}$$

Let's now calculate the tension on Leg 2.

$$\text{Tension on L2} = \text{Load} \times \frac{\text{L2} \times \text{H1}}{(\text{V1} \times \text{H2}) + (\text{V2} \times \text{H1})}$$

Again, we multiply the part that we are trying to find the tension on (now, L2) by the "low" number on the other side of the diagram. Substituting these values we get:

$$\text{Tension on L2} = \text{Load} \times \frac{\mathbf{6.7 \times 3}}{(V1 \times H2) + (V2 \times H1)}$$

$$\text{Tension on L2} = \text{Load} \times \frac{\mathbf{20.1}}{(V1 \times H2) + (V2 \times H1)}$$

Did you notice that bottom part of this equation is exactly the same as the equation for finding the tension on Leg 1? Because they are the same, we do not have to re-calculate those numbers. We can plug-in the results from our first equation (33) and we have:

$$\text{Tension on L2} = \text{Load} \times \frac{20.1}{33}$$

$$\text{Tension on L2} = \text{Load} \times .609$$

$$\text{Tension on L2} = 500 \times .609$$

Tension on L2 = 304.5 lb

This is one of the most difficult problems in this chapter. The most common mistake is multiplying when you should divide or dividing when you should multiply, so work on keeping those straight. Next, we will look at some other situations that may arise with bridles.

Tension of Bridle Legs when one Anchor Point is Below the Apex

Most bridles will have both anchor points (beams) above the apex, as we have shown so far. However, occasionally there will be a situation where one of the beams is even with or below the apex. When a bridle leg is even with the apex, it is called a Horizontal Breast-line. For now, let's discuss how to calculate the tension on the legs when one anchor point is below the apex.

The equation is identical to the one discussed earlier:

$$Tension\ on\ L1 = Load \times \frac{L1 \times H2}{(V1 \times H2) + (V2 \times H1)}$$

$$Tension\ on\ L2 = Load \times \frac{L2 \times H1}{(V1 \times H2) + (V2 \times H1)}$$

However, there is one very important twist to the equations - if an anchor point is below the apex, then the Vertical distance for the leg that is below the apex is now a negative number instead of a positive number. For example, the bridle arrangement below, V2 is a negative distance.

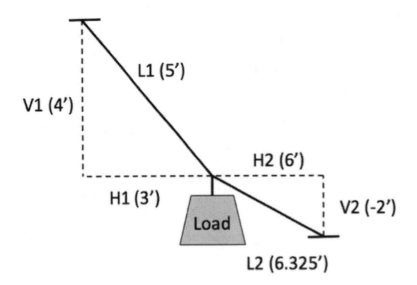

Let's calculate the tension on Leg 1 (Load is 500 lb).

$$\text{Tension on L1} = 500 \ \times \ \frac{5 \ \times \ 6}{(4 \ \times \ 6) + (-2 \ \times \ 3)}$$

$$\text{Tension on L1} = 500 \ \times \ \frac{30}{(24) + (-6)}$$

$$\text{Tension on L1} = 500 \ \times \ \frac{30}{18}$$

$$\text{Tension on L1} = 500 \ \times \ 1.66667$$

Tension on L1 $= 833.333$ lb

So, the first thing we see is that the tension on the bridle leg that is above the apex is greater than the Load. This is very important to realize because it is easy for the tension on this leg to be substantial.

Now, let's calculate the load on L2.

$$\text{Tension on L2} = 500 \ \times \ \frac{6.325 \ \times \ 3}{(4 \ \times \ 6) + (-2 \ \times \ 3)}$$

$$\text{Tension on L2} = 500 \ \times \ \frac{18.975}{(24) + (-6)}$$

$$\text{Tension on L2} = 500 \ \times \ \frac{18.975}{18}$$

Tension on L2 $= 500 \times 1.054$

Tension on L2 $= 527$ lb

Here again the tension is greater than the Load. Whenever you have a beam that is below the apex, you must calculate this tension on these beams to ensure that you are not creating a dangerous situation.

Tension on a Horizontal Breast-line

A breast-line is a unique type of bridle leg. It is a rope or cable that runs horizontally and is used to swing/breast a hanging object out from directly beneath its suspension point(s). For example, you might breast an electric upstage or downstage in order to keep another piece of scenery away from the lighting instruments. Because this line (or lines) runs horizontally, it is not lifting the load, just pulling it out of alignment. There is no vertical force on the bridle attachment point. To compute the tension on a breastline, we use this simple equation:

$$Horizontal\ Force = Load \ \times \ \frac{H1}{V1}$$

This equation is very similar to the one that was used in Chapter 6 for finding the Horizontal Force on a hanging point:

$$HF1 = VF1 \ \times \ \frac{H1}{V1}$$

Below is a diagram of this configuration.

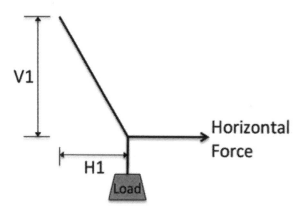

Example: Calculate the horizontal force on a breastline where V1 is 30', H1 is 2', and the Load = 700 pounds.

Before starting, note that in the earlier equations where you wanted to find the tension on the bridle, you took the length of the bridle (L) and divided it by the length of one of the other sides. Since in this problem you want to find the tension on the horizontal line, start with the length of the horizontal distance (H1) and then divide it by the length of the other side (V1). This rule for knowing which side to start your division can help make it easier to learn the equation. So, plugging the numbers into our equation, you get:

$$\text{Horizontal Force} = \text{Load} \times \frac{2}{30}$$

$$\text{Horizontal Force} = \text{Load} \times 0.0666$$

$$\text{Horizontal Force} = 700 \times 0.0666$$

Horizontal Force $= 46.62$ lb

Tension on the Supporting Leg

When you breast a load out of its normal hanging position, the tension on the supporting line will increase - the tension on the line will be greater than the load. The formula for calculating the tension on this line (or leg) is:

$$Tension\ on\ L1 = Load\ \times \frac{L1}{V1}$$

Horizontal and Vertical Tension on Anchor Points

In the Introduction to this unit, you learned that the tension on each bridle leg creates vertical and horizontal forces on anchor points. While it is not usually critical to calculate these forces, it is not difficult to do.

The equations for calculating the vertical force on the anchor points are:

$$VF1 = \frac{V1 \times H2 \times \text{Load}}{(V1 \times H2) + (V2 \times H1)}$$

$$VF2 = \text{Load} - VF1$$

Because the combined vertical forces on these two anchor points must equal the load, once you have calculated VF1, it is very easy to calculate VF2.

Using the same bridle setup as above, calculate the vertical force on each anchor point.

$$VF1 = \frac{V1 \times H2 \times \text{Load}}{(V1 \times H2) + (V2 \times H1)}$$

$$VF1 = \frac{4 \times 6 \times 500}{(4 \times 6) + (3 \times 3)}$$

$$VF1 = \frac{12000}{24 + 9}$$

$$VF1 = \frac{12000}{33}$$

VF1 = 363. 64 lb

$$VF2 = Load - VF1$$

$$VF2 = 500 - 363.64$$

VF2 = 136. 36 lb

The equations for calculating the horizontal force on the anchor points are:

$$HF1 = VF1 \times \frac{H1}{V1}$$

$$HF2 = VF2 \times \frac{H2}{V2}$$

So...

$$HF1 = VF1 \times \frac{H1}{V1}$$

$$HF1 = 363.64 \times \frac{3}{4}$$

$$HF1 = 363.64 \times .75$$

HF1 = 272. 73 lb

$$HF2 = VF2 \times \frac{H2}{V2}$$

$$HF2 = 136.36 \times \frac{6}{2}$$

$$HF2 = 136.36 \times 3$$

HF2 = 272. 72 lb

The values for HF1 and HF2 MUST be the same, or nearly the same, depending on the rounding of numbers. In this case, the values are statistically equal. Another formula for calculating the Horizontal Force (on both points) is:

$$HF = \text{Tension on L1} \times \frac{H1}{L1}$$

Pick the formula that works best for you.

Tension on a Bridle Leg when the Load is Off Center

Let's combine some of the formulas for calculating bridle tensions and horizontal breastlines. We will next look at the forces involved if the bridle load is off the center of the apex and the angles between L1 and L3, and L3 and L2 are less than 180 degrees as shown.

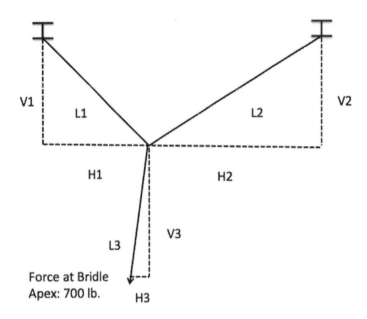

This illustration looks pretty complex, but the equation is not that much different than the equation for calculating bridle tensions we examined eariler. The equation for calculating these tensions are:

Tension L1 = Force (L1/L3) ((V3H2-V2H3)/(V1H2+V2H1))

Tension L2 = Force (L2/L3) ((V3H1+V1H3)/V1H2+V2H1))

Not too different. We have simply added a force (L3) at the bridle apex that is on the same side as Leg 1.

Example: Using the formula above, solve for the following:

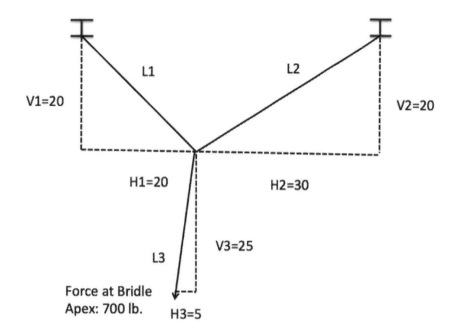

Tension L1 = 700 (28.28/25.49) ((25*30-20*5)/(20*30+20*20))
Tension L2 = 700 (36.05/25.49) ((25*20+20*5)/20*30+20*20))

Tension L1 = 700 (1.10) ((750-40)/(600+400))
Tension L2 = 700 (1.41) ((500+100)/600+400))

Tension L1 = 700 (1.10) ((710)/(1000))
Tension L2 = 700 (1.41) ((600)/1000))

Tension L1 = 700 (1.10) ((.71))
Tension L2 = 700 (1.41) ((.6))

Tension L1 = 700 (.781)
Tension L2 = 700 (.846)

Tension L1 = 546.7
Tension L2 = 592.2

Using the formula for calculating Bridle Angles discussed earlier, we get 101.3 degrees.

Flat Bridles

In our discussion on bridle angles, we said, "bridle angles greater than 120 degrees (called a "flat bridle") will put a greater force on the support point/structure than the weight load being supported." A flat bridle CAN easily create astronomical forces on the bridle legs. The illustrations below show the load on each bridle leg when the bridle angle is 120 degrees and when the angle exceeds 120 degrees.

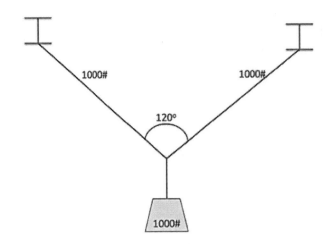

When the bridle angle is 120 degrees, the load on each of the legs will be the same as the load being lifted.

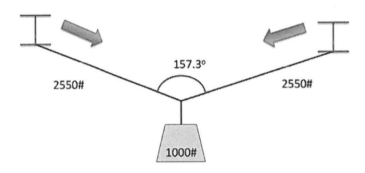

When the bridle angle exceeds 120 degrees, the load on each of the legs will become astronomical. So will the horizontal force on the beams.

So, if the rule is NOT to exceed 120 degrees, why be concerned with flat bridles, after all aren't tight–rope walkers (aerialists) are essentially walking on a flat bridle?

On extremely rare occasions, flat bridles may be unavoidable. An example of this would be a situation where headroom is extremely limited; ballroom and convention centers are a good example. In each instance, the rigging of flat bridles must be handled with extreme care. Structural engineers **must** be consulted in each case, as horizontal forces will be placed on the building's support structure that was never intended. Load cells should also be used to monitor the load forces on both the building and the hardware. Obviously, the load should be extremely "light". In addition, you're not going to be able to rig the bridle apex using your standard anchor shackle, as the bridle legs will inevitably side load the shackle. In this instance, a pear ring rigged at the bridle apex will be necessary to serve as a collector.

Now that we know why flat bridles are not recommended, let's look at the math involved. Find the tension on a slack line/cable track supporting a load.

Step 1: Assuming this slack line is a bridle, find the bridle angle. The equation for this was discussed earlier in this chapter.

Step 2: Use the equation below for finding the tension on the slack line.

Tension = Load / (Sine of Angle / ((Sine (Angle/2))

Example 1: If the Load = 200 lb and the Angle = 160 degrees, then

Tension = 200 / (Sine of 160 / Sine of 80)

Tension = 200 / (0.342020143 / 0.984807753)

Tension = 200 / 0.347296355

Tension = 575.877 pounds

Example 2: If the Load = 200 lb and the Angle = 170 degrees, then

Tension = 200 / (Sine of 170 / Sine of 85)

Tension = 200 / (0.173648178 / 0.996194698)

Tension = 200 / 0.174311485

Tension = 1,147.37 pounds

This equation does not take into consideration the weight of the rope/line. You will have to add the total weight of the line to the Load.

Also, these numbers are for static loads. If the load moves/bounces, the tension will be much greater.

Three-Legged Bridles
A two-legged bridle uses two cables (or legs) to create a new hanging point where the two legs join. This junction point (bridle point) is on the same plane as the attachment points for the two legs, just lower and somewhere between the two existing attachment points. A three-legged bridle is used when the desired bridle point is not directly between two existing attachment points and must be positioned between three points. This is common in spaces where the existing attachment points are scattered about. When the three legs are the proper length, a new hanging point is created that is in the desired location above the stage.

Calculating the lengths of the legs on a three-legged bridle is tricky, and there are several methods to do it. Here is one method.

First, start with a plan view of the beams and the points (P1, P2, P3, and P4, with P4 being the apex). I have overlaid it with three right triangles (in different shades of grey), one for each of the three bridle legs. Note: the hypotenuse of each of each triangle corresponds to the position of a bridle leg.

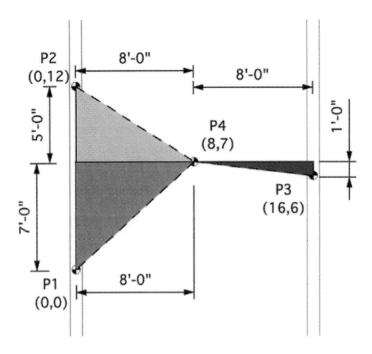

Using this drawing, Let's write down the X and Y lengths for the two non-hypotenuse sides of each triangle.

L1 X: __8__   Y: __7__

L2 X: __8__   Y: __5__

L3 X: __8__   Y: __1__

The next step is to find the Z distance for each leg. If all of these beams are 50 feet above the deck and the Apex is at 35 feet, then the Z distance is 15 feet for each. Let's complete our table.

L1 X: __8__   Y: __7__   Z: __15__

L2 X: __8__   Y: __5__   Z: __15__

L3 X: __8__   Y: __1__   Z: __15__

Now that our table is complete, let's calculate the length of each leg. The equation for doing this is:

$$Leg\ length = \sqrt{X^2 + Y^2 + Z^2}$$

Let's plug in the numbers and calculate the leg lengths.

$$Leg\ 1 = \sqrt{8^2 + 7^2 + 15^2}$$

$$Leg\ 1 = \sqrt{64 + 49 + 225}$$

$$Leg\ 1 = \sqrt{338}$$

Leg 1 = 18.38 feet

$$Leg\ 2 = \sqrt{8^2 + 5^2 + 15^2}$$

$$Leg\ 2 = \sqrt{64 + 25 + 225}$$

$$Leg\ 2 - \sqrt{314}$$

Leg 2 = 17.72 feet

$$Leg\ 3 = \sqrt{8^2 + 1^2 + 15^2}$$

$$Leg\ 3 = \sqrt{64 + 1 + 225}$$

$$Leg\ 3 = \sqrt{290}$$

Leg 3 = 117.02 feet

H-Bridles and Diamond Bridles
Although rare, H-Bridles and Diamond Bridles are rigged when there are obstructions that need to be avoided.

H-Bridles
H-Bridles utilized two apex points and are rigged when there are two equal loads to be supported on the ends of a truss. The stingers or hoist hooks are attached at the apexes just as we saw with the two-point brides. They are useful when the horizontal distance between the I-beams is too great for traditional bridling.

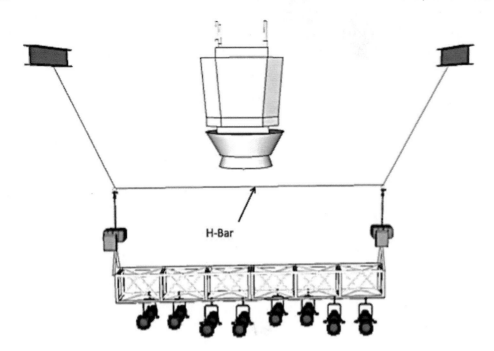

The danger with H-Bridles is that you must be careful not to exceed the 120-degree angle on the legs and plan for any obstructions above the H-Bar Leg. When raising or lowering truss, the motors must run equally to keep the truss from shifting horizontally or vertically off center. A Uniform Distributed Load or UDL is recommended in order to keep the load from shifting horizontally as well.

Calculating the Tension on the H-Bar
We discussed earlier in the chapter the formula for calculating the tension on horizontal breastlines. We will use this formula to calculate the tension on the H-bar of the H-Bridle.

If you recall, we used this simple equation to calculate the tension:

$$Horizontal\ Force = Load \ \times \ \frac{H1}{V1}$$

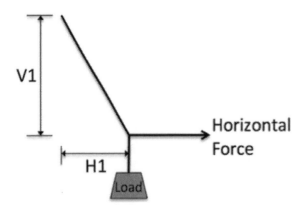

We will apply the above diagram to each of the H-Bridle Legs and simply multiply by two in order to account for each leg of the H-Bridle and get the tension on the H-Bar. Remember, the breastline runs horizontally, it is not lifting the load, just pulling it out of alignment. There is no vertical force on the bridle attachment point. The force is on the bridle junction.

Example: Calculate the horizontal force on an H-Bar where V1 and V2 is 30', H1 and H2 is 2', and the Load on each apex = 700 pounds.

$$\text{Leg 1 Horizontal Force} = \text{Load} \times \frac{2}{30}$$

$$\text{Leg 1 Horizontal Force} = \text{Load} \times 0.0666$$

$$\text{Leg1 Horizontal Force} = 700 \times 0.0666$$

Horizontal Force on Leg 1 = 46.62 lb

Since Leg 2 is identical to Leg 1, we simply multiply be 2 in order to find the tension on the H-Bar.

Horizontal Force on H Bar = 2 x 46.62 = 93.24lb
Simple enough. Let's take a look at *Diamond Bridles.*

Diamond Bridles
Like *H-Bridles, Diamond Bridles* are used when there are obstructions that must be rigged around. Again, we will the formula for *Horizontal Breastlines* to calculate the tension on the breastlines. Because there are two separate breastlines, they will not be multiplied by two as we did with the H-Bridle. Note that the breastlines are horizontal and not angled.

$$Horizontal\ Force = Load \times \frac{H1}{V1}$$

Example: Calculate the horizontal force on the *Diamond Bridle* where V1 is 20' and H1 is 5', and the Load on the apex = 1000 pounds. Since we are looking for the load on only one of the legs and both legs are supporting the load, the load on Leg 1 will be 500 lb or ½ the total load.

$$\text{Leg 1 Horizontal Force} = \text{Load} \times \frac{5}{20}$$

$$\text{Leg 1 Horizontal Force} = \text{Load} \times .25$$
$$\text{Leg1 Horizontal Force} = 500 \times .25$$

Horizontal Force on Leg 1 = 125 lb

Since Leg 2 is identical to Leg 1, the Horizontal Force will be the same.

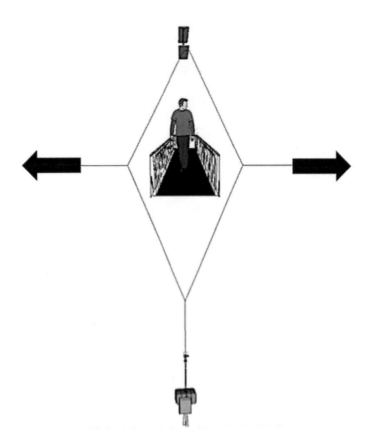

If the breastlines are angled upward as shown in the illustration below, then the forces at the apex are off-center and we will use the formula for *Calculating Leg Tensions when the Load is Off Cente*r.

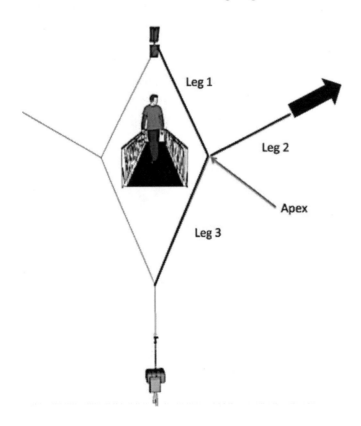

Chapter: 6
Two-Point Bridles in an Arena

In Chapter 5, we discussed using the Pythagorean Theorem to calculate the lengths of bridle legs. While it is true that you need to know the Pythagorean Theorem and its variations to calculate the lengths of bridle legs, in practice, it is a lot more complicated than was described in Chapter 5. In that chapter, we looked at the "theoretical method" of calculating bridle legs. In this chapter we will discuss the practical aspects of calculating and making a bridle for use in an arena.

Below is a diagram that illustrates a theoretical bridle problem like we looked at in Chapter 5.

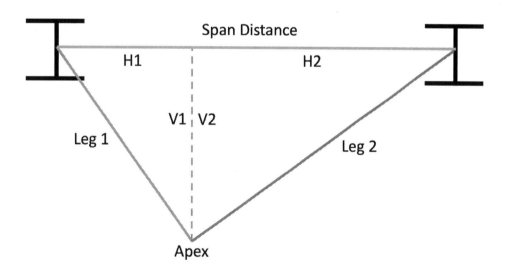

The first major issue with this problem with this illustration is that it does not accurately show how the bridle legs attach to the beams. In reality, a steel sling is wrapped around each beam, with burlap used to pad the sharp edges of the beam. As shown below.

When a tour comes to an arena, they bring lots of rigging hardware with them. Common lengths of steel slings that they typically bring may include some combination of the following slings: 5', 10', 20,' 30' and 50' lengths. They also typically bring 1.5', 2', or 2.5' lengths of steel (called "dog bones")., Baskets and bridle legs will be made from a combination of these standard-length slings. When a bridle leg is an "odd length," one that cannot just be made from the standard lengths listed above, links of Special Theatrical Alloy Chain (STAC) or Theatrical Rigging Alloy Chain (TRAC) are added to make the desired length bridle leg (or as close as possible). Screw-pin anchor shackles are used connect the slings and chains together to make the bridles, as shown in the diagram above.

To help understand how these two diagrams are related, let's overlay the last two images...

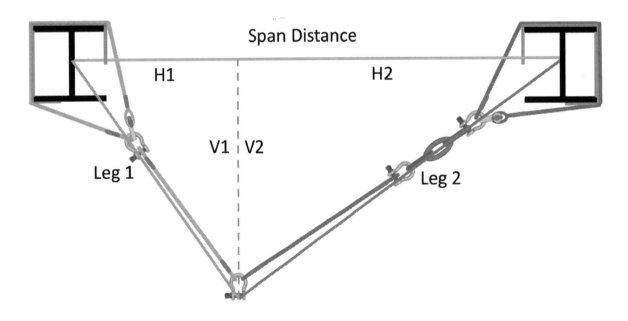

Note: STAC chain is typically ONLY used on the long leg of a bridle.

This image helps explain a few important factors:

1. While the legs do not physically connect to the center of the beams, leg measurements will assume that they are attached to these points on the beams.
2. The distance from the center of each beam to the upper shackle pin on the leg is part of the Total Leg Length.
3. The apex shackle is part of both bridle legs.

Before we move forward, you must know the Effective Length of the Hitch (ELOH) of the basket around the beam. This distance is determined by both the size and shape of the beam, and the length of the basket steel.

The Effective Length of the Hitch (ELOH) is the distance from the CENTER of the beam (no matter the shape) to the shackle pin that connects to the leg steel. This distance is generally measured in inches. Once you know this measurement, you can use it to help determine the length of Leg #1.

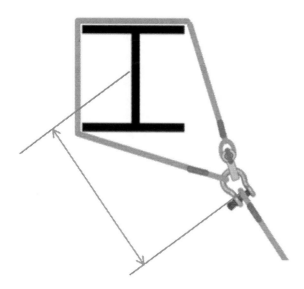

One way to know the ELOH is to physically measure it. You only need to measure this distance once for each length of steel that you use for a basket on a particular beam, then use this distance every time you use that basket length on that beam. The ELOH can be easily calculated if you have an I-beam, H-beam, or C-beam. But it is difficult to calculate if you have a Round beam, T-beam, or inverted T-beam. In the bridle problem that we will solve in this chapter, we will simply assign the ELOH a length, but in the next lesson we will look at how the calculate the ELOH. Before we get started working an example, a few important things to remember are …

- Typically, we will make the shorter of the two legs, Leg #1.
- Typically, the shorter leg will not include any Deck (STAC) Chain.
- For each piece of steel or deck chain in the leg, we will need 1 connecting shackle. If the leg has only one piece of steel, that shackle is the Apex shackle.

- For my method of calculating the leg steel, the House Rigger assigns a steel length to Leg #1 (this is typically a length that can be made up using the steel available from the steel inventory from the tour). This is typically 5', 10', 15', 20', etc. This length is typically greater than the horizontal distance from Beam #1 to the Apex shackle (H1). For example: if the horizontal distance from Beam #1 to the Apex shackle is 5'-6", I might choose a 10' long steel sling for this leg.

Now, let look at a bridle problem...

Our arena has beams that are 24 feet apart, horizontally. It has both low beams where the top of the beams are 86'-4" above the floor, and high beams where the top of the beams are 96-5" above the floor. These beams are all "T" or inverted "T" beams that are 8" tall and 13" wide. The ELOH with a 5' basket is 24" (2 feet). The show coming in has 3/8" dia. steel in the following lengths: 2', 5', 10', 20', 30'. It also has 3-foot-long deck (STAC) chains (although it is called a 3-foot-long length, it is actually 37.4 inches long). The chain hoists have chains that allow a maximum apex height of 70' above the floor. And the Production Rigger wants the apexes to be "as high as possible." So, your job is to figure out how to make each bridle.

For our bridle problem, we want the apex to be 8'-0" upstage of Beam #1 (16'-0" downstage from Beam #2). We also want the basket to be on the low steel for Beam #1 (86'-4" above the floor), but on the high steel for Beam #2 (96'-5" above the floor). Something like this...

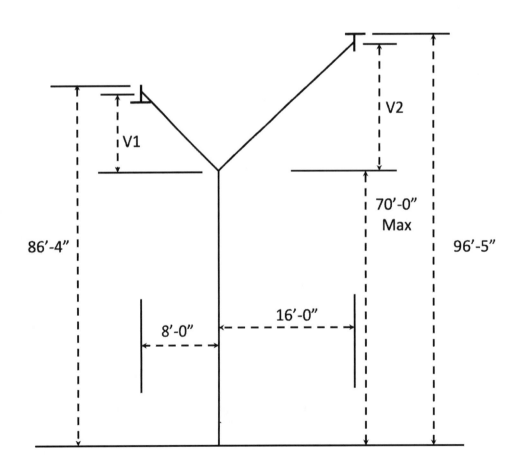

Note: Some dimensions/distances that we will use to solve this problem are in feet and others in inches (and some in both). Since calculation must be done with all of the dimensions in the same unit of measurement, that means that at different times you will have to convert feet to inches (by multiplying by 12) and inches to feet (by dividing by 12) to get all of the dimensions into the same unit of measurement. Watch closely as we go through the math in this lesson and take note of when units are converted. The first conversion takes place it the next step.

To calculate L1's length, we would need to know both H1 and V1. Unfortunately, we only currently know H1 (8'-0"). However, since we know the maximum height of the apex is 70'-0", let's set the desired apex height at 65'-0" (we know that the final apex height will be a little greater than 65', but it should be less than 70'). Now, calculate V1 using the equation:

V1 = Beam 1 height above floor – (Beam Height/2) – Apex Height.

So...

V1 = 86.33333 – (0.666667/2) – 65
V1 = 86.33333 – 0.333333 – 65
V1 = 21 feet

Now that we know both H1 and V1, we can use the Pythagorean Theorem to calculate L1.

L1 = SQRT $(8^2 + 21^2)$
L1 = SQRT (64 + 441)
L1 = SQRT (505)
L1 = 22.4722 feet

This is the TOTAL length of L1. Now, subtract the 24" (2 feet) for ELOH of the basket, to get the **Steel Length of L1 = 20.4722 feet.**

The next step is to calculate the ACTUAL length of the steel we will use for this leg.

Remember, every piece of steel requires one shackle. And a shackle is 2.375" long (inside length) or 0.1979 feet. So, the revised (actual) **L1 Steel Length would be 20.1979** (we round to this length, ignoring the rest of the calculated L1 length, because we do not want to only use existing steel (on Deck Chain) in this leg.

So, L1 will consist of a 5' backet and a 20-foot-long piece of steel.

Next, add back in the 2-foot ELOH to get the new **Total Length of L1: 22.1979 feet.**

Now that we know L1 and H1, we can recalculate the new V1.

$V1 = SQRT (22.1979^2 - 8^2)$
$V1 = SQRT (492.7467 - 64)$
$V1 = SQRT (428.7467)$
V1 = 20.7062 feet

Now, we can calculate the Apex Height.

Apex Height = Beam #1 Height above Floor – (Beam Height/2) – V1
Apex Height = 86.33333 – (0.66667/2) – 20.7062
Apex Height = 86.33333 – 0.33333 – 20.7062
Apex Height = 65.2938 or 65'- 4"

Next, calculate V2. If the height of the top pf Beam #2 above the floor is the same as Beam #1, you can skip this step because V2 will be the same as V1. In our example, they are not the same, so...

V2 = Beam #2 Height above Floor – (Beam Height/2) – Apex Height
V2 = 96.41666 – (0.66667/2) – 65.2938
V2 = 96.41666 – 0.33333 – 65.2938
V2 = 30.7896 feet

Next, we need to calculate the Total Length of L2.
$L2 = SQRT (16^2 + 30.7896^2)$
$L2 = SQRT (256 + 947.9994)$
$L2 = SQRT (1203.9974)$
L2 = 34.6987

Next, subtract the ELOH (2 feet) to get the steel needed for Leg #2.
L2 = 34.6987 – 2
L2 = 32.6987

Because L2 is less than 50' and greater than 30', subtract the length of a 30' steel plus one shackle (0.1979 feet) from L2.
L2 = 32.6987 – 30.1979
L2 = 2.5008 feet

Before we move on to the next step, we need to discuss tolerances and choices. we have a saying, "You are always looking for the BEST solution to a problem, not the PERFECT solution to the problem, because the perfect solution probably does not exist." So how does this saying apply here?

In the last step the remainder or L2 was 2.5008 feet. Since this distance is greater than 2.1979 feet, we know that we could use a 2' piece of steel as the next part of our leg. But, since this distance is also less than 37.4 inches (plus 0.1979 inches for the connecting shackle) it means that we could make up the remainder of this leg using STAC chain. Which choice do we make?

The fact is, BOTH choices are valid. My choice is to go with the STAC chain because this choice will most likely reduce the number of components in the leg. But it might not give us the closer answer (we would not know unless we did the math for both choices and compared the results). Notice that I said "closer" because it is highly unlikely that either choice will work out mathematically perfectly - with no remainder.

Let's move on at the next step using the Deck Chain. We will discuss tolerances in a bit.

To deal with the deck chain better, let's convert our remainder distance to inches.
L2 = 2.5008 x 12
L2 = 30.0096 inches

Next, subtract 2.375" for the connecting shackle.
L2 = 30.0096 – 2.375
L2 = 27.6346 inches

Finally, determine the number of links of Deck Chain by dividing remaining length by 3.74 (the inside length of one link of STAC chain).

L2 = 7.3889 (rounded to 7 Links)

So, L2 will consist of a 5' backet and a 30-foot steel, plus 7 Links of Deck Chain.

Note: The maximum number of links on a 3-foot-long piece of STAC chain is 10.
Above, we "rounded" 7.3889 to 7, because you cannot use a fraction of a chain link. But what if we had calculated that 6.5127 links were needed? This would also round to 7 links. Any number between 6.50 and 7.4999 would have rounded to 7. What this means is that there are many different calculations that would ultimately give us the same number of links. This is what I mean by "tolerance." This is important to understand, because sometimes the final result for the makeup of legs for different Horizontal Distances from Beam #1, will be the same.

Stingers
As, discussed on Chapter 1, a stinger is a piece of steel that attaches to the apex of a bridle (and hangs vertically) and makes the "hook height" lower than the apex (this is called the "Drop"). Stingers are often used when the calculated apex height is taller than the length of chain in the chain hoist (the chain length is often marked on the top of every motor box). They are often needed in venues where the steel is quite high or when hanging to the high steel in a venue. Below is a chart that provide information on different "even" bridles hung in a venue where the beams are 100' above the floor and are 30' apart, and the chain hoists have 75' of chain. This chart show some of the possible bridle combinations that might work in this situation.

Steel in each Leg	Apex Height	Bridle Angle	Stinger	Hook Height	Total Pieces of Steel
20'	83'-8"	87 degrees	10'	73'-8"	3 (50' total)
22' (20' & 2')	80'-9"	78 degrees	10'	70'-9"	5 (54' total)
25' (20' & 5')	77'-1"	68 degrees	5'	72'-1"	5 (55' total)
30'	71'-3"	56 degrees	0'	71'-5"	2 (60' total)
30' (20' & 10')	71'-3"	56 degrees	0'	71'-3"	5 (60' total)

The House Rigger will look at the steel inventory available, as well as other factors, and choose the best makeup for the bridle.

Conclusion

As promised at the beginning of this lesson, this was a lot more involved than what you learned in Chapter 7; however, you now know exactly what hardware is required to make this bridle. The House Rigger will chalk a diagram on the stage or the arena floor that will indicate how this bridle is to be made, and the down riggers will make the bridle.

There is one more thing that you might wish to calculate for the bridle – the Bridle Angle. This was also described in Chapter 7. In this example, the **Bridle Angle = 49 degrees.**

Because calculating the materials needed to make bridles is fairly time consuming, most House Riggers either use a Bridle Length Cheat Sheet or a rigging app to help them calculate what steel will be needed for the bridles. These tools will be discussed in Chapters 8 & 10. But before we get to that, let's look closer at how to calculate the Effective Length of the Hitch (ELOH) in the next chapter.

Chapter 7:
Calculating the Effective Length of a Hitch

In Chapter 6, we briefly discussed the Effective Length of a Hitch, sometimes called "giveback." In that lesson I said, "The Effective Length of the Hitch (ELOH) is the distance from the CENTER of the beam (no matter the shape) to the shackle pin that connects to the leg steel. This distance is generally measured in inches."

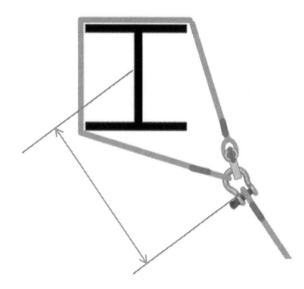

We also said, "One way to know the ELOH is to physically measure it. You only need to measure this distance once for each length of steel that you use for a basket on a particular beam, then use this distance every time you use that basket length on that beam. The ELOH can be easily calculated if you have an I-beam, H-beam, or C-beam. But it is difficult to calculate if you have a Round beam, T-beam, or inverted T-beam." In this lesson we will look at how to calculate the ELOH for all of these beams, plus round beams.

Before we begin, it is important to know the length of the basket. While this may seem simple, it is actually a little more complicated than it appears. First, let's discuss the parts of a basket.

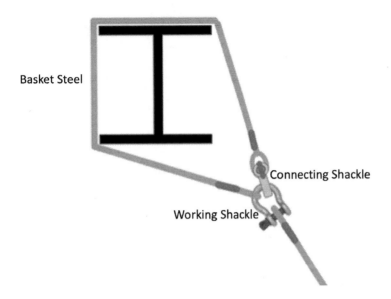

Basket Steel

Connecting Shackle

Working Shackle

A basket has three parts: the basket steel, the working shackle, and the connecting shackle. When we measure the basket's circumference, we start at the pin of the working shackle. Since a 5/8" screw pin anchor shackle has an inside distance of 2.375 inches (or 0.1999 feet) we start with that distance. Next, we add the length of the basket steel. If the basket steel is 5 feet long, we have a total of 5.1979 feet, so far. Next the add the inside length of the connecting shackle, another 0.1979 feet. This gives us a total of 5.3958 feet. Finally, we add the distance from the inside of the connecting shackle to the pin of the working shackle, another 0.1979 feet. This gives us a total of **5.5937 feet or 67.1244 inches**.

If you want to put this in an equation, it would be:

Basket Total Length = Basket Steel Length + (3 x Inside Shackle Length)

No matter the shape of size of the beam, you MUST start by knowing the Basket Length.

In this chapter we will look at three methods of calculating an ELOH. One will be for beams that have relatively rectangular sectional shape (I-beam, H-beam, C-beam, etc.). The second method will be for beams with a relative triangular sectional shape (T and inverted T beams). And the third one will be for round beams (pipe). So, let's get started.

Effective Length of the Hitch (ELOH) – for a Rectangular Beam

The first ting that we need to know to calculate the ELOH is the dimensions of the beam – its height and width. For this problem, let's make the height of the beam 14" and the width of the beam 12". Next, we need to calculate an "adjusted" height and width of the beam. This adjustment is based on two factors:

1) Since we will need to know the circumference of the steel basket wrapping around the beam, we need to consider the diameter of the cable in our calculation, so add the diameter of the cable (0.375") to both the width and the height of the beam.

2) We also need to add the thickness of the burlap padding into our calculation, so add 0.25" to both the width and the height of the beam.

So now, the **Adjusted Beam Height = 14.625"** and the **Adjusted Beam Width = 12.625"**.

To help you understand the next couple of steps look at the diagram below.

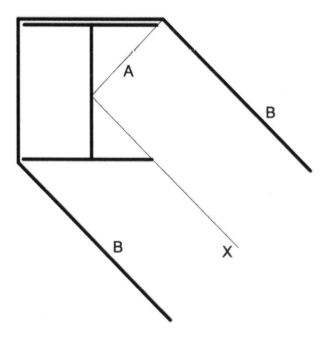

We need to find out the length of B. To do this, we use the equation:

B = (Basket Length – (Adjusted Beam Height + Adjusted Beam Width))/2

So...
B = (67.1244 – (14.625 + 12.625))/2
B = (67.1244 – 27.25)/2
B = 39.8744/2
B = 19.9372

Next, we need to calculate A, using the equation...

A = (SQRT (Adjusted Beam Height^2 + Adjusted Beam Width^2))/2

So...
A = (SQRT (14.625^2 + 12.625^2))/2
A = (SQRT (213.8906 + 159.3906))/2
A = (SQRT (373.28125))/2
A = 19.3205/2
A = 9.6602

Finally, to calculate the ELOH we use the equation:

ELOH = SQRT (B^2 - A^2)
ELOH = SQRT (19.9372^2 – 9.6602^2)
ELOH = SQRT (397.4919 – 93.3203)
ELOH = SQRT (304.1716)
ELOH = 17.44 inches

Effective Length of the Hitch (ELOH) – for a T or Inverted T Beam

Like before, you must know the height and width of the beam. Let's look at an inverted T beam with a height of 8 inches and a width of 13 inches.

Again, we need to calculi the Adjusted Beam Height and the Adjusted Beam Width. These are going to be a little different than the adjusted sizes for a rectangular beam. In this case:

Adjusted Beam Height = Beam Height + Cable Diameter + .25" for padding (or 8.625 inches)

and

Adjusted Beam Width = Beam Width + (Cable Diameter/2) + .125" for padding (or 13.3125 inches)

Start by calculating A, using the equation:

A = SQRT(Adjusted Beam Height^2 + (Adjusted Beam Width/2)^2)

So...
A = SQRT(8.625^2 + (13.3125/2)^2)
A = SQRT(8.625^2 + 6.65625^2)
A = SQRT(74.3906 + 44.30566)
A = SQRT(1186963)
A = 10.894783

Now, calculate B using the equation (using a 5-foot-long basket):

B = Basket Length – A – (Adjusted Beam Width/2)/2

So...
B = (67.1244 – 10.894783 – (13.3125/2))/2
B = (67.1244 – 10.894783 – 6.65625)/2
B = 49.573367/2
B = 24.786984

And finally, calculate the ELOH, using the equation:

ELOH = SQRT (B^2– (Adjusted Beam Height/2)^2)

So...
ELOH = SQRT (24.786984^2 – (8.625/2)^2)
ELOH = SQRT (24.786984^2 – 4.3125^2)
ELOH = SQRT (614.3945758 – 18.59765625)
ELOH = SQRT (595.7969196)
ELOH = 24.41 inches

Effective Length of the Hitch (ELOH) – for a Round Beam

While round beams are the least prevalent of the beam shapes, there are not unheard of, so I have included them in this lesson.

Like with any beam, you must know the size (diameter) of the round beam. Then calculate the Adjusted Diameter by adding the diameter of the cable, plus .025" for padding to the diameter. So, if the diameter of the beam is 16", the Adjusted Diameter would be 16.625 inches.

The next step is to calculate B, by using the following equation:

B = (Basket Length – (Pi * (Adjusted Diameter/2)))/2

So, for the 16" beam and a 5-foot-long basket ...
B = (67.1244 – (3.14159265359 x (16.625/2))/2
B = (67.1244 – (3.14159265359 x 8.3125)/2
B = (67.1244 – 26.11448893)/2
B = 41.0099/2
B = 20.5050

Next, calculate A, using the equation:

A = Adjusted Diameter/2

So...
A = 16.625/2
A = 8.3125

Finally, calculate the ELOH, using the equation:

ELOH = SQRT (B^2 − (A/2)^2)

So...
ELOH = SQRT (20.5050^2 − (8.3125/2)^2)
ELOH = SQRT (20.5050^2 − 4.15625^2)
ELOH = SQRT (420.455025 − 17.274414)
ELOH = SQRT (403.180611)
ELOH = 20.1 inches

Conclusion

So, as you have seen, calculating the ELOH takes quite a few steps. However, there is good and bad news. The good news is that most apps that calculate bridle lengths will calculate the ELOH for you, based on the size of the beam that you tell it you have. The bad news is that most of these bridle apps only calculate the ELOH for I-beams (and other rectangular beams). If you rig in a venue with inverted T beams and use one of these apps, a workaround for this problem is to find (often through trial and error) which rectangular beam has the as ELOH as your inverted T-beams, then specify this beam in the apps' setup. Bridle Pro, a bridle web app that I created (and will discuss in Chapter 10) will calculate the ELOH for all shapes of beams that I have discussed in this lesson.

Chapter 8:

Calculating Bridle Lengths Using Little or No Math

The last several chapters have been very math intensive. This chapter does some of what was covered those chapters but without the need for quite as much math. You might be wondering "why didn't you just cover this and forget about that complicated stuff?" There are two reasons: 1) much of what is covered it this chapter are "shortcuts" to what you learned earlier, and before you learn to "cut corners" you need to know as much as possible about the task; and 2) some of the methods in this chapter "round-off" or "estimate" certain things, so it is not as accurate as the methods you learned earlier. If this chapter had a subtitle, it might be "close is close enough." This will make sense as we get into the chapter.

Much of this chapter is a summary of Fred Breitfelder's book, *Bridle Dynamics for Production Riggers*. This book is available as an eBook (PDF file) that can be purchased from Fred's website http://www.bridledynamics.com. The entire premise of Fred's book is to teach riggers how to calculate bridle lengths quickly and without the need of a calculator. If you like these "old school" rigging techniques, I highly recommend that you purchase Fred's book.

ELOH
Chapter 7 of this book was devoted to leaning how to calculate the Effective Length of a Hitch (ELOH), or what Breitfelder calls the "push." Much of what I covered in that lesson Breitfelder shortens to: ELOH of a 5-foot basket is 2 feet and the ELOH of a 10-foot basket is 3 feet. There was no accounting for the size of the beam, you only have to remember these two lengths.

As you can see, the math just got <u>much</u> simpler; in fact, there is no math at all here. However, the numbers are not as accurate - see what I meant in the first paragraph above? While this may seem like a gross simplification, it is often "close enough" to the actual ELOH for many rigging situations, and it makes determining the bridle lengths much faster and easier. We will use these ELOHs throughout this lesson, so keep keep these numbers in mind.

The Give-and-Take Method of Calculating Bridle Lengths (for beams at the same height)

This method, like many of the methods discussed in this lesson, require that you compare the "desired bridle" to a "reference bridle." This reference bridle has legs that are equal length, so the apex is centered between the beams. The length of the legs is proportional to the Span distance, and are either 100% of the Span distance, 70% of the Span distance (Span distance times 0.7), or 60% of the Span distance (Span distance times 0.6). Which length you choose is dependent on the height of the steel and the minimum hook height required. However, the smaller the percentage, the flatter the bridle, and the greater the force on the beams. So, when possible, use the steepest (longest) bridle possible.

The table below shows the approximate bridle angle using the percentages of the Span discussed above. Remember, the bridle angle should NEVER exceed 120 degrees.

Leg Length compared to Span	Approximate Bridle Angle
100%	60 degrees
70%	90 degrees
60%	120 degrees

We really care about calculating the depth (vertical distance) of the bridle. It is just whatever it is. What we are concerned about is the Span and the Leg Length.

Now that you understand the reference bridles, we need to look at how we use them to calculate the Leg Lengths that will put the apex at the desired horizontal location. This method is called Give-and-Take because we will add length to one bridle leg, and take away the same distance from the other leg. What we need to calculate is the length to add and subtract. To do this we have to know the horizontal distance that the apex is from the center of the Span (where it is in our reference bridle).

Let's work out an example where the Span is 24 feet and the apex need to be 18 feet from one beam and 6 feet from the other. What we really need to see is that the apex is 6 feet from the center of the Span. Now that we have this number (let's call it the "Off-center Distance"), we can plug it into our formula.

The formulas to calculate the leg lengths are slightly different depending on which of the three reference bridles you use. The easiest one is the reference bridle whose legs are 100% of the Span.

Long Leg Length = Span + (Off-center Distance /2)

Short Leg Length = Span - (Off-center Distance /2)

So, plugging the numbers from our example into the formulas, we get:

Long Leg Length = 24 + (6/2)

Long Leg Length = 24 + 3
Long Leg Length = 27 feet

Short Leg Length = 24 - (6 /2)
Short Leg Length = 24 - 3
Short Leg Length = 21 feet

Now, to make these bridle legs we need to subtract the ELOH for the basket lengths. So if we are using 5-foot baskets, we get:

Long Leg Length = 5B/19
Short Leg Length = 5B/25

If the apex is too low when using the 100% reference bridle, then you may have to use either the 70% or 60% reference bridles. When you use these reference bridles, the formulas are:

Long Leg Length = (Span x 0.7) + (Off-center Distance x 0.7)
Short Leg Length = (Span x 0.7) - (Off-center Distance x 0.7)

and

Long Leg Length = (Span x 0.6) + (Off-center Distance x 0.6)
Short Leg Length = (Span x 0.6) - (Off-center Distance x 0.6)

respectively. So, using the same example with a 70% Reference Bridle, we get:

Long Leg Length = (24 x 0.7) + (6 x 0.7)
Long Leg Length = 16.8 + 4.2
Long Leg Length = 21 feet

Short Leg Length = (24 x 0.7) - (6 x 0.7)
Short Leg Length = 16.8 - 4.2
Short Leg Length = 12.6 feet

When we specify the bridle make up, we will probably do more rounding so that we can make them with standard length slings. Doing so, we might get:

Long Leg Length = 5B/20   Note: Remember, a 5-foot bridle gives and ELOH of 2 feet
Short Leg Length = 10B/10   Note: Remember, a 10-foot bridle gives and ELOH of 3 feet

One-Leg-Adjustment Method (for beams at the same height)

The Give-and-Take Method allows us to calculate the lengths of the bridle legs very accurately, but we have to calculate changes to both legs. The One-Leg-Adjustment Method allows us to keep one leg the same length as the Span and only adjust one leg length. While this method has half the math, it is not as accurate as the Give-and-Take Method. Plus, the more you need to move the apex from the center of the Span, the less accurate it becomes. For this reason, this method is best when you need to move the apex 30% or less of the Span distance.

This method can be used two ways:

1) Add length to one leg, or 2) Subtract length from one leg

This method is based on adding or removing a percentage of the Span to or from one leg. To understand both how this works, and the distortion that occurs, look at the tables below. In this example, will will be using a Span of 20 feet, so we start with a reference bridle that has two 20-foot long legs and show changes of one leg in 12" increments (5% changes).

Adding length to one leg

Leg length	Add Length	% of Span	Off-center Distance
20'	0"	100%	0"
21'	12"	105%	12"
22'	12"	110%	12.6"
23'	12"	115%	13.2"
24'	12"	120%	13.8"
25'	12"	125%	14.4"
Total	**60"**		**66"**

Note: Each Off-center Distance change is 5% greater than the one above it.

Subtracting length from one leg

Leg length	Add Length	% of Span	Off-center Distance
20'	0"	100%	0"
19'	12"	95%	12"
18'	12"	90%	11.4"
17'	12"	85%	10.8"
16'	12"	80%	10.2"
15'	12"	75%	9.6"
Total	**60"**		**54"**

Note: Each Off-center Distance change is 5% less than the one above it.

As you can see, this cumulative effect causes the distortion to increase as you move away from the center. In this case it is 6 inches, either long or short, depending on which method you use. Many riggers use this method as follows:

- They begin by making each leg of the bridle the same length as the Span distance. This creates an equilateral triangle with the Span and the two bridle legs.
- Then, whatever distance the apex needs to be offset from center, they add that length of Deck Chain to one leg. Example: adding 1 foot of chain to one leg moves the apex 1 foot away from the center (away from the long leg).

While this method may not always be as accurate as other methods, for short offsets it is usually accurate enough. Plus, it is a very quick and easy way to calculate bridle lengths.

The One-Eighth Bridle Trick
This is a quick and easy way to calculate the legs of a bridle that will put the apex 1/8 of the span distance from one beam and 7/8 of the span distance from the other beam, no matter the length of the Span.

Long Leg = 100% of Span
Short leg = 50% of Span

Beams at Different Heights
Up until now, we have been working with beams at the same height. While this is the most common situation, it is certainly not unusual to have beams at different heights. In this section we will look at how to calculate the lengths of legs when the apex is centered between two beams of different heights.

Let me lay out the two formulas/rules that you use for these calculations, then I will explain when to use each one. Before I do this, I need to define one term - "Rise." Rise is the difference in heights of the low and high beams. If the low beam is 80 feet above the deck and the high beam is 100 feet above the deck, the Rise is 20 feet. Got it?

The 90% Rule   The 80% Rule
Short Leg Length = Span   Short Leg Length = Span
Long Leg Length = Span + (Rise x 0.9)   Long Leg Length = Span - (Rise x 0.8)

Knowing when do to use each is important.

Use the 90% Rule if: Rise is greater than 40% of the Span
Use the 90% Rule if: Rise is 40% of the Span or less

Of course, the minimum required height of the hook (apex) is also a consideration in choosing a one rule/formula over the other.

Let's do an example. If the low beam is 80 feet above the deck and the high beam is 90 feet above the deck, the Rise is 10 feet. If the Span is 20 feet, then the Rise is 50% of the Span, so use the 90% Rule. So, the lengths of the legs will be:

Short Leg Length = 20 feet

Long Leg Length = 20 + (10 x 0.9)
Long Leg Length = 20 + 9
Long Leg Length = 29 feet

The Bridle Chart

A Bridle Chart is a Pythagorean Theorem "cheat sheet" that allows you to look-up the length of the hypotenuse of any right triangle without having to do any math. Below is an example of Bridle Chart.

SPAN	DEPTH	2	4	5	6	7	8	9	10	11	12	13	14
	10	10.2	10.8	11.2	11.7	12.2	12.8	13.5	14.1	14.9	15.6	16.4	17.2
	15	15.1	15.5	15.8	16.2	16.6	17	17.5	18	18.6	19.2	19.8	20.5
	20	20.1	20.4	20.6	20.9	21.2	21.5	21.9	22.4	22.8	23.3	23.9	24.4
	25	25.1	25.3	25.5	25.7	26	26.2	26.6	26.9	27.3	27.7	28.2	28.7

Using it is simple. First, find the Span (horizontal) distance of Leg 1 in the SPAN row. Let's choose 10 feet for this example, so look across the SPAN row until you find "10." Put your finger on it. Next, select the Depth (vertical distance that the apex is below the beam). Let's use 15 feet. Run your finger down the column until you get to the number that aligns with the "15" in the DEPTH column. Your finger should be on "18." This is the length of the leg - 18 feet.

Bridle Charts simply use the Pythagorean Theorem to show you the hypotenuse of a triangle with side of specific lengths, they do not tell you how to make the bridle legs. That you must figure out on your own.

Bridle Length Cheat Sheets

Whether the beams are at the same height or at different heights, one way to eliminate the need for doing math in the field is to create Bridle Reference Guides (aka "cheat sheets"). These cheat sheets are created for specific venues they are not a "one size fits all" like the Bridle Chart shown above.

There are many ways to create these cheat sheets, but they sometimes involve one bridle leg that can be made from common steel sling lengths (what I call the "Fixed Length Leg"), and another leg that compliments the first and horizontally positions the apex at the desired location.

To be really useful and show you how to make up each bridle leg, cheat sheets often based on a specific inventory of steel, a specific basket length (with a known ELOH that has been used to create the cheat sheet). More generic cheat sheets, a little more like the Bridle Charts described earlier can also be created.

Below is a Cheat Sheet that I created for Harrah's Cherokee Center, which has a span distance between the beams of 20'-0". It is based on all of the baskets being 5-foot in length, with an ELOH of 20.2 inches based on the beam size, and an inventory that includes 2', 5', 10' steel, as well as STAC chain that is 3-feet-long. This cheat sheet also shows the height of the apex (hook) for each bridle and the bridle angle. Multiple cheat sheets could be made for the same venue, but with a different inventory, different length of baskets (with a different ELOH), or other differences.

Rigging Cheat Sheet - Harrah's Cherokee Center

H1 Distance	Leg 1 Steel	Leg 2 Steel	Hook Height	Bridle Angle
0'-3"	5'	2' & 5' & 10' & 5L	44'-1	73
0'-6"	5'	2' & 5' & 10' & 4L	44'-1"	75
0'-9"	5'	5' & 10' & 10L	44'-1"	77
1'-0"	5'	5' & 10' & 9L	44'-1"	79
1'-3"	5'	5' & 10' & 9L	44'-2"	81
1'-6"	5'	5' & 10' & 8L	44'-3"	83
1'-9"	5'	5' & 10' & 7L	44'-3"	85
2'-0"	5'	5' & 10' & 6L	44'-4"	87
2'-3"	5'	5' & 10' & 5L	44'-5"	89
2'-6"	5'	5' & 10' & 4L	44'-6"	91
2'-9"	5'	5' & 10' & 4L	44'-7"	94
3'-0"	5'	5' & 10' & 3L	44'-9"	96
3'-3"	5'	5' & 10' & 2L	44'-10"	98
3'-6"	5'	5' & 10' & 1L	45'-0"	101
3'-9"	5'	5' & 10'	45'-2"	104
4'-0"	2' & 5'	5' & 10' & 2L	42'-9"	89
4-3"	2' & 5'	5' & 10' & 1L	42'-11"	91
4'-6"	2' & 5'	5' & 10'	43'-1"	93
4'-9"	2' & 5'	5' & 10'	43'-2"	95
5'-0"	2' & 5'	2' & 10' & 8L	43'-4"	97
5'-3"	2' & 5'	2' & 10' & 7L	43'-6"	99
5'-6"	2' & 5'	2' & 10' & 6L	43'-8"	101
5'-9"	2' & 5'	2' & 10' & 5L	43'-11"	103
6'-0"	2' & 5'	2' & 10' & 4L	44'-1"	106
6'-3"	10'	5' & 10'	44'-4"	108
6'-6"	10'	2' & 10' & 8L	41'-0"	87
6'-9"	10'	2' & 10' & 7L	41'-2"	88
7'-0"	10'	2' & 10' & 6L	41'-4"	90
7'-3"	10'	2' & 10' & 5L	41'-6"	91
7'-6"	10'	2' & 10' & 4L	41'-9"	93
7'-9"	10'	10' & 10L	41'-11"	94
8'-0"	10'	10' & 9L	42'-2"	96
8'-3"	10'	10' & 8L	42'-5"	98
8'-6"	10'	10' & 7L	42'-8"	100
8'-9"	10'	10' & 6L	42'-11"	102
9'-0"	10'	10' & 4L	43'-2"	104
9'-3"	10'	10' & 3L	43'-6"	107
9'-6"	2' & 10'	10' & 9L	40'-6"	88
9'-9"	2' & 10'	10' & 8L	40'-9"	89
10'-0"	2' & 10'	2' & 10'	41'-0"	91

Chapter 9:

Calculating the Length of Long Bridle Legs (they may be longer than you think)

When a rigger needs to calculate the length of bridle legs, a variation of the Pythagorean Theorem

$$Length\ of\ leg = \sqrt{V^2 + H^2}$$

is the go-to equation. Likewise, when the tensions on bridle legs need to be calculated, the equations

$$Tension\ on\ Leg\ 1 = Load \times \frac{Length\ of\ L1 \times H2}{(V1 \times H2) + (V2 \times H1)}$$

and

$$Tension\ on\ Leg\ 2 = Load \times \frac{Length\ of\ Leg\ 2 \times H1}{(V1 \times H2) + (V2 \times H1)}$$

are used. These are simple and easy to use equations that in most cases provide the rigger with a good, relatively accurate, answer. However, in some cases, the answers may not be accurate enough.

So, what is the problem with these equations? The answer is that they ignore the weight of the bridle legs. Actually, these equations assume that the bridle legs are weightless.

The Pythagorean Theorem calculates the length of a perfectly straight chord that runs between two points (the apex of the bridle and the anchor point of the leg, and we assume that the bridle leg lies precisely on that line. In reality, bridle legs are never perfectly straight lines, they are more accurately described as curves, specifically catenary curves. Why? Unlike weightless lines, actual bridle legs have weight, and that weight causes them to sag. A flexible cable, loaded only by its own weight, is best described by the catenary curve, although a less accurate model, the parabolic curve is sometimes used in surveying for adjusting the length of a surveying chain. The parabolic curve assumes the cable is loaded by a constant weight per foot in the horizontal direction, rather than a constant weight per foot along the cable length.

In most cases, the sag of the bridle leg is so slight that the difference in the lengths of the straight-line chord and the curve of the sagging bridle leg is not significant. But, when the bridle legs are long, and the weight of lines are relatively high compared to the load, the difference can be significant. When this occurs, the rigger must know the length of this curve in order to make the actual bridle leg the correct length.

The amount of sag in the bridle leg, and therefore the length of the bridle leg, is determined by four factors: the length of the leg, the weight per foot of the material (usually wire rope) that the leg is made from, the tension on the leg, and the angle of the chord line. As a result –

- The longer the leg, the greater the sag
- The less tension on the leg, the greater the sag
- The greater the leg weights per foot, the greater the sag
- The closer the angle of the chord is to horizontal, the greater the sag

Because we assume that the bridle legs are weightless, that leads us to another estimation – that the tension on the bridle legs is the same at the apex (the lower end) and at the anchor (the upper end). It is not. The Upper End Tension of the bridle legs is greater than the Lower End Tension because it must include part of the weight of the wire rope that makes up the bridle leg. This additional tension is calculated using the equations:

$Upper\ End\ Tension\ on\ Leg\ 1 = Lower\ End\ Tension\ on\ Leg\ 1 + (V1 \times Weight\ per\ foot\ of\ Leg\ 1)$

$Upper\ End\ Tension\ on\ Leg\ 2 = Lower\ End\ Tension\ on\ Leg\ 2 + (V2 \times Weight\ per\ foot\ of\ Leg\ 2)$

The diagram below illustrates the general relationship between the parts of the bridle.

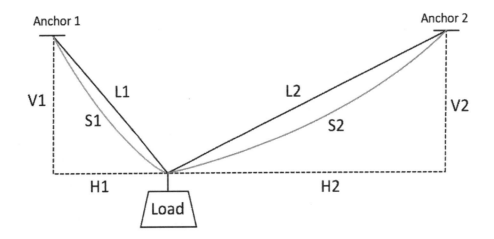

To find the length and the tension of the bridle legs (S1 and S2) we use a two-segment method that requires the equations of equilibrium be solved iteratively (the process of repeating a set of instructions a specified number of times or until a specific result is achieved). Creating a "loop" to perform these tasks can be done in Microsoft Excel by creating a VBA (Visual Basic for Applications) macro.

We have created a spreadsheet to demonstrate how such a macro works. You can download it from: www.springknollpress.com/RMMS6/SagCalc.xlsm. Note: spreadsheets that contain macros end in .XLSM instead of .XLSX. Also, when you open this spreadsheet, Excel will warn you that it contains a macro and ask you if you want to enable or disable the macro. Of course, you want it enabled.

To calculate the length of the bridle legs, we model the two bridles as catenary curves and identify the line tensions to produce horizontal and vertical equilibrium for the specified load position. We start with the weightless line estimate for the lower end tension on the bridle legs. This is not the true lower end tension under the catenary model. Because of the line weight of the cable, the angle of the LINE TENSION is LOWER than the chord slope at the load. Thus, to produce adequate vertical force, the line tension must be higher than that of the weightless line estimate, so that vertical force on Leg 1 plus the vertical force on Leg 2 is equal to the Load. Because vertical force on Leg 1 must be equal to the true lower end tension of Leg 1 multiplied by the sine of the true angle, our algorithm methodically increases the line tension until these equilibrium conditions are satisfied. When the algorithm has determined that the horizontal forces on the apex are equal and the sum of the vertical forces at the apex equal the load, the process is terminated and the calculated lengths and tensions, along with the message "Equilibrium Conditions Satisfied" are displayed in the spreadsheet. If macro also checks to ensure that there are no calculation errors that would cause the program to freeze. If so, the message "Solution could not be Found" is displayed.

Our macro also calculates and displays the weight of each leg, the angle of the chord for each leg, and the mid-span perpendicular deflection distance for each leg in order to help the user understand more about each leg. Let's look at the four sections of the spreadsheet.

The upper left section is the diagram of the bridle setup displayed above. This diagram relates to the upper right section of the spreadsheet – the part where the user enters the data for the bridle.

(d1)	(h1)	(d2)	(h2)	(w)	(w1)	(w2)
H1 (feet)	V1 (feet)	H2 (feet)	V2 (feet)	Load (lb)	Cable Wt 1 (lb/ft)	Cable Wt 2 (lb/ft)
10	10	10	10	300	0.26	0.26

Click to Calculate Bridle Length	*Cable Weight	
	1/2" dia. wire rope =	0.46 lb/ft
	3/8" dia. wire rope =	0.26 lb/ft
	1/4" dia. wire rope =	0.12 lb/ft

Equilibrium Conditions Satisfied

The user must enter seven data items, three related to Leg 1 (Blue), three related to Leg 2 (Orange), and the Load on the apex (Green). We have given you the weight per foot of three sizes of wire rope. Each leg can be made of a single size of wire rope, but the two legs do not have to be from the same size wire rope. After the user has filled-in these cells, the user needs to click on the button that is labeled "Click to Calculate Bridle Length." Doing this runs the macro and updates the cells the third and fourth sections. Remember, anytime any of the seven data entry is changed, you must re-click on this button to re-run the macro.

Note: The notations in parenthesis above the seven data entry cells are the variables names used in the macro, for each data item. You can look at the actual macro by going to Tools>Macro>Visual Basic Editor.

The code in this spreadsheet is complex and beyond the scope of this book.

Sections three and four of this spreadsheet provide the output about the bridle legs Leg 1 (Blue) and Leg 2 (Orange). These sections look like this.

Bridle Leg 1 Data			
L1 Length (ft)	S1 Length (ft)	Lower End Tension (lb)	Upper End Tension (lb)
14.14	14.14	213.28	215.88

Weight of Leg (lb)	Angle of Leg (deg)	S1 Mid-Span Perpendicular Deflection (ft)
3.68	45.00	0.03

Bridle Leg 2 Data			
L2 Length (ft)	S2 Length (ft)	Lower End Tension (lb)	Upper End Tension (lb)
14.14	14.14	213.28	215.88

Weight of Leg (lb)	Angle of Leg (deg)	S2 Mid-Span Perpendicular Deflection (ft)
3.68	45.00	0.03

These sections show the length of the chords (L) along with the length of the bridle legs (S). They also show the Lower End Tension, the Upper End Tension, the Weight of each leg, the Angle of each leg from horizontal, and the Mid-Span Perpendicular Deflection length.

We might call this a "normal" bridle. The legs are at 45 degrees to horizontal and their lengths are relatively short. When we compare the lengths of the chords (L) to the calculated bridle lengths (S) we see that they are the same. In other words, the Pythagorean Theorem would work perfectly for this bridle. But, let's look at an example where one leg is long (200 feet) and the wire rope is heavier.

(d1)	(h1)	(d2)	(h2)	(w)	(w1)	(w2)
H1 (feet)	V1 (feet)	H2 (feet)	V2 (feet)	Load (lb)	Cable Wt 1 (lb/ft)	Cable Wt 2 (lb/ft)
10	30	200	30	300	0.46	0.46

Bridle Leg 1 Data			
L1 Length (ft)	S1 Length (ft)	Lower End Tension (lb)	Upper End Tension (lb)
31.62	31.62	348.62	362.42

Weight of Leg (lb)	Angle of Leg (deg)	S1 Mid-Span Perpendicular Deflection (ft)
14.55	71.57	0.16

Bridle Leg 2 Data			
L2 Length (ft)	S2 Length (ft)	Lower End Tension (lb)	Upper End Tension (lb)
202.24	207.81	116.34	130.14

Weight of Leg (lb)	Angle of Leg (deg)	S2 Mid-Span Perpendicular Deflection (ft)
95.59	8.53	20.96

Let's look at the results for Bridle Leg 2. In this example we can see that the calculated bridle leg length (S2) is over five and a half feet longer than the chord length (L2). Without adding this additional length of cable to this bridle leg, the apex would not hang at the desired location. You should also note that making Leg 2 longer significantly decreases the tensions on Leg 2, but significantly increases the tension on Leg 1.

Conclusion

It is important that riggers understand the amount of sag in the bridle leg is determined by four factors: the length of the leg, the weight per foot of the material (usually wire rope) that the leg is made from, the amount of tension on the leg, and the angle of the chord. In many instances, the simple weightless method of calculating the length of the bridle leg works fine, but there are times it does not. We have created a free tool/spreadsheet that allows riggers to easily use a more accurate method of calculating the length of bridle legs, as well is the tension on those legs.

Chapter 10:
Bridle Apps

While being able to do a rigging math problem from memory is good, in the real world, calculating loads, bridle lengths, etc. is not a "hand operation." The job is too serious, and the result of a mistake can be far too costly. There are several tools that help make your calculations faster and help ensure accuracy. Remember, these are tools for riggers, and not tools that make you a rigger.

Let's look at some of the popular native operating system apps and web apps for entertainment rigging.

Apps for Calculating Bridle Legs

Bridle by Production Innovators ($15.99) is a popular rigging app for the iOS (Apple) operating system. This app quickly calculates the lengths of bridles (including the number of links of deck chain) needed for any bridle setup. One of the things that I do not like about this app is that it tends to use a lot of "dog bones" for making bridle legs. Unless the tour has a lot of these short slings, there can be an issue with running out these short slings before all of the points are hung. Big problem!

Bridle by Tricky-Design is a $3.99 bridle app for Google Android devices. This app looks a lot like the *Bridle* app by Production Innovators. I have not used it because I do not own an Android device.

Rig Chalk by Sweet Merch: This $4.99 app is for Google Android devices. While I have heard a lot of good things about this app, I have not used it because I do not own an Android device.

Bridle Pro by Delbert Hall (http://springknollpress.com/BP.html) is a free web app for calculating bridle legs. When you start this app, you begin by selecting one of versions of the app: one version asks users to specify the desired apex height, and the other version ask users to specify the steel length in Leg #1 (the short leg). This app is optimized to use as few dog bones as possible and will calculate the ELOH any shape of beam. Most bridle apps are not designed to do either of these things.

PocketRigger by Delbert Hall: *PocketRigger* is a free rigging app. It has more than 48 calculators and reference charts to help you solve rigging problems of all types, including a basic bridle calculator. This is a web app, which means in can run on any device (computer, tablet, or smartphone) with a web browser. Learn more about PocketRigger at http://springknollpress.com/PR/Index.html

LD Calculator Lite by Paul Pettetier Software: This free downloadable app for Windows (only) is a collection of tools primarily for people who work in the lighting field. However, it includes an excellent "Rigging formula" calculator for two-point bridle legs. While this app was last update in 2005, it is still an excellent app.

Creating Your Own Rigging Tools

Creating your rigging math tools is not as difficult as it may sound. Plus, they can be as simple or as complex as you want them to be. And, because YOU are creating them, they can be organized in a way that makes the most sense to you. So how can you create these tools?

Probably the easiest and most power tool for creating your own rigging apps is Microsoft Excel or another spreadsheet program. Excel (and other spreadsheet program) can run on both computers and tablets, like the iPad. Although these programs can run of smart phones, I have never felt the small screens on most smart phones work well for spreadsheets. In my book *Rigging Math Made Simple*, I will discuss how to create your own rigging apps with Excel.

This book also includes a lesson on how to create web apps using HTML and JavaScript. If you have a basic knowledge of HTML, you can create a web page with a built-in app/rigging calculator.

Part III:

Truss and Chain Hoists

Chapter 11:
Aluminum Truss

In this chapter, we will discuss the various types of aluminum truss and truss components that are available for the entertainment industry and how they are used. We will not be discussing steel truss, but many of the same considerations apply. We will also discuss orientation, installation and inspection. ANSI E1.2 2012 covers all the design, manufacture, inspection, and use of aluminum trusses, structural components and towers. This chapter will follow these ANSI guidelines and recommendations. ANSI guidelines related to the entertainment industry are available for free download at: http://tsp.plasa.org/tsp/documents/index.html

In addition, this is a partial list of the factors used by engineers in performing structural analysis:

- Section properties of the members
- Allowable buckling stress
- Slenderness of the tubes
- Radius of gyration
- Factored axial resistance
- Maximum factored load on the truss
- Slenderness of the girder
- Maximum force which can be transmitted through top and bottom tubes
- Permissible design stresses:
- Axial tension or compression
- Bending and Shear
- Bearing (crushing)
- Stresses within reduced stress zones (HAZ)
- Permissible stresses in the fillet welds (traverse & longitudinal)
- Allowable stresses in the pins and bolts
- That all welds are made by certified welders in accordance with established design procedures
- Loading limitations to comply with maximum shear capacity
- Assessment of the lateral stability

Parts of a Truss and Truss Terminology

Truss comes in a variety of shapes and sizes. However, the terminology remains basically the same. To start, let's look at the basic parts of an I-beam for comparison. An I-beam consists of a top flange, a bottom flange, and a web. The top and bottom flanges are the flat part at the top and bottom of the beam. They directly correspond to the top and bottom chords on the truss. Their function is to maintain the stability of the web. The chords of the truss do the same thing; they maintain the stability of the diagonals/spreaders.

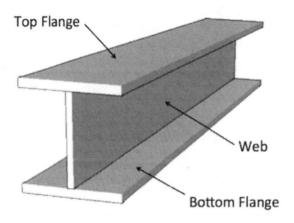

Parts of an I-Beam

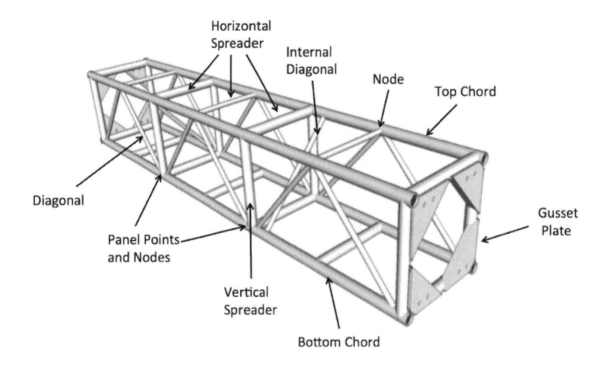

The web of the I-beam is the vertical member that supports the top and bottom flanges. It is similar to the diagonal and vertical supports of the truss. The web's function is to spread the applied forces to the flanges. The truss diagonals perform a similar function in that they transfer the vertical forces horizontally to the chords. There always will be *tension* and *compression* in about 50% to 50% of all of the truss members.

Truss Orientation

The design of box truss typically has the horizontal cross members on the two top and bottom faces. The diagonal and vertical members are typically on the other two side faces. *Truss orientation* needs to be such that the diagonals form a continuous pattern - usually forming the letter **A**. This differs with pre-rigged truss. Truss load data is only valid if the truss is oriented in the manner.

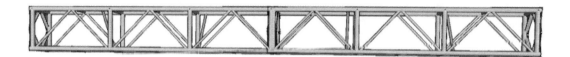

Some riggers may argue that orientation on general box truss doesn't matter. All that is important is to ensure that the diagonals are on the sides and form the same letter pattern between sections. This may be true on some general box truss, but if you examine the horizontal spreaders on the top chord of some truss, you will note that some struts are narrow while some are wide. Because truss is used to hang equipment from the lower cords and spreaders, it is best to keep the truss in the letter **A** orientation.

Truss hung on its side may seem structurally sound, however, hanging a truss in this manner would change the load characteristics considerably. Manufacturers would not stand by their product if the truss should fail.

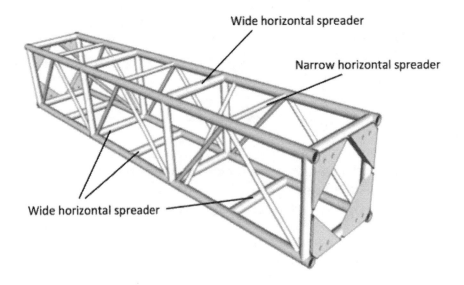

Wide horizontal spreader

Narrow horizontal spreader

Wide horizontal spreader

Truss configured correctly. If there is any doubt about orientation, check with the manufacturer.

Panel Points and Nodes

Panel Points and Nodes form the point where the diagonal, vertical and horizontal spreaders are welded to the chords. Structurally, they are the strongest point on the truss to apply a vertical force. They allow for the vertical force to be distributed horizontally from diagonal to diagonal.

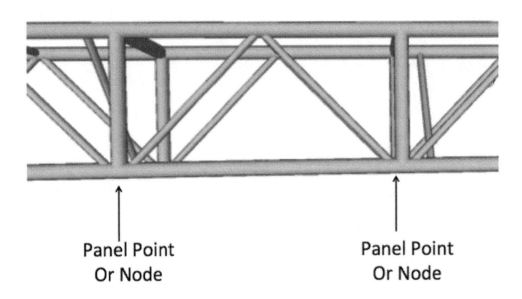

Panel Point
Or Node

Panel Point
Or Node

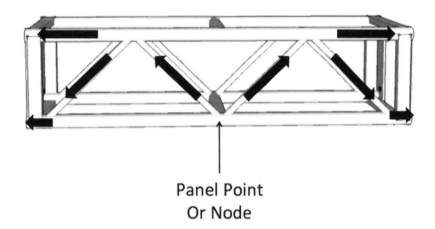

Panel Point
Or Node

Some of the Forces that are distributed on a truss

When loads are applied at a panel point, the forces are distributed horizontally from diagonal to diagonal.

When applying a force at the panel point, forces on the structure needs to be kept in *compression*. The *internal diagonals* are not that integral to the structure of the truss. If present, they help to maintain the form of the truss during construction. *Connecting points* are where one truss is joined to another. These points are considered to be strong connections, however some manufacturers may recommend not hanging a substantial load at these junctures. Again, it's always best to check with the manufacturer.

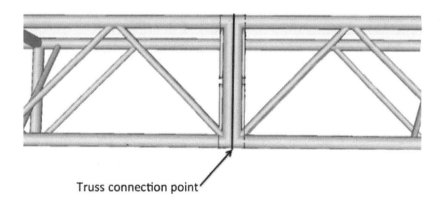

Truss connection point

Terms:
Before we begin examining truss loading, lets become familiar with some terminology.

Allowable load: maximum static equivalent load that can be safely imposed on truss / tower in addition to the self-weight.

Competent person (OSHA definition)"Competent person" means one who is capable of identifying existing and predictable hazards in the surroundings or working conditions, which are unsanitary, hazardous, or dangerous to employees, and who has authorization to take prompt corrective measures to eliminate them.

Compression: when forces on an object are pressed together toward the center of the object. Compression is best on panel points.

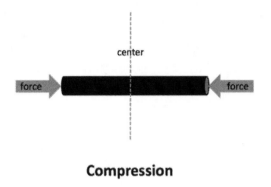

Compression

CPL (center point load): a concentrated load that is applied at the mid-span of a beam.

Deflection: the degree or angle to which a structural element is displaced under a load.

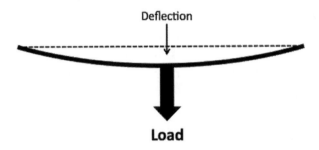

Dynamic loading: forces caused by the acceleration or deceleration of an object.

Panel point (node): The point of intersection where the spreaders (stretchers) and diagonals meet a chord.

Point load: a load which is localized to a specific location on a beam.

Qualified person (OSHA definition) "Qualified" means one who, by possession of a recognized degree, certificate, or professional standing, or who by extensive knowledge, training and experience, has successfully demonstrated his ability to solve or resolve problems relating to the subject matter, the work, or the project.

Shear: arises from a force that is applied perpendicularly to the material cross section on which it acts.

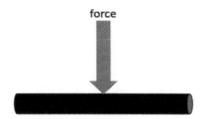

Shear

Span: the distance between the supporting points.

Tension: when the forces on the object stretch or pull away from the center.

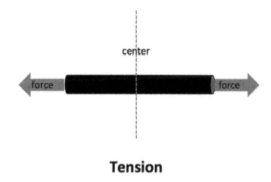

Tension

Torque: a measurement of how much force acting on an object which causes the object to rotate. The object rotates about an axis. We call this axis the pivot point.

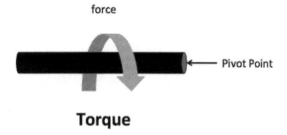

Torque

UDL (uniform distributed load): a load that is evenly spread over the length of a beam.

Working with truss requires a familiarity with all of these terms. It also requires a working knowledge of the size and make of the truss and a familiarity with the manufacturer and engineer's limitations of the particular truss you are working with.

Truss Loading
Manufacturers provide truss-loading data charts that give detailed information relative to the truss type, truss span, and load type. Manufactures provide load data charts for every type of truss they manufacture. These charts are available on their website and should be referred to when loading their truss. Truss loading will be covered in detail in Chapter 16.

Truss Connections
There are two basic connections for truss sections. These are bolted (plated) and spigoted (with eggs and fork). The strength of these connections are based on the load data for each type and size of truss. The strongest of these connections is the spigoted, but each connection is suitable for the size and type of truss.

Bolted Truss

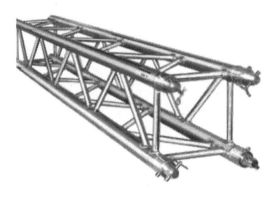

Spigoted Truss with eggs or nipples

Spigoted Forked Truss
photo courtesy of James Thomas Engineering

Bolted truss uses four grade 8 truss bolts with washers and nuts. These are attached at the gusset plates. Grade 8 bolts are stronger than the more conventional grade 5 bolt and are identified by the six radial lines at the bolt head. They are made from carbon alloy steel, which allows for greater *torque* strength in the bolt threads. Grade 8 nuts are used along with high alloy washers. When attaching these bolts to the end plates, a truss bolt socket and ratchet is used to snug the bolts. Snug them as you would lug nuts on the rim of a tire. Do not over tighten-and, most importantly, do not use an impact driver!

Grade 8 truss bolt
photo courtesy of TomCat

Grade 8 truss bolt markings

Spigoted Truss has steel nipples (sometimes called eggs) that are inserted at one side of the truss chords. When the truss sections are in alignment, the spigots mate and are secured with a hitch pin and clip. Do not force the eggs into place. They should fit easily.

Spigoted Truss using forks has steel male and female forks that mate at each end of the truss chords. When the truss sections are in alignment, the forks mate and are secured with hitch pins and clips.

Towers and Truss Components

As concerts began making the transition from indoor venues to outdoor spaces, there arose a need for supporting the horizontal truss structures from the ground. Truss manufacturers started beefing up their horizontal truss so that it could support loads vertically. This set up became known as *ground supported truss.*

Floating sleeve blocks were created as a means of connecting the horizontal truss to the vertical towers while enabling the truss to be raised and lowered by chain hoists. The sleeve blocks surround the towers enabling the truss to slide up and down (Chain hoists will be discussed in another chapter). Head blocks with sheaves mounted inside allowed the chain to run from the hoist over the head block to the horizontal truss.

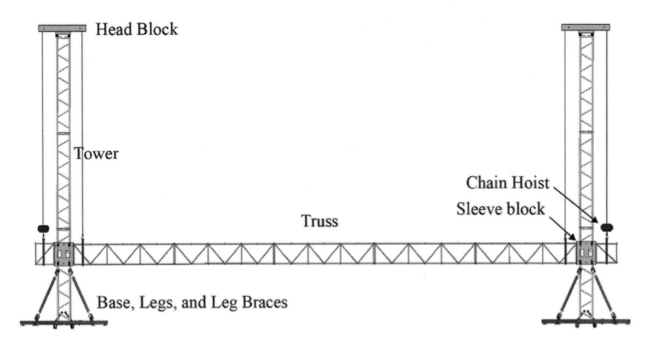

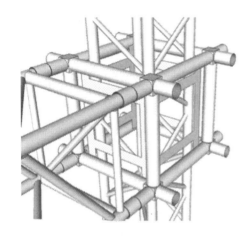

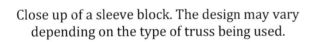

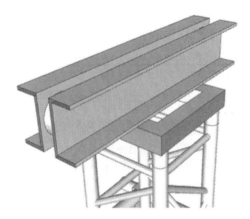

Close up of a sleeve block. The design may vary depending on the type of truss being used.

Close up of an aluminum head block. Note the chain sheaves at the top.

The future of the design and manufacture of truss will always be based on the demands of the industry. As production demands change, so will truss design. Today, the most important factors are span, loading, lifting, ease of assembly, and transport. Customer demand is based on:

- the length of truss needed for the job
- the amount of weight that will be used on the truss
- points on the truss needed to lift the truss into position
- speed and ease of assembly
- transportation costs to and from venues

Most manufactures have multiple designs, both lightweight and heavyweight, for a wide variety of customer needs. Truss catalogues are a great resource for available truss and truss products.

A few catalogs that are available online are:

James Thomas Engineering -
http://jthomaseng.com/pdffiles/Product%20Range%202014_merged.pdf

TomCat Truss -
http://www.tomcatglobal.com/Tomcat/media/tomcat/Catalogue/TOMCAT-CAT-(pdf).pdf?ext=.pdf

Tyler Truss-
http://www.tylertruss.com

The reference to truss and truss types discussed here are based on the James Thomas Engineering Catalogue, but you should note that there are many other reputable truss manufacturers.

The some of the basic truss types available on the market today include:

- Ladder
- Box
- Supertruss
- Super Mega-Truss
- Moving Light Truss
- Pre-Rigged Truss

- Triangle truss
- Folding Truss
- Swing truss
- Trapezoid
- Octagonal
- Round

Some manufacturers have both light-duty and heavy-duty versions of each. Be sure you use the correct load data charts as light-duty and heavy-duty vary greatly.

Truss Types
Ladder Truss is a two-dimensional version of box truss. It is strong when placed in the vertical position as shown, but weak when placed on its side. This truss is great where there is little space on each side of the truss as it fits well into narrow width spaces.

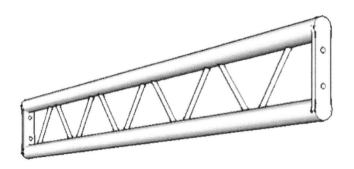

Ladder Truss

General Purpose Box Truss is the most popular truss on the market today. It is easy to assemble and can accommodate many different lighting rigs, PA systems, and video walls. They come in a variety of sizes (a few are shown below) and can be used in both indoor and outdoor venues.

12"x 12" Box Truss   18"x 12" Box Truss

Super Truss is stronger than standard box truss. It is portable and easy to assemble and can handle a variety of lighting, PA and video systems.

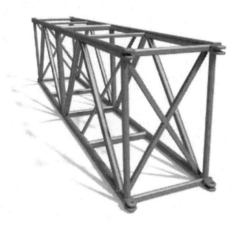

20.5" x 30" Super Truss

Super Mega-Truss is often used for supporting large roof or "mother grid" systems. It is extremely strong and is for use when heavy lifting or support is required. Casters are added for maneuverability.

Super Mega-Truss

Moving Light Truss is very similar to pre-rigged truss. It is designed to hold moving light fixtures up in the truss while in transit. Movers are then lowered once the truss once in position. Truss size is generally around 91" x 30" x 26". Other sizes are available. Casters are added for maneuverability.

Moving Light Truss

General Purpose Pre-rigged truss is 30"x26"in size and can carry two lighting bars inside the truss for storage. Once in hung, the lighting bars can be lowered into position.

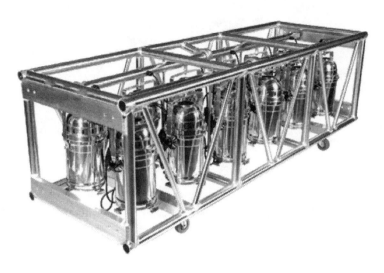

Pre-rigged Truss

Other Truss Types

Triangle truss must be oriented so that the apex is at the top. The hinged portion of a bi-fold truss must be kept toward the top as well. Flipping it over significantly reduces it load capacity.

Triangle

Tri fold

Latest Developments – HUD Truss

The latest development in the industry (2008) is the use of HUD Truss or (High-Performance Utility Design) Truss. Similar to Pre-Rigged Truss, HUD truss was developed as the need arose to maximize the stacking and cargo capacity in tractor-trailers. As fuel and trucking costs increased, HUD truss was developed as a strong, pre-rigged, and compact alternative to other pre-rigged truss. Designed and manufactured by Tyler Truss, it is light weight, durable, easy to stack for transport, and assembles using spigots and hitch pins. When the legs are attached, the lighting instruments are raised off the floor and store up inside each truss section. Netting is used around the lights to provide additional support during transit. Cables are secured in their positions on each section. As the truss is rolled out to their floor marks, the spigoted sections are pinned and the cables are mated. Once the truss is attached to the hoists, the legs can be removed for storage or mounted in the upright position on the truss forming handrails. The lights never have to be lowered into position. Everything is performance ready.

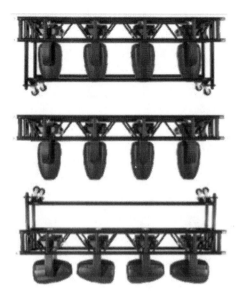

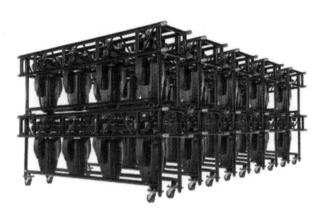

photos courtesy of Tyler Truss

HUD truss designed to be suspended with grapples secured to the top chord at the end panel points. Although round slings can be used, the attachment must be with two slings rather than one continuous sling as there are no horizontal spreaders across the bottom. Each round sling MUST attach to the bottom chord with a choker hitch that also wraps the top chord.

Inspection

ANSI E1.2 - 2012 covers the design, engineering, manufacturing, loading and inspection of aluminum truss in the entertainment industry. It recommends that a *qualified person* perform periodic inspections at least once a year and that the owner keep inspection records on file for each truss component. This does not mean that truss inspection should be limited to just the owner and to once a year. A *competent person* has the responsibility to perform a visual inspection before each use.

The following is a partial list of items that need to be visually inspected prior to use:

- Truss geometry. Check for twisting or bending of the truss or tower units

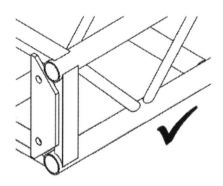

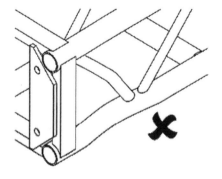

- Unusual bending in the truss chords. Camber
- Dents, abrasion or wear in the cords, diagonals or spreaders

  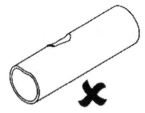

- Missing diagonals or connecting plates (if used)

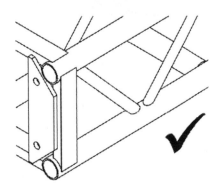 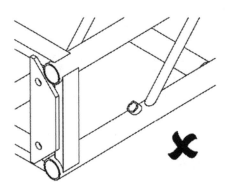

- Deformation, corrosion, or excessive wear around the truss bolt-holes or pin-holes.
- Proper grade fasteners. Check for wear and corrosion.
- Check for cracks and abrasions around the welds

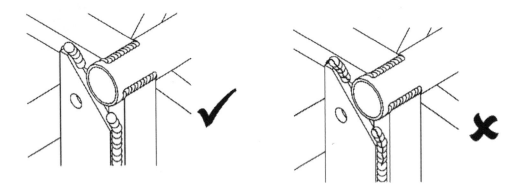

If any of these problems are noted, then the truss must be labeled DO NOT USE and removed from service until a *qualified person* can perform a more complete inspection or make repairs to the system. For a free copy of this and other ANSI recommendations for the entertainment industry, please visit:
http://tsp.plasa.org/tsp/documents/published_docs.php

Summary

In this chapter, we discussed the various types of aluminum truss and truss components. The comparison between an I-beam and a truss showed us that the top and bottom flanges of an I-beam directly correspond to the top and bottom chords on a truss and that the chords maintain the stability of the diagonals and spreaders similar to the web of an I-beam. We learned that a truss, when under load, is always in a state of either tension or compression. *The panel points and nodes are the strongest point on the truss to apply a vertical force.* They allow for the vertical force to be distributed horizontally from diagonal to diagonal. To aid in the loading of various truss types, manufacturers provide us with truss-loading data charts that give detailed information relative to the truss type, truss span, and load type. They provide load data charts for every type of truss they manufacture. These charts are available on their website and should be referred to when loading their truss. In addition, there are two basic connections for truss sections, *bolted (or plated)* and *spigoted.* The strength of these connections is based on the load data for each type and size of truss.

Today there are many different trusses available on the market. Some of the basic truss types today include:

- Ladder
- Box
- Supertruss
- Super Mega-Truss
- Moving Light Truss
- Pre-Rigged Truss

- Triangle truss
- Folding Truss
- Swing truss
- Trapezoid
- Octagonal
- Round

As concerts began making the transition from indoor venues to outdoor spaces, there arose a need for supporting the horizontal truss structures from the ground. Truss manufacturers started beefing up their horizontal truss so that it could support loads vertically. This set up became known as *ground supported truss.*

Lastly, we learned the importance of truss inspection. ANSI E1.2 - 2012 covers the design, engineering, manufacturing, loading and inspection of aluminum truss in the entertainment industry. It recommends that a *qualified person* perform periodic inspections at least once a year and that the owner keep inspection records on file for each truss component. A *competent person* has the responsibility to perform a visual inspection before each use.

Credits: James Thomas Engineering, TomCat and Tyler Truss for allowing the use of photos and drawing from their catalogues.

Chapter 12:

Rigging Hardware

This chapter will examine the equipment and methods used for properly preparing a truss prior to suspending in a venue. We will discuss everything in preparing the truss up to the chain hoist, while Chapter 6 will explore methods used to hang the truss from the hoist to the hanging point. Before we begin, let's examine some of the hardware used in the industry.

Introduction - Working Load Limits and Design Factors
Most of the hardware we use in the entertainment industry falls into one of two categories: industrial hardware (i.e., shackles and slings) and recreational hardware (i.e., carabineers and climbing loops). Most industrial hardware is stamped with a Working Load Limit (WLL) or Safe Working Load (SWL), whereas recreational hardware is mark with it Minimum Breaking Strength (MBS), usually expressed in kiloNewtons (kN). To understand the WLL of a piece of hardware, you must first understand its MBS, and how it is derived.

Most hardware manufacturers use a statistical method called "3 sigma" to determine the MBS of their products. Cancord Inc., a manufacturer of fiber rope, explains 3 sigma this way,

> *This means the minimum breaking strength is calculated by taking the mean or average breaking strength of 5 rope samples and subtracting 3 standard deviations. Statistically, this creates a confidence level of 99.87% that any sample of rope will be stronger than the quoted minimum breaking strength.*

Got it? Probably not, so let's look at the theoretical results of a destructive test done on five samples of a fictional new product - a "Rigging Widget."

Sample #	BS (kN)
1	31
2	31
3	30
4	30
5	29.5

Now that we have the results of the five samples, we need to find the Mean (average) of these tests.

Mean = 30.3

Next, we find the <u>Variance</u>. To find the Variance, we need to do several things. First, find the difference from the Mean for each sample. We do this by subtracting the Mean from the BS. Next, we square each difference (BS-Mean)^2. Third, we total this column for the five samples - giving us 1.8. See table below.

Sample #	BS (kN)	BS - Mean	(BS - Mean)^2
1	31	0.7	0.49
2	31	0.7	0.49
3	30	- 0.3	0.09
4	30	- 0.3	0.09
5	29.5	- 0.8	0.64

Total = 1.8

The final step is to divide this total by the number of samples.

Variance = 0.36

The Standard Deviation is the square root of the Variance, so

Standard Deviation = 0.6

Since Standard Deviation is often denoted by the Greek letter sigma, 3 sigma is three times the Standard Deviation.

3-Sigma = 1.8

Now that we know 3-Sigma we can calculate the Minimum Breaking Strength. It is the Mean minus 3 Sigma (three Standard Deviations).

Minimum Breaking Strength = (30.3 - 1.8) or **28.5 kN**

Since manufacturers always round to a whole number when listing the MBS, we would round this down and stamp **MBS 28 kN** on our rigging widgets.

It may seem odd that the rated MBS on our rigging widget is **28 kN**, while our lowest test result was **29.5 kN**, the Mean was **30.3 kN**, and just under half of our samples broke at **31 kN**, but that is how the MBS is calculated. It is possible for there to be test results that are lower than MBS derived with the 3-Sigma method, but statically it is a very small number.

Now, the manufacturers of industrial hardware will assign their equipment a *Working Load Limit (WLL)* or *Safe Working Load Limit (SWL)* based on the calculated MBS and what they determine to be a safe operational margin or *Design Factor.*

The Design Factor creates a margin of safety to compensate for normal wear and less than optimal working conditions. Design Factors do NOT compensate for extreme shock loads, extensive wear/damage, or other factors that might cause the hardware to fail. All hardware used in rigging should be inspected before every install to ensure that it is not damaged.

All hardware does not have the same Design Factor. Below is a list of common Design Factors that are used by manufactures of different types of hardware for determining the working load limit.

- Synthetic Slings: 5:1
- Wire rope slings: 5:1
- Stage rigging (counterweight rigging system, including the wire rope): 8:1
- Shackles: 6:1
- Base mounted drum hoists: 7:1
- Personnel lifts: 7:1 to 10:1
- Fiber ropes: 7:1 to 12:1
- Chain (except grade 43): 4:1
- Grade 43 chain: 3:1
- Ratchet straps: 3:1
- Most Sailing hardware (including stainless steel shackles): 2:1

The Design Factor that the WLL is based on is not commonly displayed on the hardware's packaging or even in literature from the manufacturer. Therefore, it is important that riggers be familiar with the common Design Factors above. If you are not sure of the Design Factor used to derive the WLL, you need to check with the manufacturer. Knowing the Design Factor for all rigging hardware is very important.

Whereas the Working Load Limit is the maximum force that may be applied to the product, the *Design Factor* or DF is a number assigned by the manufacturer that determines the Working Load Limit. Design Factors are a percentage of the Breaking Strength and are often expressed as a ratio, such as 5:1 or sometimes as a single number, such as 5.

Example 1:

A piece of rigging hardware has a Breaking Strength of 1,400 lb. The manufacturer gives the hardware a Working Load Limit of 280 lb. What is the Design Factor being used?

To calculate this, simply divide 1,400 by 280. Design Factor is 5.

Example 2:

A shackle has a Working Load Limit of 6,500 lb. Using a Design Factor of 6, what is the Breaking Strength of the shackle?

6,500 x 6 = 39,000 lb

Remember, recreational hardware, such as carabiners, are marked with the breaking strength (usually in kiloNewtons) instead of a WLL. Note: Newtons and kiloNewtons are a measurement of Force. Sometimes weight and force are given in pounds, which can be confusing to the beginner or expert alike.

To convert kiloNewtons to pounds, multiply the MBS by 224.8. Example: If a carabineer has a rated MBS of 53 kN, it's MBS is 11,914.4 lb.

You now have to apply a Design Factor to the MBS. The General Rules of Thumb below are a good guideline.

General Rules of Thumb

- DF of 5:1 for Standing Rigging (i.e. rigging that does not move)
- DF of 8:1 for Running Rigging (rigging that moves)
- DF of 10:1 for rigging used in flying of people or moving over the heads of people

Slings

Round slings are used to wrap truss. They are soft, non-abrasive, and do not damage the aluminum chords when used properly. There are many different types of slings on the market, each are designed for a specific purpose. In this chapter, we will discuss two basic types of round slings. These are synthetic core and wire rope core. Both consist of an endless core loop that is covered with a protective, synthetic fabric jacket. Note: Round slings are sometimes called "Spansets." It should be noted that "Spanset" is a brand name, like "BandAid" and not the correct name of the product.

photo courtesy of TomCat Truss

Synthetic core slings are made from 100% polyester strands. These strands are looped around forming a continuous core of strands. The core is then covered with a synthetic fabric sleeve that serves to hold the strands together and to protect them from wear.

A tag is then sewn onto the sleeve containing the basic product information about the sling. OSHA regulations require the tag to be in place and the information legible. If this tag is missing or the writing is illegible, do not use the round sling.

Wire rope core slings, called GAC Flex or Steel-Flex, are made from steel Galvanized Aircraft Cable that is wound in an endless configuration forming an Independent Wire Rope Core (IWRC). They are then covered with a double-wall polyester jacket. A Velcro tag may be opened allowing the inspection of the wire rope core. Wire rope core slings tend to be less flexible than polyester core slings, but have greater resistant to heat damage.

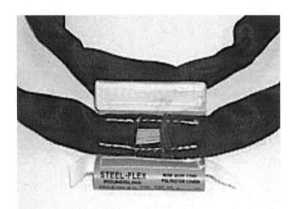

photo courtesy of LiftAll, Lift-It® Manufacturing Company, Inc.

Color-coding identifies the sling and its load rating in various configurations. It's the commercial industry that uses colored slings that are color coded according to load capacity in Figure 3.

Color Code	Approx. Body Diameter	Approx. Weight/Foot	Rated Capacity in Pounds					Minimum Length
			Vertical	Choker	Basket	60°	45°	
Purple	0.60"	0.20 LB	2,600	2,100	5,200	4,500	3,700	3'
Green	0.80"	0.30 LB	5,300	4,200	10,600	9,200	7,500	3'
Yellow	1.00"	0.50 LB	8,400	6,700	16,800	14,500	11,900	3'
Tan	1.20"	0.60 LB	10,600	8,500	21,200	18,400	15,000	3'
Red	1.30"	0.75 LB	13,200	10,600	26,400	22,900	18,700	3'
White	1.40"	0.90 LB	16,800	13,400	33,600	29,100	23,800	6'
Blue	1.75"	1.15 LB	21,200	17,000	42,400	36,700	30,000	6'
Orange	2.00"	1.30 LB	25,000	20,000	50,000	43,300	35,400	6'
Orange	2.25"	1.50 LB	31,000	24,800	62,000	53,700	43,800	6'
Black	2.50"	2.00 LB	40,000	32,000	80,000	69,300	56,600	6'
Black	3.00"	2.50 LB	53,000	42,400	106,000	91,800	74,900	7'
Black	3.25"	3.50 LB	66,000	52,800	132,000	114,300	93,300	7'
Black	3.75"	4.00 LB	90,000	72,000	180,000	155,900	127,300	7'
Black	4.00"	4.50 LB	100,000	80,000	200,000	173,200	141,400	7'

Load Capacity Charts for Round Slings

photo courtesy of CoreSlings.com

It is only in the entertainment industry that we find the sling jackets colored black. The load data on the attached chart is for a *specific* brand of round sling so be sure you are using the correct manufacturer's data chart. It shows the Working Load Limits (or WLL) that are assigned to the various sling colors. You can see that there are a variety of "black colored" slings with their corresponding load ratings. Always be sure to check the load rating data found on the sling tag. Note: that the load capacities change as the sling is used in a vertical, choker, basket, and angled configurations. These configurations are also printed on the tag for convenience. (Figure 1) Working Load Limits will be discussed further at the end of this chapter.

Inspection. OSHA 1910.184 covers the safe use and inspection of round slings. Specifically, OSHA 1910.184(d) states,

> *Each day before being used, the sling and all fastenings and attachments shall be inspected for damage or defects by a competent person designated by the employer. Additional inspections shall be performed during sling use, where service conditions warrant. Damaged or defective slings shall be immediately removed from service.*

Thing to look for are:
- Heat/ chemical damage
- Abrasion/wear/hard, stiff or crunchy to the touch
- Knots
- Frayed jacket/ open exposed core
- Cuts in the jacket
- Damaged/ illegible or missing tags

Measuring a round sling. To correctly measure the length of a sling, stretch out the sling and measure from the inside edge of the sling to its opposite inside edge. Slings generally come in lengths of 1.5-feet to 8-feet.

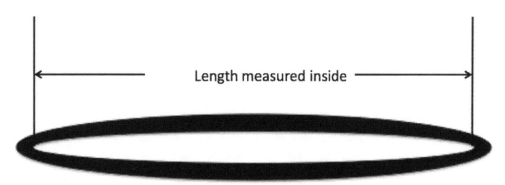

Length measured inside

Measuring a Round Sling

Steel slings (often called legs) are used to make baskets and bridles that run up from the chain hoist to the I-beams and suspend the truss into its final trim position. In the arena industry 3/8" and 1/2" wire rope slings are the choice. 3/8" diameter steel slings are load rated for loads up to 1.4 tons while 1/2" diameter steel slings are rated for loads up to 2.5 tons. These are made from 6x19 XIPS,

IWRC steel. This means that there are 6 strands in the cable with 19 wires in the strand. XIPS means Extra Improved Plow Steel and IWRC refers to Independent Wire Rope Core. Steel slings have an increased wire diameter and flexibility.

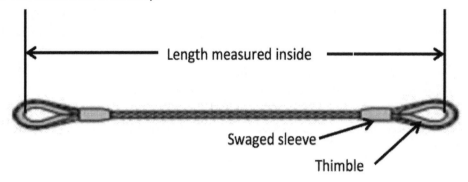

Length color-coding of steel slings. Many rigging production companies in the United States color-code the ends of their wire rope slings for ease of *length* identification. This is not to be confused with load data charts, nor is this to be recognized as any industry standard. It is done simply to make it easy for the "down-rigger" to quickly identify the length of the steel when pulling slings from a road box. The ends of the steel are spray painted with a color to designate their length:

- No color for 1.5-foot, 2-foot, and 2.5-foot-long steel slings (called dog bones)
- Red for 5-foot-long slings
- White for 10-foot-long slings
- Blue for 20-foot-long slings

Other colors for 30-foot and 50-foot steel may vary, but generally green for 30' and yellow for 50'.

Note: In other countries, other colors may be used. Some rigging companies may simply spray paint their steel all one color for identification that it is their steel and not to be confused with someone else's.

Shackles

Shackles are commonly used in arena rigging for connecting slings to other slings or connecting slings to the hooks on a chain hoist. Before we get into how shackles are used, look at the figure below to understand the two body shapes for shackles and the three types of pins.

Anchor Shackle   Chain Shackle

Anchor shackles, aka Bow shackles, are the most common type shackle used in arena rigging because the "bell shaped" allows this type of shackle to be used as a "collector ring" so that multiple lines, can be connected at a single point. Chain shackles, aka D shackles, cannot be used as collector rings - the loads must always be aligned with the centerline of the shackle. This makes them less useful for arena rigging.

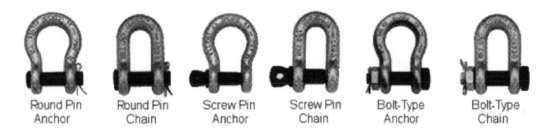

| Round Pin Anchor | Round Pin Chain | Screw Pin Anchor | Screw Pin Chain | Bolt-Type Anchor | Bolt-Type Chain |

Shackles pins are be "round pins" - that use a cotter pin to hold them into place, "screw pins" - where a threaded end screws into a threaded "ear" on the shackle's body, or a bolt - that uses a captive nut to keep it in place. Arena rigging is done almost exclusively with Screw Pin Anchor Shackles.

Multiple lines (bridle legs) are commonly connected to another piece of steel with an anchor shackle at the bridle's apex, as shown below.

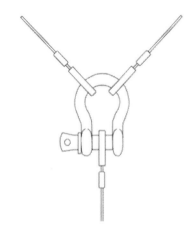

This is allowed, within limits. The Crosby Group says...

> SHACKLES, RINGS, LINKS AND MASTER LINKS CAN BE USED AS A COLLECTOR RING. DO NOT EXCEED AN INCLUDED ANGLE OF 120 DEGREES ON ANY COLLECTOR RING (60 DEGREES EITHER SIDE).

It should be noted that users are not limited to the number of legs that can be connected to a connector ring (including a shackle) as long as the rule above is followed, and the load on the shackle is "reasonably centered."

Below is an image showing an example of off-center loading of a shackle. (Note: off-centering of the load is ONLY permitting on screw pin and bolt type shackles, NEVER on round pin shackles).

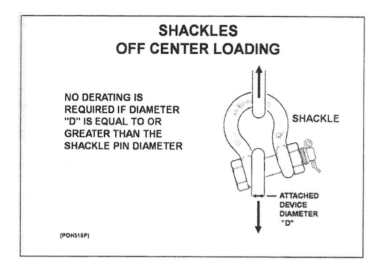

Related to off center loading, Crosby states...

IF THE ATTACHING LINKS' DIAMETER ARE EQUAL TO OR LARGER THAN THE SHACKLE PIN DIAMETER, NO REDUCTION OF THE WLL IS REQUIRED, REGARDLESS OF THE LOCATION ON THE PIN.

and

IF THE LOAD IS NOT CENTERED ON THE SHACKLE PIN AND THE ATTACHING LINK IS SMALLER THAN THE SHACKLE PIN DIAMETER, THE WLL SHOULD BE REDUCED 15% DUE TO THE RESULTING ANGULAR LOADING.

Another situation that sometimes arises with shackles is "side loading." When a rigger says that a shackle is "side loaded," he means that the load on the shackle is on opposites sides of the shackle and none of the load is on the pin of the shackle, as in the illustration below.

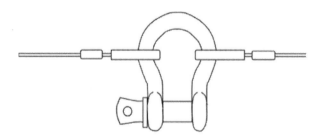

But this is not what shackle manufacturers mean when they use the term "side loaded." According to *The Crosby Group Product Application Seminar Workbook (ASME/OSHA BASED), Edition 7A,* Crosby would define this as an Incorrect Shackle Alignment" and say that it is not allowed. See below.

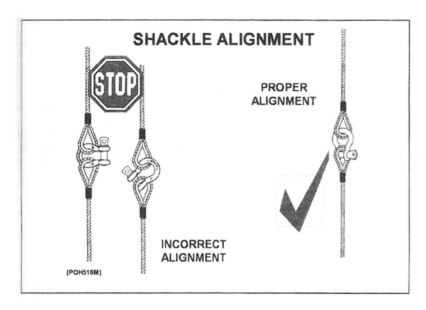

Shackles should be inspected for wear before being installed.

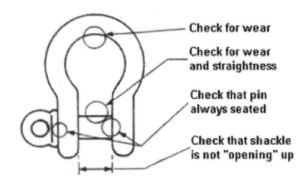

Check for wear
Check for wear and straightness
Check that pin always seated
Check that shackle is not "opening" up

1. Inspect the body of the shackle for excess wear. Wear of 10% or more of the original diameter is where the shackle needs to be replaced.
2. Inspect the shackle body for bending. A bent shackle often indicates excessive side-loading.
3. Inspect the shackle eye and pin holes for stretching or elongation.
4. Inspect the shackle pin for distortion, surface blemishes, wear and fractures.
5. Inspect the seating of the pin.

General Notes on Shackles

- Shackles should always be larger than the cable size
- Pin should only be finger-tight
- Mouse shackles on long term or permanent installs
- Different manufacturers have different ratings
- Shackle does not care if it's pin up or pin down
- Back off pin 1/8-1/4 turn
- If a shackle is very hard to open it might have been overloaded

Round Ring, Pear Rings and Oval Rings

Round rings, pear rings, and oval rings (aka Master Links) are often used as collector points for multiple lines.

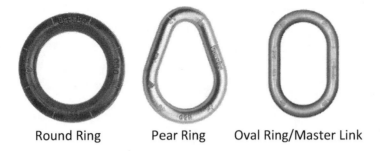

Round Ring   Pear Ring   Oval Ring/Master Link

These rings can be forged or welded. Always check the manufacturer's WLL for the particular ring that you are using.

Truss-Lifting Points

Truss-Lifting Points (or grapples) are designed as an alternative to round slings. They provide a "hard" attachment point to either to top or bottom cords and are rated for around 2000 pounds.

photo courtesy of James Thomas Engineering

However, these should be used with caution, as mounting from the bottom chords may cause the truss to rotate due to uneven loading, and mounting from the top chords on certain truss types may cause distortion. Contact the manufacturer to see if *grapples* can be used instead of round slings.

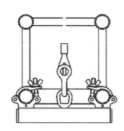

12" Lifting Point mounted to bottom chords

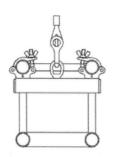

12" Lifting Point mounted to top chords

photo courtesy of James Thomas Engineering

Chain Hoists

Chain Hoists are a staple of the entertainment industry and will be discussed further in Chapter 4. They are the "muscle" for the lifting overhead truss systems off the ground and into position.

photo courtesy of Columbus McKinnon

They are used to hang and secure such things as lighting equipment, speaker arrays, video walls and projection equipment. Like so many other tools and equipment borrowed from other industries, the electric chain hoist found its way into entertainment rigging to satisfy a need- to hoist lighting, sound and video equipment into the air. In the early days of arena rigging, up-riggers had to haul up both the chain and the hoist to a position on the beams. Considering the amount of weight that the up-rigger has to haul up, this became "out of fashion" very quickly. The chain hoist was soon modified to run inverted, so that up-riggers only had to haul up the chain and the bridle legs. Now, the hoist is connected directly to the truss round slings by means of a shackle. Essentially, a chain hoist *is* an electric motor that climbs a chain while pulling a load up.

One Ton hoists attached to a section of box truss. Note how the round slings are wrapped at the panel point.
photo courtesy of Mountain Productions

Chain Hoist capacities range from 1/8 Ton to 3 Ton. However, the most common capacities used in the entertainment industry are ¼ Ton, ½ Ton, 1 Ton and 2 Ton.

Attaching the chain bag to the hoist. When attaching the bag hooks to the chain hoist, the hooks need to be placed facing out. This avoids the links of the chain from snagging the points of the hook. Always check to be sure you are using the correct size bag for the correct length of chain. Nothing can be more embarrassing and dangerous than to have a hoist nearing its trim height and hear,

" chink.....chink...chink..chink. chink.chink.chink.chink!"

as the excess chain brings all of the remaining chain crashing to the stage floor. Make sure you are using the correct size bag for the correct length of chain.

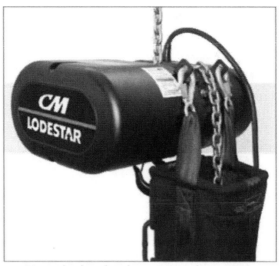

Note the bag hooks point to the outside

photo courtesy of Mountain Productions

STAC Chain (sometimes called Deck Chain)

STAC chain stands for Special Theatrical Alloy Chain is a product of Columbus McKinnon (CM), which is known for its chain hoists. This chain has an inside link dimension of 3.74 inches, and a working load limit of 12,000 pounds. This chain is used to adjust the length of the bridle legs so that the bridle point or apex will fall at the rigging point chalk mark below on the floor. This chain is usually available in 3-foot length (10 links), 4-foot lengths (13 links), and 5-foot lengths (16 links). The 3-foot length (actually 37.4 inches) is the most common length for touring productions.

TRAC Chain (Theatrical Rigging Alloy Chain) is made by Peerless and has the same specifications as STAC Chain.

Bolts

Bolts are "graded" based on the hardness of their steel. The most common grades are Grade 2, Grade 5 and Grade 8. The chart below describes each of these grades.

No Markings	**Grade 2** Low or medium carbon steel
3 Radial Lines	**Grade 5** Medium Carbon Steel, Quenched and Tempered
6 Radial Lines	**Grade 8** Medium Carbon Alloy Steel, Quenched and Tempered

The higher the grade, the stronger the bolt, but also the more brittle. Grade 5 or higher is recommended for rigging applications.

Equally important as the grade of the bolt is the torque to which the nuts are tightened. Truss bolts should be around 90 ft/lbs for temporary structures and around 110 ft/lbs for long term installs. Also, make sure you have a washer on both sides of the truss. Do not use impact guns when assembling truss. They can damage the threads, plus they are very noisy.

Hanging the Truss

Now that we have looked at the equipment, lets discuss some of the methods used in hanging truss. In Chapter 1 we discussed proper truss orientation and the importance of panel points. There are several methods used to wrap a truss with round slings; four of which we will discuss here. The important points to remember when wrapping truss are:

1. Always keep the panel points in compression
2. Load the truss evenly so as to avoid rotation
3. Wrap the chords evenly so as to avoid rotation and support the chords
4. Never wrap the sling on a splice or a fitting

Wrapping the truss with round slings.

There are four *basic* methods for wrapping the truss. There are many others, but these are the most common. What method you use will be determined by the diameter of the truss (size), sling length, and headroom.[1]

Choking the lower chords using two slings is often chosen for larger diameter truss. Two 3 to 6-foot slings form a choker hitch on the lower chords. Note the choker faces to the outside. Wrapping to the inside may affect stability especially if the truss is loaded unevenly. The upper chords can be wrapped if necessary to reduce the length of the sling and shorten headroom or they can run to the outside of the upper chord joining at the shackle.

---

[1] *Headroom is the measured distance between the trim height and the drop. See Chapter 7 for a further discussion*

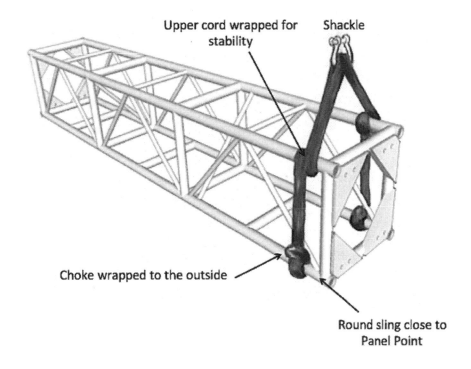

Upper cord wrapped for
stability

Shackle

Choke wrapped to the outside

Round sling close to
Panel Point

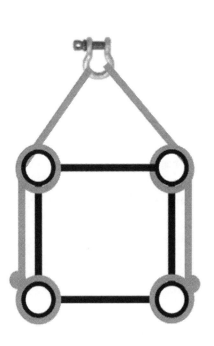

Section View

Upper chords wrapped

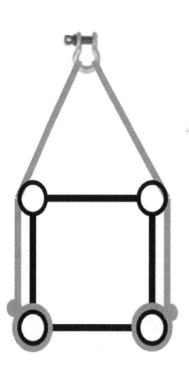

Section View

Upper chords un-wrapped

Wrapping the entire panel point with one sling is often done with smaller truss and a longer 8-foot sling. The sling is run under the bottom chords, wrapped one turn, run on the outside, wraps the upper chords, before meeting to join at the shackle. The upper chords can be wrapped if necessary to reduce the length of the sling and shorten headroom or they can run to the outside of the upper chord joining at the shackle.

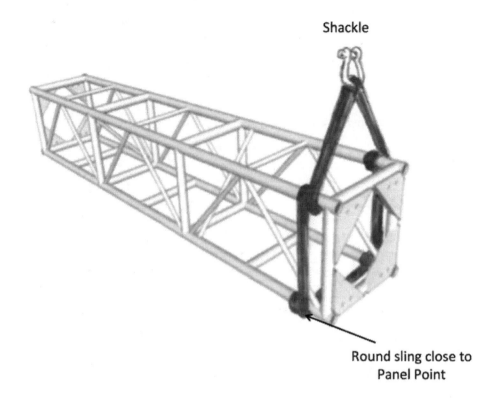

Shackle

**Round sling close to
Panel Point**

The X wrap is another very stable wrap that is used around the panel point of a truss. The illustration below shows two round slings that are used to hang the truss. Each sling is choked to the lower chords and then crosses each other to the upper chords. At this point they can either wrap the upper chords (as shown) or they can just run around the outside of the top chord to the shackle. Wrapping the upper chord is optional, but it is often done to shorten the length of the round sling and add additional stability.

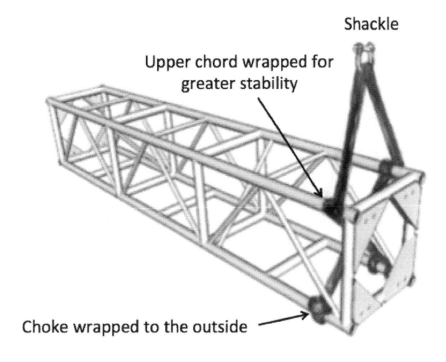

Shackle

Upper chord wrapped for greater stability

Choke wrapped to the outside

The X wrap is a very stable wrap

The illustrations below show variations of an X wrap using both single and double round slings.

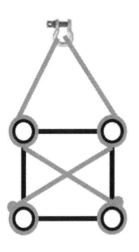

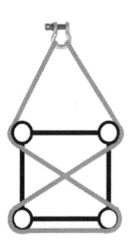

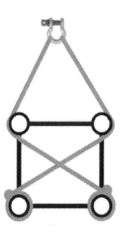

Two round slings with wrap at the upper chords

Single round sling

Section Views

Two round slings   with no wrap at the upper chords

The last wrap we will discuss is to be used when there is very little headroom between the hoist and the ceiling. This is typical when hanging truss in ballrooms and convention centers. In this situation, only the lower chords are wrapped using 2-short or 1-medium length round slings. This enables the hoist to be positioned down into the truss minimizing headroom distance. As with grapples, hanging a truss in this manner requires a certain amount of care. When hanging equipment and cables on the truss, the rigger must ensure that the load on the truss is evenly balanced. With the round slings connected only to the bottom chords, the *Center of Gravity* at the shackle is very low and the truss can become *out of balance* very easily.

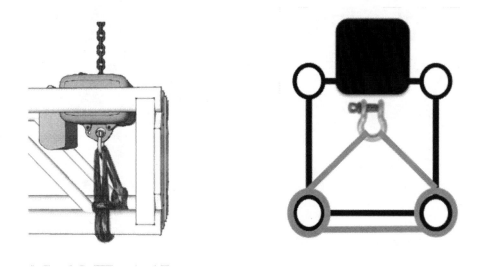

Bridle Angle at the Shackle. The bridle angle at the shackle should be no more than 90 degrees. A higher angle puts too much stress on the sling and upper chords.

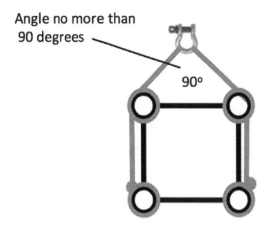

Tag Location. Round sling tags provide manufacturer's information about the make-up and load rating of the round sling.

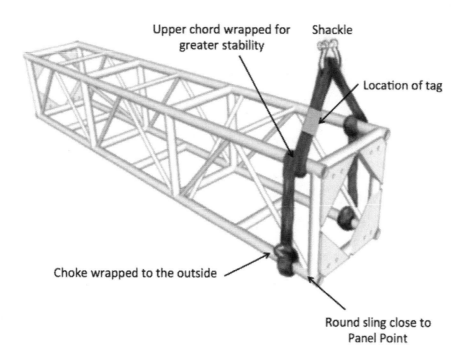

Upper chord wrapped for greater stability

Shackle

Location of tag

Choke wrapped to the outside

Round sling close to Panel Point

On steel core or Steel Flex slings, the tags are attached with Velcro at the juncture where the sleeve is stitched. The Velcro can be opened if requested by the Fire Marshall allowing inspection of the core. Polyester core slings have the label stitched on. Too often stagehands will correctly wrap the chords of a truss only to incorrectly wrap the tags around the chords or shackle.

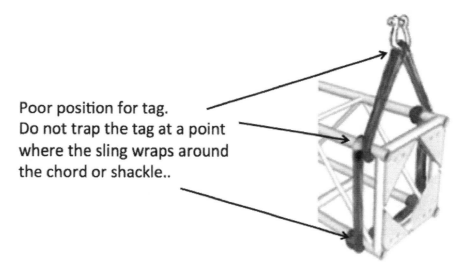

Poor position for tag. Do not trap the tag at a point where the sling wraps around the chord or shackle..

Slings should be wrapped so the tag is positioned on a "straight run", usually at the top- just below where the shackle attaches so it's out of audience view. This allows inspection of the tag if required, but it also prevents the information on the tag from being worn off. OSHA does NOT have a regulation for the *placement* of slings on truss. They do, however, have a regulation that requires the tag of a lifting sling to be legible. ASME (American Society of Mechanical Engineers) B30.9-2010 Rigging Practices also states not to have the cover splice located within the choke when using round slings. If the information on the label is not legible then you cannot use the sling. If you place the label inside the choke or wrap, the writing on the tag will eventually wear off.

Safeties

Steel safeties are run from the hoist hook through the truss to the other hoist hooks or from the truss to an I-beam. They are used as a back-up should there be a failure of the synthetic round slings due to excessive heat or fire. Steel Flex was created due to concerns over the synthetic slings. The Steel-Flex sling does not usually require a backup safety based on heat related issues. In the United States the decision to use a safety back up for a Steel-Flex sling is determined by the venue or the Fire Marshall. However, redundancy is always a good thing in the event of some unforeseen disaster.

Summary

This chapter examined the equipment and methods used for properly preparing a truss prior to suspending in a venue. Most of the hardware we use in the entertainment industry falls into one of two categories: industrial hardware (i.e., shackles and slings) and recreational hardware (i.e., carabineers and climbing loops). Most industrial hardware is stamped with a Working Load Limit (WLL) or Safe Working Load (SWL), whereas recreational hardware is mark with it Minimum Breaking Strength (MBS), usually expressed in kiloNewtons (kN). To understand the WLL of a piece of hardware, you must first understand its MBS, and how it is derived.

Chapter 13:

Chain Hoists

Introduction

Electric chain hoists are extremely versatile motors that can be used to lift loads within their rated capacities. Chapter Two examined the rigging hardware and truss connections. This chapter will examine electric chain hoists, electricity and power distribution. Guidelines for the use of Electric Chain Hoists and Chain Hoist Systems are available for free download at the PLASA web site:

http://tsp.plasa.org/tsp/documents/published_docs.php

- **ANSI E1.6-1** Entertainment Technology – Powered Hoist Systems
- **ANSI E1.6-2** Hoist Inspection and Maintenance
- **ANSI E1.6-3** Safe Use Electric Chain Hoists
- **ANSI E1.6-4** Portable Control of Fixed-Speed Electric Chain Hoists in the Entertainment Industry

Types of Hoists

Since ancient times, hoists have been made up of two basic components: the lifting media, used to lift the load, and the power, or the force used to operate the drum. The typical media used for lifting a load can be anything from hemp rope, wire rope to chain. Power can include anything from human exertion, hydraulics, and pneumatics to electric power. Today, the most common chain type hoists are either manually operated, such as a chain fall hoist seen left, or electric shown right.

photos courtesy of Columbus McKinnon

Hoists utilizing the media of wire rope can be as simple as the "come-along" shown below left, to the more complex automated line shaft winch shown below right.

The "come along" is a simple manually operated hoist.

PowerLine™ Line Shaft Hoist
photo courtesy of JR Clancy

Since the electric chain hoist is a staple of arena rigging industry, this chapter will introduce you to the key components and operation of this very versatile rigging component. *This book is NOT a service or operation manual! Please consult the service manual of the hoist you are using for more comprehensive information and refer to the ANSI Standards listed above.*

The classic Lodestar.

photo courtesy of Columbus McKinnon

The chain hoist, often called a "chain motor," is a hoisting system using differential pulleys to enable the operator to effectively manage a load. Essentially, it is a compound pulley system with different radii engaging a chain. The exerted forces are multiplied according to the ratio of the radii. The photo below shows an old-style, manual chain fall hoist with the lifting wheel and operating chain and how it is connected to the reduction gears and chain sprocket. Essentially, an electric hoist operates on the same principle.

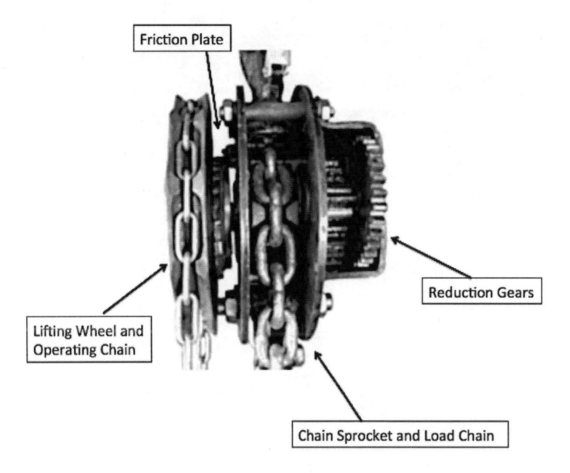

An old-style manual hoist showing internal parts

A classic 1 Ton Model L Loadstar will have a 7.67:1 reduction for its first stage and a 7.90:1 reduction for its second stage for a total lifting ratio of 60.593:1. Quite a lot of lifting power!

Key components of the Electric Hoist
Let's look at a few of the basic components of a typical electric chain hoist. We will be using the **CM Lodestar, Model L** for our example, but you should be aware that there are many other manufactures of chain hoists for the entertainment industry and not all of them will have the same exact features. *Please contact the manufacturer for the Service and Operating Manuals for the hoist you are using.*

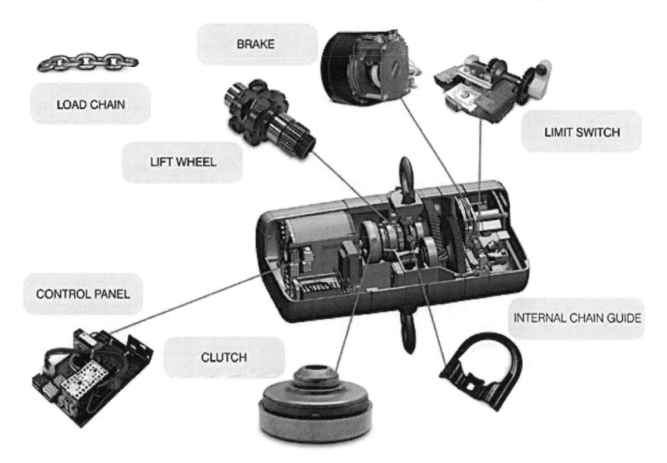

photos courtesy of Columbus McKinnon

Control Panel

The Control Panel is located under the motor housing cover and allows the user to make a quick voltage change adjustment on the color-coded voltage change board. Any voltage change should be noted on the voltage tag attached to the power cord. Because the motor can rotate in either direction with a three-phase hoist, the chain direction should be checked before each use.

Load Chain

The *load chain* is what lifts the load. It is made up of high carbon, alloy, grade 80 (G80) steel. G80 was the first chain approved by OSHA for overhead lifting. The number refers to the ultimate breaking strength of the chain.

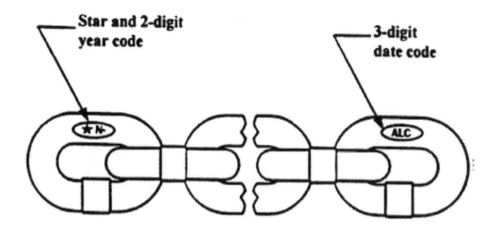

G80 means that the maximum stress on the chain is 800 newtons per millimeter squared. Columbus McKinnon simplifies this by labeling their chain with a "star" for Star Grade. Each link is case hardened with carbon for additional strength and longevity. When replacing chain, always purchase directly from the manufacturer of the hoist you are using, never from another source. Their lift wheels are specially designed for their chain. Always make sure the chain is clean and lubricated. Never let the load chain the run dry. CM recommends Lubriplate Bar and Chain Oil 10-4 (Fiske Bros. Refining Co.) or equal lubricant. One way to check to see if the chain is properly lubricated is to observe how the chain folds into the chain bag. The chain should lay into the bag evenly; if it stacks to one side, then it could be lacking proper lubrication. Lastly, always check the chain for nicks, gouges and wear.

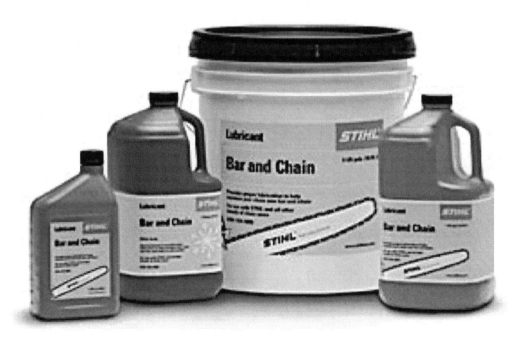

Lift Wheel

The *Lift Wheel* connects to the clutch pinion and the clutch gear connects to the drive shaft where it engages the chain links. The Classic Loadstar has a 4 sprocket Lift Wheel. The Next Generation Loadstars have 5 sprockets.

Internal Chain Guide

The internal chain guide insures that the chain is guided through the lift wheel and remains in the lift wheel when there is no load on the chain.

Brake

CM Hoists utilize two forms of braking:

1. Mechanical Braking is mechanical device (seen right) that uses a magnetic field to release the clamps on the brake drum allowing the shaft to rotate freely. Normally, the clamps are engaged when there is no power to the hoist and released when the hoist is being raised or lowered.

2. Regenerative braking occurs when a load is being lowered. The load on the hoist over powers the rotors on the hoist and the motor serves as a speed reduction generator limiting the rate of decent.

Clutch

A friction clutch is employed to protect the hoist motor from an extreme overload condition. The friction clutch is temporarily disengaged when the hoist reaches a higher torque than the motor is designed to handle.

Limit Switch

Most chain hoists have chain limit switches. Being able to set the limit switches is an important part of hoist operation. The limit switch is found on all electric chain hoists except the Prostar. Its purpose is to limit the extent of the run of chain in both the upper and lower direction. As the hoist is raised and approaches the hook, it will automatically stop when its pre-set, upper limit is reached, thus preventing the hook from burying itself in the chain guide and damaging the hook, chain, and hoist. A similar limit is set for the opposite direction. As the hoist is lowered and reaches the end of its pre-set lower limit, the hoist automatically stops.

Setting the Limit Switches

The dimensions in the "A" column are the highest allowable hook position in mm or inches that can be set for safe operation between the top of the hook and the bottom of the hoist. The chart shown below covers most Columbus McKinnon models.

MODELS	MAX. LENGTH OF LIFT (ft.)	HOOK TRAVEL Per Notch (inch)	UPPER LIMIT "A" POSITION (links)	LOWER LIMIT "B" POSITION (inches)
B	102	11/16	8	12
C	204	1-5/16	8	12
F	102	11/16	8	12
L	125	3/4	8	12
LL	254	1-15/32	8	12
R	66	3/8	8	12
RR	125	3/4	8	12

Table courtesy of Columbus McKinnon

Procedure for setting limit switches

Columbus McKinnon recommends the following procedure for setting both the upper and lower limit switch settings. The following is copied with permission from the Columbus McKinnon Maintenance Manual:

1. *Disconnect hoist from power supply.*
2. *Remove back frame cover*
3. *The position of the upper and lower limit switches are indicated on the fiber insulator.*
4. *Loosen the screws to permit guide plate to be moved   out of engagement with the traveling nuts, refer to Figures 18 and 19.*

Setting the Upper Limit Switch

5. *Reconnect hoist to power supply.*
6. *Run hook to the desired upper position, cautiously operating the hoist without a load.*
7. *Disconnect hoist from power supply.*
8. *Moving one traveling nut toward the other increases hook   travel and away from the other decreases the travel. Now, turn the nut nearest the switch indicated as the "UPPER LIMIT SWITCH" until it just breaks the limit switch contacts. An audible click will be heard as the switch opens. Continue to rotate the nut toward the switch an additional one full tooth.*
9. *Reposition the guide plate in the next slot and securely tighten screws.*
10. *Reconnect hoist to power supply and check the stopping point of hook by first lowering the hook about 61 cm (2 Foot), then raise the hook by jogging cautiously until the upper limit switch stops upward motion. The stopping point of hook should be the desired upper position. If not, repeat the above instructions.*
11. *Double check setting by lowering the hook about 61cm (2 feet) and then run the hook into the upper limit with (UP) control held depressed.*

12. *Fine adjustment of the upper limit setting may be obtained by inverting the guide plate in Step 5. The offset on the plate gives adjustments equivalent to 1/2 notch, see Table 6 for the "Hook Travel Per Notch of Limit Switch Nut" When inverting the plate, it may be necessary to use the notch adjacent to the one used in the preliminary setting.*

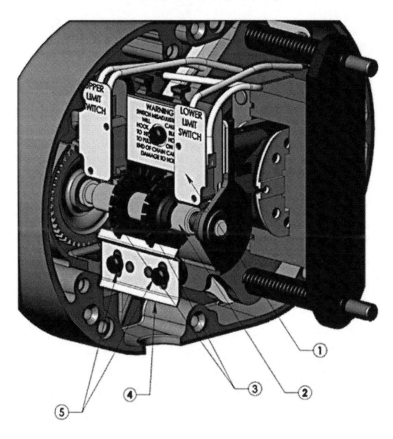

Figure 18. Limit Switches, Models B, C & F

1. **Limit switch sub-assy**
2. **Limit switch shaft**
3. **Traveling nuts**
4. **Guide plate**
5. **Screws**

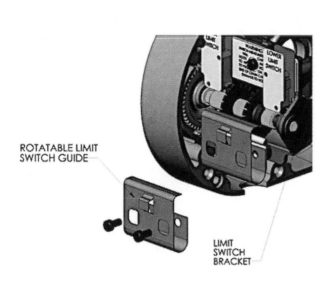

Figure 18A. Rotatable Limit Switches, Models B, C & F

Figure 19. Limit Switches, Models J, L, R, LL & RR
1. Limit switch sub-assy   4. Guide plate
2. Limit switch shaft   5. Screws
3. Traveling nuts

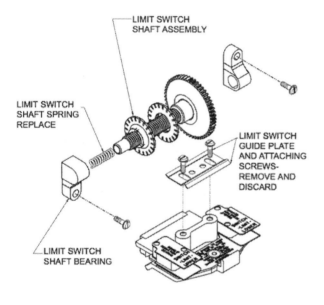

Figure 19A. Industrial Limit Switches, Models J, L, R, LL & RR

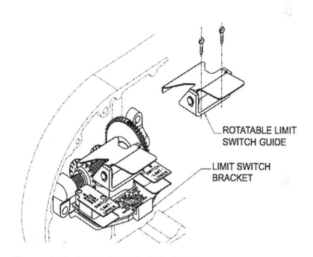

Figure 19B. Rotatable Limit Switches, Models J, L, R, LL & RR

Illustrations courtesy of Columbus McKinnon

Setting the Lower Limit Switch

1. *Again, refer to Table 6 shown above. The "B" dimension column shows the minimal link distance between the top of the hook and the bottom of the hoist.*
2. *Disconnect hoist from power supply.*
3. *Remove back frame cover*

4. The position of upper and lower limit switches is indicated on the fiber insulator.

5. Loosen the screws to permit guide plate to be moved   out of engagement with the traveling nuts, refer to Figures 18 and 19.

6. Run hook to the desired lower position, cautiously operating the hoist without a load.

7. Disconnect hoist from power supply.

8. Moving one traveling nut toward the other increases hook   travel and away from the other decreases the travel. Now, turn the nut nearest the switch indicated as the "LOWER LIMIT SWITCH" until it just breaks the limit switch contacts. An audible click will be heard as the switch opens. Continue to rotate the nut toward the switch an additional one full tooth.

9. Reposition the guide plate in the next slot and securely tighten screws.

10. Reconnect hoist to power supply and check the stopping point of hook by first raising the hook about 61 Centimeters (2 feet) then lower the hook by jogging cautiously until the lower limit switch stops downward motion. The stopping point of hook should be the desired lower position. If not, repeat the above instructions.

11. Double check setting by raising the hook about 61 cm (2 feet) and then run the hook into the lower limit with (DOWN) control held depressed.

12. Fine adjustment of the lower limit setting may be obtained by inverting the guide plate in Step 10. The offset on the plate gives adjustments equivalent to 1/2 notch, see Table 6 for the "Hook Travel Per Notch of Limit Switch Nut" When inverting the plate, it may be necessary to use the notch adjacent to the one used in the preliminary setting

13. Reconnect hoist to power supply.

One Notch will move the load chain ¾" on a Model L Motor

photo courtesy of Columbus McKinnon

Label
Hoists can be configured to many different carrying capacities, speeds and voltages. An electrical data label is attached to every hoist displaying information relevant to that specific hoist. If the label is worn or missing, do not use the hoist.

The label should contain the following information:
- Model Number
- Load Capacity in tons or Kg
- Horse Power
- Hoist Speed(s) in feet per minute
- Power Supply and conversions
- Amps
- Manufacturer Information including Date of Manufacture
- Special Warnings
- Quality Assurance

 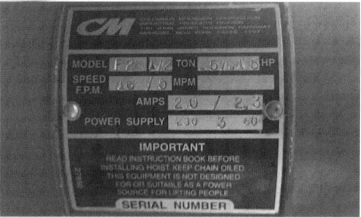

Understanding Rated Loads and Design Factors
Most industrial hardware is rated with a Working Load Limit (WLL) or Safe Working Load (SWL). This rated load limit is the absolute maximum load that a manufacturer recommends be applied to a piece of hardware. In the case of chain hoists, this number is usually expressed in Tons (or Kgs). The Working Load Limit is a fraction of the breaking strength and is based on an application of the Design Factor. Design Factors are a percentage of the breaking strength and are expressed as a ratio, such as 5:1, or sometimes as a single number, such as 5. The Design Factor of the CM Loadstar is 5:1.

Example: What is the working load limit (WLL) of a of chain hoist with a breaking strength of 10,000 pounds based on a Design Factor of 5:1?

Working Load Limit = Breaking Strength/ Design Factor
Working Load Limit = 10,000 / 5

Working Load Limit = 2000 lb or 1 Ton

The Design Factor creates a margin of safety to compensate for normal wear and less than optimal working conditions. Design Factors do NOT compensate for extreme shock loads, extensive wear/damage, or other factors that might cause the hardware to fail. All hardware used in rigging should be inspected before every install to ensure that it is not damaged.

1 TON-MAX-1000 Kg

⚠ WARNING -TO AVOID INJURY

- DO NOT OPERATE HOIST WHEN LOAD IS NOT CENTERED UNDER HOIST.
- DO NOT OPERATE UNLESS TRAVEL LIMIT DEVICES FUNCTION. TEST EACH SHIFT.
- DO NOT REMOVE OR OBSCURE THIS WARNING LABEL.
- DO REPLACE DAMAGED OR MAL- FUNCTIONING HOOK LATCH.

- DO NOT LIFT MORE THAN 1 TON, 1000 KG.
- DO NOT OPERATE WITH TWISTED, KINKED OR DAMAGED CHAIN.
- DO NOT OPERATE DAMAGED OR MALFUNCTIONING HOIST.
- DO NOT LIFT PEOPLE OR LOADS OVER PEOPLE.

-- KEEP CHAIN WELL OILED AND READ --

ANSI B30.16 SAFETY CODE FOR HOIST AND APPROPRIATE CM HOIST INSTRUCTION, MAINTENANCE AND PARTS MANUAL.

35201

Inspection and testing

Minimum inspection and testing of electric chain hoists are based on ANSI E1.6-2 – 2013, *Design, Inspection, and Maintenance of Electric Chain Hoists for the Entertainment Industry*. Following ANSI recommendations, Columbus-McKinnon defines the type of "wear and tear" an electric chain hoist is subjected to as *Normal, Heavy, and Severe*.

- *Normal Service: Involves operation with randomly distributed loads within the rated load limit, or uniform loads less than 65 percent of rated load for not more than 25 percent of the time.*
- *Heavy Service: Involves operating the hoist within the rated load limit which exceeds normal service.*
- *Severe Service: Normal or heavy service with abnormal operating conditions.*

In addition, frequent and periodic inspections MUST be performed on all hoists. *Frequent inspections* involve a visual inspection by a competent person before each use, but may also include weekly and monthly inspections based on normal, heavy or severe service. Records are not required for frequent inspections. *Periodic Inspections* must be performed by qualified personnel and require that inspection records be kept. These inspections are to be performed yearly for normal service, semi-annually for heavy service, and quarterly for severe service. Failure of any component must be corrected before the hoist can be returned to service.

Load Testing

Any hoist that has been repaired or has had its components replaced, must be load tested to insure proper operation. In addition, any hoist that has not seen service for at least twelve months must also be load tested. Follow manufactures recommendations regarding the types of loads to be used during the testing. ANSI recommendations on load testing are as follows:

- ***4.3 Testing*** *4.3.1 An operational test of the hoist must be performed before a dynamic load test of that hoist.*
- ***4.3.1.1*** *Lifting and lowering functions shall be tested under no-load conditions. (Testing through complete rated lift length is not required).*
- ***4.3.1.2*** *Brake(s) operation shall be tested under no-load conditions.*
- ***4.3.2*** *Dynamic load testing shall be at 125% of the hoist's rated capacity, if approved by the manufacturer. If the operation of an overload protection device prevents lifting a 125% load, then the load shall be reduced to the rated capacity and the test completed. If the manufacturer prohibits load testing at 125% of the rated capacity, the load testing shall be done with the load specified by the manufacturer.*
- ***4.3.3*** *Testing of the overload protection device shall be performed according to the manufacturer's recommendations.*
- ***4.3.4*** *Dynamic load testing shall be required whenever a load bearing component, as identified by the manufacturer is altered, repaired, or replaced.*
- ***4.3.5*** *The replacement of load chain is specifically excluded from requiring dynamic load testing; however, an operational test shall be made prior to returning the hoist to service.*

Operation and Safety Procedures

Before lifting any load, check for the following:

- That the load being lifted is within the rated load limits of the hoist. Overloading can cause failure of the hoist components and danger to personnel. When using three or more hoists to raise a truss, be aware of the phenomenon known *as statically indeterminate structure*, which can cause unintentional overloading. This will be discussed more in detail in the chapter on Static and Dynamic Loads.
- That the upper and lower limits are set.
- That the hooks on the chain bag are facing out.
- That the working shackle or sling is firmly seated in the saddle of the hook and that the hook latch is closed. Off-center loading of the hook is not permitted.
- Do not wrap the load chain around the load and do not wrap the hook onto itself as a choker chain.
- When the load is ready to be lifted, raise the load only about six inches off the ground. This will insure that the load is firmly seated in the hook.

When lifting the load

- Check "bumping" is often done to allow the load to settle. Wait 4 to 5 seconds before bumping the hoist again. This will allow any residual "shock" load frequencies to dissipate.
- Do not use the hoist to lift people.
- Warn all personnel in the area of your intension to lift the load.
- Only competent personnel are permitted to operate the equipment.
- When using a double-reeved chain hoist, be sure the chain is not twisted. A twist can occur is the hook block has capsized through the chain itself.
- Do not allow the load to swing while being raised.
- Be aware of your surroundings whenever operating a hoist.

Summary

Always be familiar with the equipment you are using. Hoists are no exception. The manufacturer's instruction manual provides excellent information as to the use, inspection, and operation of the specific type, make and model. Many hoist manufacturers like Columbus McKinnon offer training in the operation and maintenance of their equipment. The ANSI guidelines for the use of Electric Chain Hoists and Chain Hoist Systems are available for free download at the PLASA web site:

http://tsp.plasa.org/tsp/documents/published_docs.php

- **ANSI E1.6-1** Entertainment Technology – Powered Hoist Systems
- **ANSI E1.6-2** Hoist Inspection and Maintenance
- **ANSI E1.6-3** Safe Use Electric Chain Hoists
- **ANSI E1.6-4** Portable Control of Fixed-Speed Electric Chain Hoists in the Entertainment Industry

Chapter 14:

Basic Electricity and Power Distribution

In Chapter 13 we discussed electric chain hoists. In this chapter we will start with basic electricity, circuits, fuses and connectors. Finally, we will examine how electricity is distributed and how power is supplied to the hoists.

Electrical Theory
Simply defined, electricity is the flow of electrons down a conductor. So, what is a conductor? Basically, conductors are most commonly the "metals"; but a conductor can be any material that will allow electrons to flow from one point to another.

"Good" Conductors
- Gold
- Silver
- Copper
- Aluminum
- Iron

"Poor" Conductors
- Water
- Earth or ground
- Human Body

Some conductors allow electrons to flow more easily than others. Gold and silver, for example, are excellent conductors of electricity, but their cost is prohibitive for common electrical wiring. Copper is not as good a conductor as gold and silver as there is some resistance to the flow of electrons naturally occurring in the metal, but it is inexpensive and readily available. The resistance to flow increases with metals like aluminum and iron.

Insulators are materials that do not allow electrons to flow at all. These are used to cover conductors to prevent the electrons from flowing into the earth (grounding). Some common insulators are:
- Glass
- Rubber
- Plastic

So, how does electricity work?

Without going into atomic theory, basically, for every proton (+ charge) centered in the nucleus, there is an equal number of electrons (- charge) orbiting around the nucleus. There is a balance between positive charged protons and negative charged electrons. Electrons, however, are not all that bound to the atom. In the case of the metals (conductors) the electron in the last orbit is called a valence electron. If an outside pressure or force is applied, this last electron is essentially "kicked out" of orbit and is essentially "free" to roam about. This creates an imbalance in the atom, as there are now more protons (+ charge) than there are electrons (- charge). The atom is going to be looking for any free electrons to balance itself out. Any free electron will attach itself to the new atom until a force or pressure causes it to move on. This is what electricity is: the flow of free electrons jumping from atom to atom down a conductor. The copper atoms essentially pass the electrons down the wire.

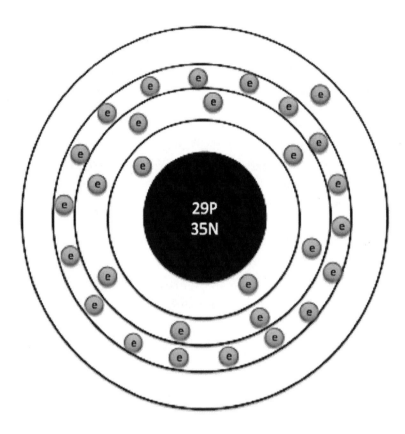

The Bohr model of a copper atom is very useful atomic model in our understanding of electricity. Note the single valance electron in the last orbit.

If this sounds almost like water flowing down a hose, it is. The free electrons flowing down the conductor are comparable to water flowing down a tube (current). The force or pressure that causes the electrons to flow can be compared to the force behind the water (Electro-Motive Force).

Let's examine some of these common terms and their inter-relationship to each other.

- Electro-Motive Force (EMF)- is the force or pressure behind the flow of electrons. It is measured in *Volts*.
- Current- is the flow of electrons. It is measured in *Amperage* (or *Amps*).
- *Watts*- is a measurement of the energy created or how much work is done. It is referred to as Power.
- *Ohms*- is the resistance to the flow of electrons. Slows the flow.

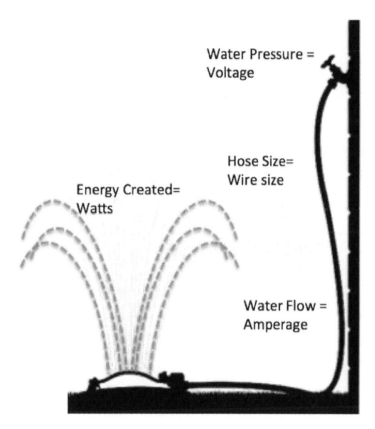

Water Pressure = Voltage

Hose Size= Wire size

Energy Created= Watts

Water Flow = Amperage

Resistance to Flow= Ohms

The water sprinkler example best describes this inter-relationship. As faucet is turned on, water begins to flow down the hose. Think of this as the force or pressure behind the flow of water (volts). A lawn sprinkler connected to our hose begins to rotate and squirt water as a result of the pressure or force of water in the hose (amperage). The current slows due to the resistance of the sprinkler (ohms). As the faucet is turned on to full, the flow of water increases, and the lawn sprinkler rotates faster and faster. Notice the relationship between the current flow, the water pressure, resistance, and the sprinkler? The same relationship is true with electricity.

A Volt is the force required to push 1 Amp through 1 Ohm of resistance. As the electrons flow down a conductor, it encounters resistance. This resistance is caused by a natural resistance in the copper wire and a resistance (effort) performing work. This work, called Power, may be in the form of electro-magnetism (as a rotor spinning in a motor) or heat (as a lamp glowing in a lighting instrument).

Power is measured in Watts. A Watt is equal to one Amp being pushed down a conductor by one Volt. This relationship is expressed by two basic formulas: Ohms Law and the PIE Formula. Let's look at both of these formulas and how they work.

Ohms Law

Ohm's law states that the current through a conductor between two points is directly proportional to the potential difference across the two points. Introducing the constant of proportionality, the resistance, one arrives at the usual mathematical equation that describes this relationship:

$$Amps\ (I) = Volts\ (V)\ /\ Ohms\ (R)$$

where I is the Amperage through the conductor in units of amperes, Volts is the potential difference measured across the conductor in units of volts, and Ohms is the resistance of the conductor in units of ohms. More specifically, Ohm's law states that the R in this relation is constant, independent of the current.[1]

Example 1: A resistance of 12 Ω is placed across a 9 V battery. What is the current flow in Amps? Using the formula

$$I = V/R$$

we get: I=9/12
or
0.75 Amps

Example 2: In a circuit, there is a resistance of 100 Ω and a current of 0. 05 A, what is the voltage?

Restating the formula:

$$V = I \times R$$

we get: V= 100 x 0.05
or 5 Volts

[1] Reference: Wikipedia, the free encyclopedia.

PIE Formula

The PIE formula expresses the relationship between Watts (Power), Volts (E) and Amps (I). It is often referred to the West Virginia formula because it can be rephrased as Watts= Volts x Amps or W=VA making it easy to remember. All electrical equipment has a limit as to how much electricity (or amperage) it can handle. This formula allows us to safely keep track of the Amps, Watts and Volts in an electrical circuit.

Example 1:

A model L chain hoist will draw 13A at full load. The Voltage is 120V. What is the Wattage or Power of the hoist?

Using the formula

$$P = I \times E \text{ (or } W = V \times A)$$

we get: P= 120 x 13

or

1,560W

Example 2:

A chain hoist is able to produce 2,500W of power. The voltage is 230V. What is the Amperage?

Using the formula

$$I = P/E \text{ or } (A = W/V)$$

we get: A= 2,500/230

or

10.86 Amps

Circuits

Think of a circuit as a loop. It starts with a power source such as an outlet or battery. Electrons flow down a wire to a *load*, such as a lamp or motor. Another wire runs from the load back to the source completing the circuit. A switch is often inserted into the circuit, allowing the operator to *open* or *close* the circuit. If the switch is open, the load will not function; if closed, the load will engage. The diagram below illustrates a simple circuit.

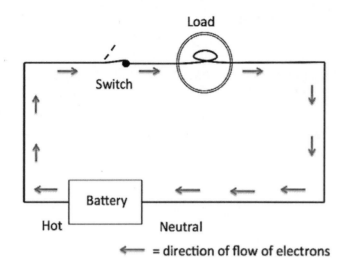

A simple circuit

Series and Parallel Circuits

Ever work with those Holiday Tree lights where one light goes out and they all go out? That is typical of a *series circuit*.

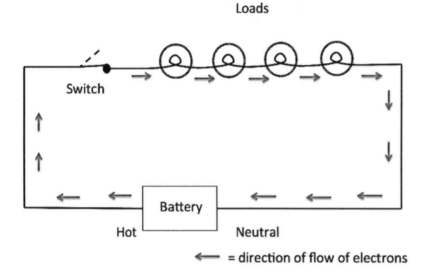

A series circuit

Loads

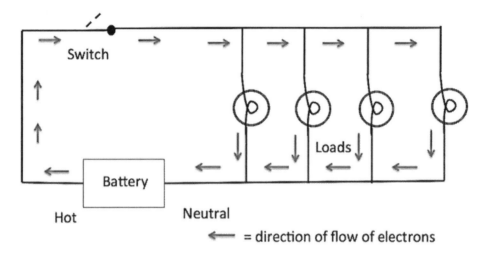

A series circuit is shown with a break in the filament wire. The flow of electrons stops when the circuit is broken.

In a series circuit, the electrons must pass through each consecutive lamp filament. The voltage is reduced consecutively. If one lamp goes out, they will all go out!
With parallel circuits, the electrons pass thru each lamp filament individually while getting full voltage. If one filament breaks, the rest stay on.

A Parallel Circuit.

Combination Circuits
Most circuits are combinations of series and parallel. Fuses, circuit breakers and switches are always used in series with multiple loads in parallel. Switches enable the operator to turn the circuit on and off, while fuses and circuit breakers protect the circuit from experiencing an overload.

Fuses and Circuit Breakers

Essentially, fuses and circuit breakers are electricity's safety valve. Should a circuit rated at 20-amps experience a sudden 30-amp surge in the flow of electrons, this excessive electrical current could cause damage to the entire circuit and even fire. Fuses and circuit breakers are placed in series and are rated at the same amperage as the circuit. A fuse has a low resistance metal wire or strip that melts when too much current flows through it. A circuit breaker is made up a bi-metal strip that will disengage the circuit when it experiences too much current.

Direct Current vs Alternating Current

Electricity comes in basically two forms: *Direct Current (DC)* and *Alternating Current (AC)*. *Direct Current* is the only type of electricity that can be stored and used at a later time. Batteries are a good means of producing and storing *Direct Current*. In a *Direct Current* circuit, the electrons flow along a wire in one direction from one terminal (+) to the other (-). Unfortunately, *Direct Current* does not travel very well over long distances. The natural resistance in the transmission wires use up the current flow very quickly and you are left with 0 voltage at the end if the line.

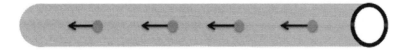

Flow of electrons in a Direct Current.
Electrons flow in one direction.

Unlike *Direct Current*, *Alternating Current* **can** be transmitted over long distances. Because the current changes direction (or polarity), the electrons do not have far to travel. They simply reverse direction. If there is a resistance encountered during transmission, transformers are able to "step" the voltage back up, thus *Alternating Current* is what is used today in transmission lines and power stations. The down side to *Alternating Current*, is that it must be used immediately.

Flow of electrons in an Alternating Current.
Electrons alternate direction.

In the U.S., the change in the direction (or polarity) of the electrons happen very quickly- 120 times per second per each leg, or 60 full cycles per second.

Otherwise, there is not a lot of difference between the two types of currents. *Voltage* is still the pressure or force, *amperage* is still the electrical current, *watts* is still a measurement of the work done and *Ohms* still measures the resistance to the flow. The formulas discussed earlier, still work.

Power Distribution

Electricity is created by a variety of different sources. Power plants generate power from such resources as nuclear, hydroelectric, solar, hydrocarbon and wind. These generating plants are generally located close to these resources, so the power they generate must be transported at high voltages and low amps across long distances. The power produced consists of three conductors or legs called phases. These phases are 120 degrees "out of phase" with each other. The alternating current produced is at the same frequency and voltage amplitude, but the phase differential is 1/3rd to each leg. In other words, each phase reaches its peak voltage 1/3rd of a cycle after the previous leg reached its peak and 1/3rd of a cycle before the next leg reaches its peak. Three hot wires deliver the power. The voltage across any two hot wires will measure 208V. The manner in which this power is delivered is called a service.

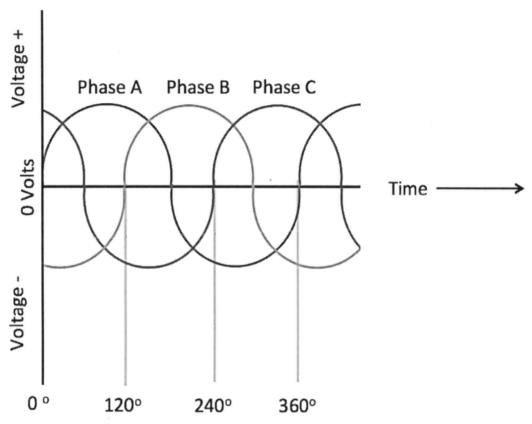

This 3-phase sine wave shows each phase plotted in time. Note each sine wave is 120° out of phase to one another.

The Delta Service

The drawing shown below is referred to as the "Delta Service" after its similarity to the Greek Letter Δ. It best illustrates how electricity is produced and delivered down transmission lines. It has four wires: three "hot" legs, plus a ground. Notice each leg is 120° to each other and is labeled A, B, and C just as the illustration shows above. At lower voltages, the Delta configuration can be perfect for producing rotating magnetic fields such as those found in chain hoists motors.

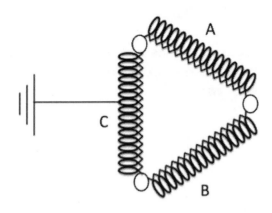

A Delta Configuration- Three "hot" legs plus a ground

The Wye Service

But how is this power delivered to building, particularly an arena venue?

As mentioned earlier, AC voltage can be "stepped up" or "stepped down" by means of line transformers. This is done through a series of sub-stations until the electricity reaches the line transformers outside the venue. Once inside the building, the electricity is converted from a Delta service to a Wye service where it is made more useable.

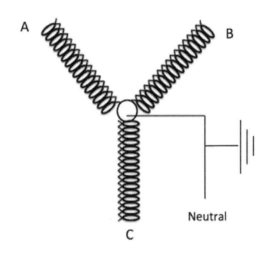

Three Phase Wye Configuration

Notice the Wye service has the same three "hot" legs A, B, and C, that were present in the Delta service, but now it has the addition of a neutral leg (and ground) that was created at the transformer for a total of five wires. The ground is bonded to the Neutral, which in turn runs into the earth outside. With the Delta service, all three legs were connected to each other. With the Wye service, all three legs share a common neutral. Here the voltage is 208V between any two "hot" wires, but also 120V can be measured between any "hot" wire and the Neutral. This means that the Wye system can provide two separate voltages; three phase (208V) and single phase (120V). This is much more convenient for use by a wide variety of appliances and equipment.

Single-Phase

Single-phase electricity is the power we find in our homes. It is simply not practical to use in industry. A single-phase service has two "Hots" that are drawn off one of the legs of a Delta service. Each of the "new" legs measures 120V from the "hot" to the Neutral and 240V between them. The neutral is again created at the transformer. The ground is bonded to the Neutral where it is attached to an electrode and run to the earth outside the home.

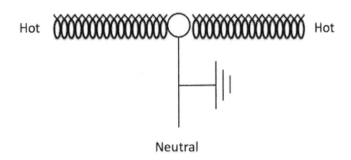

Single-Phase Configuration

Grounding vs Grounded

Electricity will always try and find its way to the earth. This is where the term "ground" originates. Although a poor conductor, the human body IS none-the-less a conductor of electricity. If you are the only means available for electrons to reach the earth, then the electrons will travel through you. However, if given a choice between you and a grounded conductor, such as copper, then the electrons will travel down the ground wire to reach the earth. Remember: electrons will always travel down the path of least resistance to reach the earth.

In order to understand the differences between the terms *grounded* vs. *grounding*, let's look at what these two words mean. In any electrical circuit, we need two wires to complete the circuit; one is called the *hot* and the other is called the *neutral*. In some instances, the neutral wire is called the *grounded neutral wire* or *grounded neutral.* This neutral is grounded to the earth so as to establish the earth as a reference for the electrical system. A *grounding wire* serves as a "safety" wire by connecting the equipment directly to the earth in the event of a short circuit.

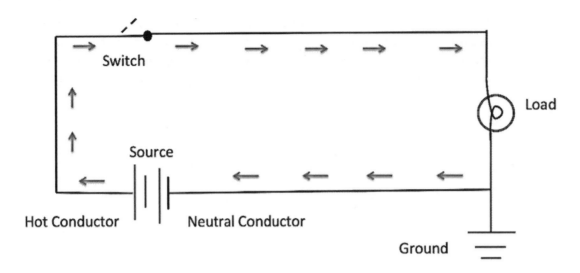

There are three uses to the term "ground".
- Equipment grounding
- Grounded neutral
- System ground

Equipment Grounding.
The Equipment Ground wire is not part of the electrical circuit. Its purpose is to form a connection between the chassis or body of the electrical equipment and the earth. If there should be an electrical *short circuit*, then the electrons will follow along the ground wire (the path of least resistance).

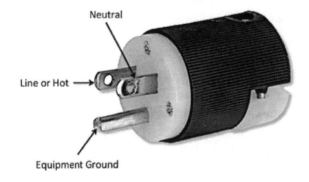

Edison Plug with Ground

Grounded Neutral
How does the equipment ground wire connect to the ground? It does so at the service panel where the neutral wire and the grounding wire are bonded at the neutral buss. This is called the *Grounded Neutral*. Should too much current flow through the grounding wire, then the circuit breaker at the electrical panel will blow.

System Ground
The system ground occurs when the neutral buss of an electrical panel or service is connected to the earth by an electrode that runs from the panel to the ground. The neutral buss now has the potential of serving as a ground as well. It may seem strange that a neutral, which is part of an electrical circuit and carries an electrical current, also serve as a ground. Wouldn't this also make the ground "live"? Not so. What this does is gives the electrical source a reference to the earth.
A good example would be with portable generators. The generator frame is bonded to the neutral buss. Unless the frame is sitting on the earth, it has no connection reference to the earth. The generator frame may need to be grounded to the earth by a separate electrode to give it a reference to the earth.

To summarize, think about that electrical short circuit. A technician is focusing a lighting instrument; the lighting instrument short circuits. Rather than having the electrons flow through the technician, the electrons flow through the ground wire (*equipment grounding*). The ground wire is grounded at the neutral buss (*grounded neutral*). The neutral buss is grounded at the panel to the earth by an electrode (*system grounding*).

Hooking up the Power
Whether In a theatre or arena, road shows come into the venue with their own dimmer racks, amplifiers and power distribution boxes. All require hook up to the venue's power supply. Electrical codes require that only licensed electricians be allowed to work on power distribution panels. However, because entertainment wiring is temporary, codes do allow for "qualified persons" to hook up power supplies in this instance. OSHA's definition for "qualified" is:

> *"Qualified" means one who, by possession of a recognized degree, certificate, or professional standing, or who by extensive knowledge, training, and experience, has successfully demonstrated his ability to solve or resolve problems relating to the subject matter, the work, or the project.*

Stagehands who are ETCP certified can meet this qualification. Unqualified personnel should not touch the power.

Locating the Power distrubution panels
Theatre power distribution is usually located stage right or left of the proscenium. In arenas, it is generally located near the service entrance. Once the power is ready to be connected, there is a proceedure to follow for properly connecting the feeder cables to the power source. Again, only a qualified stage technician may connect the feeder cables to the panel.

Connecting Power
Cam-locs are considered temporary feeder cables and are run from the power distrubution panel to the show distribution boxes(called *distros*). More discussion on Cam-locs will follow at the end of this chapter.

Prior to connection

1. Find the build's power distribution panel and turn the master switch (Bull Switch) to the OFF position. The master circuit breaker at the show's distrubtion box (*distro*) should be OFF as well. Use a test meter to insure that the power is indeed OFF.

2. Lay the feeder cables out, making sure there is enough cable to make the run from the power panel to the show distribution box. Do not connect the feeder cables to the show distribution box at this time.

3. Make sure the feeder cables are the correct gauge and the show is not drawing more amps than the panel can provide. (*This should have been done before the show left the shop, but it never hurts to check it again*).

4. Account for all the Cam-loc feeder cables and note their color markings. There should be five. The Cam-loc connector ends will be colored- black, red, blue for Hot, white for Neutral, and green for Ground. These will run to the show's distro. The opposite ends of the Cam-locs, called tails, will be bare wires with color coded tape to match their respective ends. It will be these tails that connect to the lug nuts of the building's power distribution panel.

Note the location of the lug nuts in the building's power supply panel. There will be lug nuts for the three hots, one neutral, and a connection for the ground. The bare wire ends will connect to these lugs. Note, that there are fuses for each one of the "Hot" legs and that each are rated in amps. These are typically indentified as leg A, leg B, and leg C. The Neutral buss will not have a fuse, but will be identified with a white Neutral wire running to it. The legs may have colored wires connecting them to the panel or they may be all black. They will NOT be white (light grey) or green, as these colors are reserved for the Neutral wire (white, light grey), or green for Ground.

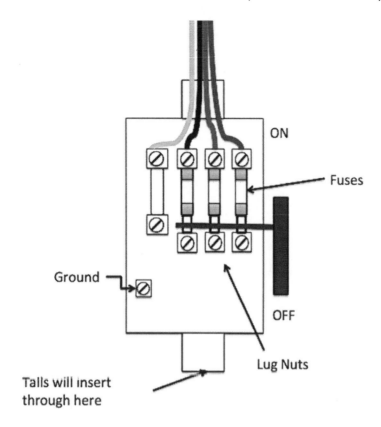

5. Locate the access hole at the base of the electrical panel. It will be through this hole that the feeder cables will pass. There should be nothing sharp that can cut the rubber insulation. Once attached, it may be necessary to tie a strain relief rope to the feeder bundle to prevent the cables from being pulled out.

It is *extremely* important that the procedure for connecting the feeder cables to the building's power distribution panel be followed in the correct order and by a "qualified" electrician. Any deviations or short-cuts may result in electrocution and even death.

1. Run the green (Ground) feeder cable through the hole at the base of the electrical panel and insert it into the Ground lug. Securely tighten the lug with a 17mm Allen Key.
2. Next, run the white (Neutral) feeder cable through the hole at the base of the electrical panel and insert it into the lug for the Neutral. Securely tighten the lug with a 17mm Allen Key.
3. Lastly, run the remaining feeder cables through the hole at the base of the electrical panel and attach them to the A, B, and C lugs. It does not matter the order, but usually the sequence is Black, Red, Blue. Securely tighten each lug with a 17mm Allen Key.
4. Close the panel door and attach a strain relief device around the feeder bundle if necessary.
5. Turn the power bull switch to the on position.
6. Test each leg with a test meter.
   • The volt meter should read 0 volts between the Ground and the Neutral
   • 120 volts between each Hot leg and the Neutral
   • 120 volts between the Hot leg and the Ground

- 208 volts between each Hot leg.
7. If you do not get these readings on the meter, re-check your connections.
8. Notify the show electrician that the power is ON.

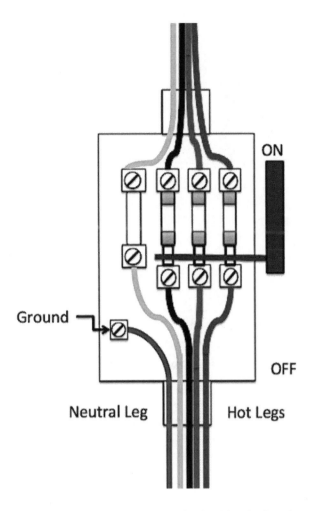

ON

OFF

Ground

Neutral Leg   Hot Legs

Feeder connections made at the building's distribution
panel. Power is turned ON.

Safety Hint: Sometimes feeder cables maybe extremely long and will require coiling to save space. Anytime power is running through a cable, an electro-magnetic field is created. Coiling a cable will create unwanted HEAT. Many times, electricians will reduce the electro-magnetic field created by coiling the cable in a figure eight pattern.

Once the power have been verified by the test meter and the show electrician has been notified, turn the power OFF at the panel. Power is now ready to be connected to the show's distro boxes. Make sure the master circuit breaker is in the OFF position too. The Cam-loc connections are made to the show's distro in the same order as was made at the panel: Green first, then White, then Black, Red, and Blue (the sequence of Black, Red, Blue doesn't matter). *Never deviate from this order as electrocution may result if the power should somehow be ON and somehow the legs cross connect.* Once the connections to the show distribution box have been made, then the power at the panel can be turned ON and the master circuit breaker can be turned ON.

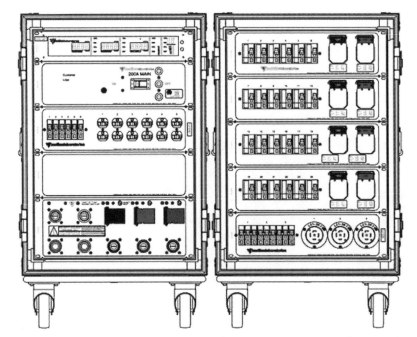

Safety Hint: when making any connection, it is always a good idea to *assume* that all the feeder cables are "Hot" to ensure "caution" when handling.

A Dual Power Distribution Box. Note the connection points for Cam-loc connector at the lower left.
photo courtesy of Mountain Productions

Disconnecting the Power

Disconnecting the power is simply a matter of reversing the process.
1. Turn the power OFF at the show's distro box.
2. Turn the power OFF at the building's power distribution panel
3. Disconnect the feeder cable at the show's distro in the following order:
   a) Black, Red and Blue (again sequence doesn't matter).
   b) Neutral
   c) Ground
4. Once disconnected from the distro, the feeder cables can be disconnected form the building's power supply panel in the same order.

Hooking Up Power to the Chain Hoist

A power station for the chain hoist motors will run separately from the show's distro box. Delta configurations provide 240V phase to phase; Wye configurations provide 208V phase to phase. The illustration on the next page shows one type of power supply station to the hoists as well as the controllers. We will discuss the power supply cable to the hoists in more detail at the end of this chapter. A hoist controller allows you to run individual hoists or groups of hoists by simply switching the numbered ON or OFF buttons for a specific hoist or groups of hoists. This may seem easy enough, but when raising or lowering a truss, always be aware of your surroundings. No one should ever stand under a hoist or truss while it is being moved.

Motors that run in Reverse

We mentioned earlier that three-phase motors run in a Delta configuration. That is, three "Hot" legs and no neutral. Chain hoist motors, we said, are no exception. There are times when a chain hoist motor WILL run backwards. This is an easy fix. Simply reverse any two of the "Hot" legs with each other. The hoist motor will now run in the correct direction.

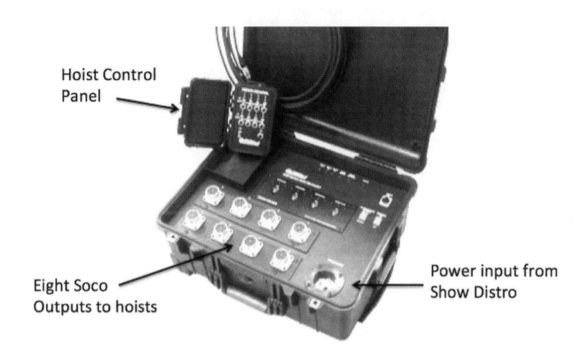

Hoist Control Panel

Eight Soco Outputs to hoists

Power input from Show Distro

A 12-channel hoist controller
photo courtesy of Allied Electronics

A "pickle" allows the user to connect to an individual chain hoist at the motor
photo courtesy of Columbus-McKinnon

CABLE AND CONNECTORS

Cable used in the entertainment industry must be strong and durable and yet flexible enough to withstand a wide variety of uses/ abuses. In its lifetime, cable will
be dragged, hoisted, pulled, squeezed, run over by scenery carts, road cases and forklifts. And yet, it must be dragged down at the end of every show, coiled and placed in road cases only to be unpacked and re-hung for the next show.

Single conductor, portable cable is often referred to as EISL (Entertainment Industry Stage Lighting)* cable. It has the durability and flexibility to withstand the abuses noted above. Code classifications for EISL cable is noted on the cable jacket of the cable. The table below will help you to decipher those cryptic codes printed on the cable sheathing. Please note that cable with the J or V designation is not recommended for use in the entertainment industry.

Type	Description
S	Severe Service Cord - 600 volts (also 277/480 or 480)
O	Oil Resistant Neoprene Outer Jacket Material
C	Temperature Rated Jacket (with temperature limit shown)
J	Junior Service cord (thin outer jacket)
V	Junior Service (thinner jacket than the one noted above)
E	Thermoplastic elastomer jacket
T	Thermoplastic jacket
W	Extra-hard usage, weather-resistant

Example: a cable with the designation of SO means that the cable is rated for severe service had has an oil resistant outer jacket. SCE cable means a severe service, temperature rated cable with a thermoplastic elastomer jacket. SOW will be the code we will find on all 7 pin Chain Hoist Motor Control Fly Cable. SOW means severe service, rubber jacketed portable cord with oil and water-resistant outer jacket.

Wire Size

All cable is rated in amps according to size (gauge). The following table shows the wire gauge size and its associated amperage based on the American Wire Gauge (AWG) standard. Note that the smaller the number, the larger the wire diameter. Wires that are greater than 1 AWG are written as #0, #00, #000 and so on. For example, the table below shows a #00 wire which is shown as 2/0 (or two-ought).

---

*EISL was the designation of these cable types before being adopted by the NEC. Before the creation of EISL, the only available cable was type W. It should be noted that Type W is **not** welding cable. Welding cable is not permitted for use where the voltage is 120v or greater.

Multi-connector cable is cable with several wire conductors inside the sheathing. This is labeled on the sheathing of the cable with the gauge of the wire and the number of conductors. A cable with three ten-gauge conductors would be shown as 10/3.

Wire gauge (AWG)	Amperage
#18	7 amp
#16	10 amp
#14	15 amp
#12	20 amp
#10	25 amp
#00 (2/0)	300 amp
#0000 (4/0)	405 amp

Color Coding of Wires

Multi-cable conductors are color-coded. Each color represents a specific purpose assigned to that particular conductor. The next chapter will discuss in depth what the purpose of each color means.

Color	Purpose
Red	Hot
Yellow	Hot
Blue	Hot
Black	Hot
White	Neutral
Green	Ground

Note: Orange is specifically reserved for the B phase (the high leg) in a Delta system.

Connector Types

Connectors allow for cable to be quickly, and safety connected or disconnected to the hoist. They come in both male and female gender. The male connector has exposed contacts that carry no power. It must be connected to the female in order to become charged. The female connector has all its contacts internal. It carries all the power.

There are many types of electrical connectors used in both theatre and arena. These include:
- Edison or parallel blade
- Stage Pin
- Twist-lock

Since this book is focusing specifically on Arena Rigging and hoist operation, we will focus only those connectors specific to hoist operation and power distribution.

Cam-Loc

A cam-loc is a singe wire connector used primarily for connecting a power source to a distribution box. It comes in sizes 2/0 for 300 amps and 4/0 for 400 amps and is color-coded to indicate legs: Red, Blue and Black for Hot legs, White for Neutral legs, and Green for ground. They lock in place by a clock-wise, half-turn rotation. There is also a mini #0 cam-loc for 100-amp connections.

Five Cam-loc connectors. The ends shown will be connected to a power distribution box, the bare ends will be connected to the lugs at a source panel.

photo courtesy of LEX Products Corporation

Hubble

Hubble manufactures a very durable, twist lock connector. The male end will attach to the hoist supplying power, while the female will connect to the pickle. These are available in either three phase or single phase.

Three-phase Hubble male and female twist lock connector

photo courtesy of Hubble Incorporated

Socapex

Socapex or (Soca) is the brand name for a type of multi-cable connectors used in the entertainment industry. Originally manufactured by a company called Amphenol Socapex, its slang name "Soca" has become synonymous with any similarly manufactured "generic" multi-cable. It primarily comes in 7 and 19 pin, 250V. The electrical connectors are male and female. The 7-pin, connector, more commonly used to power chain hoists, is configured for single or three phase voltage. 19-pin Soca is more commonly used to supply power to lighting fixtures on the truss, as the multi-cable is lighter than conventional cables.

6/7 SOW Cord, 7-Pin Motor Hoist Cable w/ 7PM-MCFL Connectors, Rating: 10 Amps, 250 VAC

photo courtesy of LEX Products Corporation

Summary

This chapter introduced you to basic electricity, how the power is generated and delivered to a theatre or arena venue. Again, it is important to remember that with permanent electrical installations, only licensed electricians can perform such work. In the entertainment industry, provisions are made for temporary installations. Only "qualified" personnel" can attach feeder cables to the building's power. In addition, we examined how Delta power is delivered to the show's distro and how that power is ultimately sent to the hoist.

Chapter 15:

Truss Math

In this chapter we will look at how to compute the vertical force on each end of a truss when the loads are spread out in different locations along the truss. This chapter starts with a single load placed somewhere along the truss. Here is a diagram of the problem.

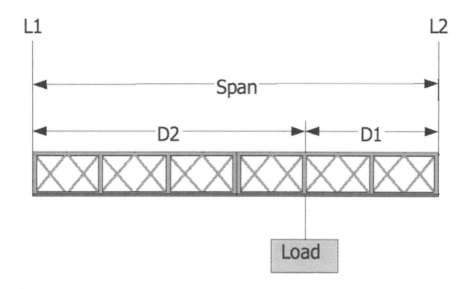

You might have noticed that I use D1 and D2 in the illustration above instead of H1 and H2 as I have used in previous chapters. Why? Maybe it is not a great reason, but it is because this type of problem does not contain a V1 or V2. This will also be true for the problems in Chapters 12 and 13, so I have substituted "D" for "H" in these chapters. I have also switched the numbering of D1 and D2, so do not get confused by this. It does not really make any difference what you label these distances, as long as you understand the concept of which parts you multiply by or divide by to solve the problem.

Our desire is to find the vertical force on the two supporting Legs (L1 and L2). In many cases you can easily determine what percentage of the Span D1 and D2 represents. If so, the load on each end of the truss will correspond inversely to this percentage. For example, if D1 is 25% of the Span, then the load on L2 is 75% of the Load. However, if it is difficult to determine these percentages, then the equations below can be used for solving this type of problem.

$$Tension\ on\ L1 = \frac{Load \times D1}{Span}$$

Note: You can also think of it as L1 = Load x (D1/Span) if that is easier for you to remember.

$$Tension\ on\ L2 = \frac{Load \times D2}{Span}$$

Note: You can also think of it as L2 = Load x (D2/Span) if that is easier for you to remember.

or

Tension on L2 = Load – L1

The trick I use to remember the method of solving this problem is to remember that to find the tension on one leg, you multiply the Load by the distance of the Load from the OPPOSITE leg, and then divide by the Span. We used the trick of "multiplying opposites" and then dividing in Chapter 7 on "Tension on Bridle Legs," and the same idea is used with this problem.

So, let's work a problem.

Example: If the Span is 20 feet, D1 is 5 feet and D2 is 15 feet (note: D1 + D2 must equal Span), and the Load 1 is 200 lb, what is the tension on L1 and L2?

$$Tension\ on\ L1 = \frac{Load \times D1}{Span}$$

$$Tension\ on\ L1 = \frac{200 \times 5}{20}$$

$$Tension\ on\ L1 = \frac{1000}{20}$$

Tension on L1 = 50 lb

$$Tension\ on\ L2 = \frac{Load \times D2}{Span}$$

$$\text{Tension on L2} = \frac{200 \times 15}{20}$$

$$\text{Tension on L2} = \frac{3000}{20}$$

Tension on L2 = 150 lb

Also, Tension on L1 + L2 must always equal the Load, which is one way to check your work. But, since that is true, once you find L1 you can compute the tension on L2 by using the simple equation Tension on L2 = Load – Tension on L1. Another easy check of your math is to make certain that the leg that is closest to the load has the most tension. Practice these simple problems before going to the next chapter, which puts multiple loads on the truss.

In Chapter 11, you learned how to compute the tension on L1 and L2 when there was a single load on the beam/truss. In this chapter, you will learn how to compute the loads when you have multiple loads that are spread out along the truss. Here is a diagram of the problem.

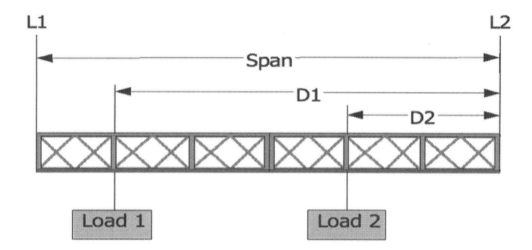

As in Chapter 11, our desire is to find the vertical force on the two supporting Legs (L1 and L2). The equations for solving this problem are:

$$Tension\ on\ L1 = \frac{(Load\ 1\ \times\ D1) + (Load\ 2\ \times\ D2)}{Span}$$

$$Tension\ on\ L2 = (Load\ 1 + Load\ 2) - Tension\ on\ L1$$

Note: Instead of using the equations above, you can use the equations in Chapter 10, and find the tensions on the legs for each load, then add the two tensions for each leg to get the total tension. Before we begin calculating the tensions, it should be noted that, unlike the problem in Chapter 13, D1 + D2 will NOT equal the Span. The equation for determining the tension on L1 uses L2 as the starting point for D1 and D2. Let me say this again – both D1 and D2 are measured from L2 to their respective loads. This is confusing to some people, but this is correct.

Example: If the Span is 20 feet, D1 is 17.5 feet, D2 is 5 feet, Load 1 is 100 lb and Load 2 is 200 lb, what is the tension on L1 and L2?

$$\text{Tension on L1} = \frac{(100 \times 17.5) + (200 \times 5)}{20}$$

$$\text{Tension on L1} = \frac{1750 + 1000}{20}$$

$$\text{Tension on L1} = \frac{2750}{20}$$

Tension on L1 = 137.5 lb

And because the Tension on L1 + Tension on L2 must equal Load1 + Load 2 we can use the simple equation to determine L2.

Tension on L2 = (Load1 + Load 2) – Tension on L1
Tension on L2= (100 + 200) - 137.5
Tension on L2= 300 - 137.5
Tension on L2 = 162.5 lb

Although this may seem complicated at first, remember that you keep the 1s together (Load1 x D1) and the 2s together (Load2 x D2), then add them and divide the result by the Span. If you have more than two loads, just add "(Load 3 x D3)" and so on to the first part of the equation and divide the total by the Span. Practice the sample problems before going on to the next chapter, which is even more complex.

Multiple Loads on a Truss
Next, you will learn how to compute the loads when you have multiple loads that are spread out along the truss. Here is a diagram of the problem.

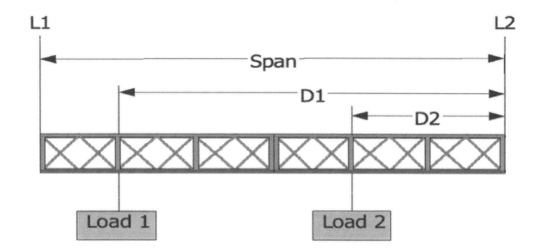

As in Chapter 11, our desire is to find the vertical force on the two supporting Legs (L1 and L2). The equations for solving this problem are:

$$Tension\ on\ L1 = \frac{(Load\ 1\ \times\ D1) + (Load\ 2\ \times\ D2)}{Span}$$

$$Tension\ on\ L2 = (Load\ 1 + Load\ 2) - Tension\ on\ L1$$

Note: Instead of using the equations above, you can use the equations in Chapter 10, and find the tensions on the legs for each load, then add the two tensions for each leg to get the total tension. Before we begin calculating the tensions, it should be noted that, unlike the problem in Chapter 13, D1 + D2 will NOT equal the Span. The equation for determining the tension on L1 uses L2 as the starting point for D1 and D2. Let me say this again – both D1 and D2 are measured from L2 to their respective loads. This is confusing to some people, but this is correct.

Example: If the Span is 20 feet, D1 is 17.5 feet, D2 is 5 feet, Load 1 is 100 lb and Load 2 is 200 lb, what is the tension on L1 and L2?

$$Tension\ on\ L1 = \frac{(100\ \times\ 17.5) + (200\ \times\ 5)}{20}$$

$$Tension\ on\ L1 = \frac{1750 + 1000}{20}$$

$$Tension\ on\ L1 = \frac{2750}{20}$$

Tension on L1 = 137.5 lb

And because the Tension on L1 + Tension on L2 must equal Load1 + Load 2 we can use the simple equation to determine L2.

Tension on L2 = (Load1 + Load 2) – Tension on L1
Tension on L2= (100 + 200) - 137.5
Tension on L2= 300 - 137.5
Tension on L2 = 162.5 lb

Although this may seem complicated at first, remember that you keep the 1s together (Load1 x D1) and the 2s together (Load2 x D2), then add them and divide the result by the Span. If you have more than two loads, just add "(Load 3 x D3)" and so on to the first part of the equation and divide the total by the Span. Practice the sample problems before going on to the next chapter, which is even more complex.

Cantilevered Truss

Finally you will learn how to compute the loads when one or more of the loads are cantilevered outside of the legs. Here is a diagram of the problem.

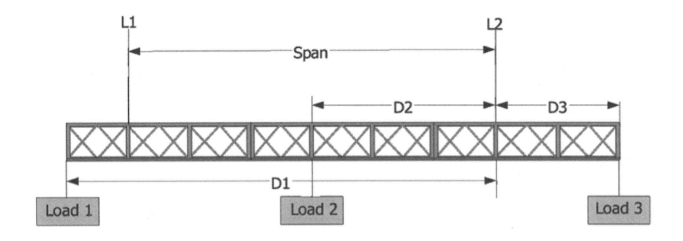

The equations for solving this problem are similar to the ones you learned in Chapter 14, except now we must deal with the Load that is cantilevered outside of the leg that is opposite the leg on which we are computing the tension. This sounds a bit confusing, but will explain shortly. The equations for solving this problem are:

$$Tension\ on\ L1 = \frac{(Load\ 1 \times D1) + (Load\ 2 \times D2) - (Load\ 3 \times D3)}{Span}$$

$$Tension\ on\ L2 = (Load1 + Load\ 2 + Load3) - L1$$

Before we begin, let's note that, as in the previous chapter, the Span has no relevance to D1, D2 or D3. But, as in the previous Chapter, all of the distances (D1, D2 and D3) will be measured from L2. I also want to explain the "− (Load 3 x D3)" part of this equation.

You need to think of this rig as a teeter-totter or a lever, where the fulcrum is at the point where the Leg attaches to the truss. When we are computing L1, the fulcrum is where L2 attaches to the truss. If Loads 1 and 2 did not exist, the L1 end of the truss would pivot up (at the point where L2 attached to the truss) because Load 3 would not have anything counterbalancing it on the other side (and the L1 cable, chain, or round sling would not provide any resistance).

This would tell you that there is a positive force on L2 but a negative force on L1. (Remember: downward forces are "positive" and upward forces are "negative.") Because this is true, we need to include this negative force when we calculate the load on L1. When all of the loads were between the two Legs, you only had positive forces, so all of the forces were "added." Since we now have a negative force, we need to "subtract" it. That is why we have "− (Load 3 x D3)" in this equation. "− (Load 3 x D3)" is the negative force on L1.

Example: If the Span is 30 feet, Load 1 is 200 lb, D1 is 35 feet, Load 2 is 150 lb, D2 is 15 feet, Load 3 is 100 lb, and D3 is 10 feet, what is the tension on L1 and L2?

$$Tension\ on\ L1 = \frac{(Load\ 1 \times D1) + (Load\ 2 \times D2) - (Load\ 3 \times D3)}{Span}$$

$$Tension\ on\ L1 = \frac{(200 \times 35) + (150 \times 15) - (100 \times 10)}{30}$$

$$Tension\ on\ L1 = \frac{7,000 + 2,250 - 1,000}{30}$$

$$Tension\ on\ L1 = \frac{8,250}{30}$$

Tension on L1 = 275 lb

$$Tension\ on\ L2 = (Load1 + Load\ 2 + Load3) - L1$$

Tension on L2= (200 + 150 + 100) - 275
Tension on L2= 450 - 275
Tension on L2 = 175 lb

The most common mistake in solving these types of problems is adding instead of subtracting for the Load that is cantilevered. With a little practice, you can master these equations.

Although the equations in this chapter are for three Loads on a truss – with two of them cantilevered – in reality, most truss problems will involve many more Loads on the truss. In these cases, you can use variations of these equations to find the tension on the legs.

Statically Indeterminate Structures

So far in this chapter, we have only looked at truss that were supported by two legs/pick points. However, in the real world, trusses are often supported by three or more points. Beams/trusses that are supported by three or more points are called *statically indeterminate structures*.

One important thing to know about a beam that is supported by three or more points is that EVERY load on the beam affects the tension on EVERY supporting point on the beam, no matter where that load is placed on the beam or the number of supporting points. Sometimes the load will have a positive effect on a supporting point (a downward force) and sometimes it will be a negative effect on the supporting point (an upward force), but it WILL affect EVERY point. This means that it is much more complicated to calculate the load on any point supporting a truss supported by three or more points.

If the load on a truss supported by three or more points is uniformly loaded, the distance between the pick points is exactly the same, there are support points on the ends of the truss, and the truss is perfectly level, then there are tables that can show you the loads on each support point on the truss. Below is an example.

Statically Indeterminate Structures is beyond the scope of this book, but they are covered in detail in *Rigging Math Made Simple*.

TRUSS LOAD ANAYLZER-EOT

Jon Sogoian and I created a spreadsheet called TRUSS LOAD ANAYLZER-EOT that is intended to help professional entertainment riggers make decisions about the use of truss. Specifically, this application will help riggers answer four questions:

1) Is the span length between the points supporting the truss (or of the cantilever) acceptable or too long, based on a specified truss?
2) Is the total load on each span (or cantilever) acceptable or too great, based on the specified truss and the span length?
3) How much load is on each point supporting the truss?
4) Is the Total Static Load on the chain hoist less than or greater than the capacity of the chain hoist?

You can download the latest version of TRUSS LOAD ANAYLZER-EOT (2.1) for free from http://springknollpress.com/TLA-EOT/Truss Load Analyzer-EOT - 2.1.xlsm.zip. This is a compressed file that when be uncompressed gives you the Truss Load Analyzer EOT-2.1.xlsm file.

How to use this spreadsheet is discussed in my book *Rigging Math made Simple*.

More information on truss loading in discussed in Chapter 16.

Chapter 16:
Truss Loading

When installing a truss, there are four major questions about overloading that need to be answered:

1) Have I overloaded the span between any two truss suspension points?

2) Have I overloaded a truss suspension point?

3) Have I overloaded the chain hoist?

4) Have I overloaded the hanging point?

Since this lesson deals with truss overloading, we will concentrate on answering questions 1 and 2. In fact, let's address question 2 now. The fact is, if you have not overloaded the span between the truss suspension points and if you have placed the truss suspension point at a panel point (as required by all truss manufacturers) it is highly unlikely that you have overloaded the truss suspension point. Placing the truss suspension points at panel points is a critical step in safely rigging a truss.

To answer question 1, you will need to begin by looking at the truss loading table for the truss you are using. Below is an example of a typical loading table for a 20.5 x 20.5 general purpose plated truss.

Span feet (meters)	Maximum allowable uniform loads			Maximum allowable point loads						
				center point		third point		quarter point		
	Load lbs/ft	Load lbs (kgs)	Max Defl in.	Load lbs (kgs)	Max Defl. in.	Load lbs (kgs)	Max Defl. in.	Load lbs (kgs)	Max Defl. in.	
10 (3.05)	839	8390 (3806)	0.08	4744 (2152)	0.07	3558 (1614)	0.09	2372 (1076)	0.08	
20 (6.09)	230	4600 (2087)	0.34	2306 (1046)	0.27	1729 (784)	0.35	1153 (523)	0.32	
30 (9.14)	97	2910 (1320)	0.76	1464 (664)	0.62	1098 (498)	0.78	732 (332)	0.73	
40 (12.21)	51	2040 (925)	1.36	1021 (463)	1.13	765 (347)	1.39	510 (231)	1.30	
50 (15.24)	29	1450 (658)	2.10	737 (334)	1.80	553 (251)	2.16	369 (167)	2.05	

The truss loading tables provided by most US truss manufacturers are setup to display the data based on span lengths of 10 feet, as shown above. However, some truss load tables are based of 5-foot spans, which can be very useful because it provides you with more information.

ANSI E1.2 - 2012 Entertainment Technology— Design, Manufacture and Use of Aluminum Trusses and Towers requires truss manufacturers to list the max total load, the max uniformly distributed load, the maximum center point load and maximum deflection distances on their loading tables. Some manufacturers list the maximum allowable load and deflection distance for additional span distances: third point, fourth (quarter) point and sometimes fifth point. So, truss manufacturers will provide the maximum loading numbers for (at most) five possible loading situations of a truss. If the user has distributed the load on the truss in one of these configurations, the user can compare his/her loads to the maximum loads for that situation in the table. If his/her load is equal to or less than the maximum allowable load listed, then the span is not overloaded.

But, what about loading configurations that are not listed in the table? The truss manufacturers' general reply to this question is that the user should consult with the manufacturer to ensure that the loading situation does not overload the truss. While this seems like good advice, is it always necessary?

A generally recognized rule for determining if a span of a truss is overloaded is:

If the total load on the span is less than the Maximum UDL/2 for the specified span distance, then the span is not overloaded.

While this rule is straight-forward and easy to understand, is it an accurate equation that we want to follow? My answer is "Most of the time - yes, but not always." To find out why I say this, let's look at the chart below that uses the data from the truss load table from earlier in this lesson.

Span	Max UDL	Max CPL	Max UDL/2	Difference
10	8,390	4,744	4,195	549
20	4,600	2,306	2,300	6
30	2,910	1,464	1,455	9
40	2,040	1,021	1,020	1
50	1,450	737	725	12

In every case for this truss, the Max UDL/2 is less than the Max CPL for the same span distance. However, while most of these differences are fairly insignificant (1 – 12 pounds), the difference for a 10-foot span is quite significant - 549 pounds. So, while the load table says that you can safely place a single 4,744-pound load at the center point of a 10-foot span of this truss, the overloading rule stated above says that you cannot put a total of more than 4,195 pounds of load on the truss. This, of course, makes no sense.

An engineer at Tyler Truss tells me that it is safe to place the Max CPL at any point on the span. This gets us around the exception for short spans of truss that we see in the chart above. Also, looking at the data for the Third Point and Quarter Point in the loading table, we can see that there can be many situations where the total load on the span can be greater than the Maximum CPL for the specified span and yet not overload the truss. However, if the total load on a span does not exceed the Max CPL listed for a specific span in the load table, you the span will NEVER be overloaded.

Sometimes a truss might have a UDL and at least one point-load on the same span of a truss. If you have this situation, you need to calculate a revised Maximum CPL based on the Ratio of Consumed Capacity of a suspended UDL on a span. The steps to doing this are:

Step 1: Divide the weight of the suspended UDL on the span by the Maximum UDL listed in the load table for the specified span length. This gives you used capacity (as a decimal number).

Step 2: Subtract the used capacity (as a decimal number) from 1 to get the remaining capacity.

Step 3: Multiple the Maximum CPL for the specified span by the remaining capacity (specified as a decimal number) to get the new/revised Maximum CPL capacity.

There are standard WLLs for most types of hardware: DF = 5 for chain hoist and round slings, DF = 4 for the chain in the hoist, and DF = 6 for shackles. But what Design Factor is used for determining the WLL of the truss?

For truss made in the United States, the DF is the one dictated by the Aluminum Association's "Aluminum Design Manual" (ADM), which is 1.95 for a brittle failure mode and 1.65 for a ductile failure mode. To put this in perspective, at best, the MBS of aluminum truss is less than one-third as strong as a shackle, less than two-fifths as strong as the hoist and the round slings, and less than half as strong as the chain, with the same WLL. This is why great care must be taken with truss.

Reading the notes on the truss tables will provide you with important information. For example, truss manufacturers typically subtract the weight of the truss from the rating so that the riggers do not have to include it in their calculations (although the riggers will have to add the weight of the truss when calculating the load on the point.) Also, some truss tables include a 15% reduction in the loads based on repetitive use, as specified by the ANSI standard. If this reduction has been made, it will be indicated in the notes.

Here are answers to some common questions related to rigging truss and truss strength:

Q. Can I rig something from the horizonal spreaders on a truss?
A. Yes, you can rig from the 2" diameter horizontal spreaders, but not smaller spreaders on the truss. The horizontal spreaders on XSF's trusses are designed to hold 2,000 lb each. If higher loads are expected, the rigger should rig from the chords of the truss, instead of the horizontal spreaders.

Q. Can truss suspension points be rigged in tension (from the upper chords) or must it always be rigged in compression (from the lower chords)?

A. Most truss manufacturers say that the truss is just as strong when suspended from the top chord and from the bottom chord (and flat truss must always be suspended from the top chord). However, when truss is overloaded in tension the diagonals will snap, but in compression they will buckle. If a failure occurs when the truss is supported by the bottom chord, consequences are less catastrophic.

Q. I have been told to always hang at or near a panel point, is this important?

A. Truss is stronger at the panel points than between the panel points. Manufacturers specifically require that a truss suspension point be made at a panel point.

Truss should be inspected during each install to ensure that there are no broken welds or bent or damaged members of the truss. It should also be inspected after it is loaded (gaps at the gusset plates can indicate overloading). Truss should also be inspected once per year by a competent person with expertise in inspecting truss. ANSI E1.2 - 2012 Entertainment Technology— Design, Manufacture and Use of Aluminum Trusses and Towers should be consulted for more information on inspecting truss. The video listed below is an excellent source of information on inspecting truss. https://www.youtube.com/watch?v=nDmw7nm6Y0c&feature=emb_rel_pause

Maximum Load on a Cantilevered Truss

The information below was provided by Adrian Forbes-Black with Tomcat USA.

Our general company policy on cantilevered standard truss is as follows:

The total weight to be placed on the cantilevered truss must be less than the allowable CPL for a span 4 times the length of the cantilever.

Therefore, the first thing to do is to times the length of the cantilever by four. If that new length is more than the load tables for that truss allow or account for, then the cantilever is too long. For instance, if you want to cantilever a 12" x 12" nut and bolt connection truss 15 feet then you would need to look at what it could do at a span of 60 feet. However, that isn't covered by the load tables, so the cantilever is too long. However, if we reduce the cantilever to 10 feet then we would need to look at the 40-ft span length, which is something we do have in the engineering. Now that the length is approved, we can look at the center point load at that span to see what we can put on the end of the cantilever.

If you look at the attached load table for our Light Duty 12" x 12" nut and bolt truss for reference you can see that the maximum span allowable is 40-ft, which means a maximum cantilever length of 10 feet. The CPL at 40 feet is 426 pounds, which also means we can allow up to that much on the end of our 10-ft cantilever.

Obviously, this is a rough rule of thumb & should only be used as a guide, with advice taken from a professional engineer where applicable or deemed necessary, especially with dynamic loads or outdoor applications, etc.

Conclusion

Truss are complex systems of components. Truss manufacturer's load tables are created to help you determine the maximum load you can put on a span depending on where you place the load. However, users should understand all of the factors used to create these truss loading tables (they are typically appended to each truss table). And always remember that truss should be inspected before each use to ensure that it is not damaged.

Part IV:

Appendices

Appendix 1:

Reference Data

Sometimes you just need data about a piece of equipment or hardware. While manufacturers provide data on their products, some things you should just know as a rigger. Below are tables of reference data that may be helpful.

Round Slings

Code	Color	Capacity Vertical (lb)	Capacity Choker (lb)	Capacity Basket (lb)
EN30	Purple	2,600	2,100	5,200
EN60	Green	5,300	4,200	10,600
EN90	Yellow	8,400	6,700	16,800
EN120	Tan	10,600	8,500	21,200
EN150	Red	13.200	10,600	26,400
EN180	White	16,800	13,400	33,600
EN240	Blue	21,200	17,000	42,400
EN360	Grey	31,000	24,800	62,000
EN600	Brown	53,000	42,400	106,000
EN800	Olive	66,000	52,800	132,000
EN1000	Black	90,000	72,000	180,000

Pipe Weight

Size	Schedule 40 LB per Foot	Schedule 80 LB per Foot
1"	1.68	2.17
1-1/4"	2.27	3
1-1/2"	2.72	3.63
2"	3.65	5.02

Bolt Markings/Data

Grade	Radial Bolt Markings	Material	Nominal Size Diameter/Inches	Proof Load psi	Tensile Strength minimum psi	Yield Strength minimum psi
Grade 2 No Radial Lines		Low or Medium Carbon Steel	1/4" to 3/4"	55,000	74,000	57,000
			Over 3/4" thru 1 1/2"	33,000	60,000	36,000
Grade 5 3 Radial Lines		Medium Carbon Steel	1/4" to 1"	85,000	120,000	92,000
			Over 1" thru 1 1/2"	74,000	105,000	81,000
Grade 8 6 Radial Lines		Medium Carbon Alloy Steel	1/4" thru 1 1/2"	120,000	150,000	130,000
Metric 8.8		Medium Carbon Steel	All sizes under 16mm	580	800	640
			16mm thru 72mm	600	830	660
Metric 10.9		Alloy Steel	5mm thru 100mm	830	1040	940

Swaging

Nicopress Cavity Code	Wire Rope Size	Number of Nicopress Swages	Number of Lococloc Swages
C	3/32"	1	2
G	1/8"	3	3
M	5/32	3	3
P	3/16"	4	4
F2	7/32	2	4
F6	1/4"	3	4
G9	5/16"	3 or 4	5A/4C

Wire Rope

7X19
Galvanized Aircraft Cable

Diameter (in)	Min. Breaking Strength (lb)	WT/1000 feet (lb)
3/32	920	17.5
1/8	2,000	29
5/32	2,800	45
3/16	4,200	65
7/32	5,600	86
1/4	7,000	110
5/16	9,800	173
3/8	14,400	243
Meets Fed. Spec. RR-W-410D for dimension		
Meets MIL-W83420D for strength		

7X7
Galvanized Aircraft Cable

Diameter (in)	Min. Breaking Strength (lb)	WT/1000 feet (lb)
3/64	270	-
1/16	480	7.5
3/32	920	16
1/8	2,000	28.5
5/32	2,800	43
3/16	4,200	62
7/32	5,600	86
1/4	7,000	106
Meets Fed. Spec. RR-W-410D for dimension		
Meets MIL-W83420D for strength		

6X25
Galvanized Wire Rope
IWRC EXIPS

Diameter (in)	Min. Breaking Strength (lb)	WT/Ft (lb)
3/8	6.8 T	0.26
7/16	9.2 T	0.35
1/2	12 T	0.46
9/16	15.1 T	0.59
5/8	18.5 T	0.72
3/4	26.5 T	1.04
7/8	35.8 T	1.42
1	46.5 T	1.85
Meets Fed. Spec. RR-W-410D		

6X37
Galvanized Wire Rope
IWRC EXIPS

Diameter (in)	Min. Breaking Strength (lb)	WT/Ft (lb)
1/4	3.1 T	0.116
5/16	4.7 T	0.18
3/8	6.8 T	0.26
7/16	9.12 T	0.35
1/2	12 T	0.46
9/16	15.1 T	0.59
5/8	18.5 T	0.72
3/4	26.5 T	1.04
7/8	35.8 T	1.42
1	46.5 T	1.85
Meets Fed. Spec. RR-W-410D		

Shackles

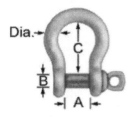

Black-Oxide Steel Shackles

Dia.	A	B	C	WLL (lb)
1/4"	15/32"	5/16"	1-1/8"	1,000
5/16"	17/32"	3/8"	1-1/4"	1,500
3/8"	21/32"	7/16"	1-7/16"	2,000
7/16"	23/32"	1/2"	1-11/16"	3,000
1/2"	13/16"	/8"	1-15/16"	4,000
5/8"	1-1/16"	3/4"	2-1/2"	6,500
3/4"	1-1/4"	7/8"	3"	9,500
7/8"	1-7/16"	1"	3-1/4"	13,000
1"	1-11/16"	1-1/8"	3-3/4"	17,000

DF = 6

Hot-Dipped Galvanized Carbon Steel Shackles

Dia.	A	B	C	WLL (lb)
3/16"	3/8"	1/4"	7/8"	666
1/4"	7/16"	5/16"	1-1/8"	1,102
5/16"	1/2"	3/8"	1-1/4"	1,500
3/8"	5/8"	7/16"	1-7/16"	2,204
7/16"	3/4"	1/2"	1-11/16"	3,306
1/2"	13/16"	5/8"	1-7/8"	4,409
5/8"	1-1/16"	3/4"	2-3/8"	7,165
3/4"	1-1/4"	7/8"	2-13/16"	10,471
7/8"	1-7/16"	1"	3-5/16"	14,330
1"	1-11/16"	1-1/8"	3-3/4"	18,739
1-1/8"	1-13/16"	1-1/4"	4-1/4"	20,943
1-1/4"	2"	1-3/8"	4-11/16"	26,455
1-3/8"	2-1/4"	1-1/2"	5-1/4"	29,762
1-1/2"	2-3/8"	1-5/8"	5-3/4"	34,000
1-3/4"	2-7/8"	2"	7"	50,000
2"	3-1/4"	2-1/4"	7-3/4"	70,000

DF = 6

Hot-Dipped Galvanized Alloy Steel Shackles

Dia.	A	B	C	WLL (lb)
3/8"	5/8"	7/16"	1-7/16"	4,000
1/2"	13/16"	5/8"	1-7/8"	6,600
5/8"	1-1/16"	3/4"	2-3/8"	10,000
3/4"	1-1/4"	7/8"	2-13/16"	14,000
7/8"	1-7/16"	1"	3-5/16"	19,000
1"	1-11/16"	1-1/8"	3-3/4"	25,000
1-1/4"	2"	1-3/8"	4-11/16"	36,000
1-1/2"	2-3/8"	1-5/8"	5-3/4"	50,000
1-3/4"	2-7/8"	2"	7"	68,000
2"	3-1/4"	2-1/4"	7-3/4"	86,000

DF = 6

Welded Chain

Grade 30

Nominal Chain Size		Material Diameter		Minimum Breaking Strength		Working Load Limit	
in	mm	in	mm	lb	kN	lb	kg
1/8	4.0	0.156	4.0	1,600	7.2	400	180
3/16	5.5	0.217	5.5	3,200	14.4	800	365
1/4	7.0	0.276	7.0	5,200	23.2	1,300	580
5/16	8.0	0.331	8.0	7,600	33.8	1,900	860
3/8	10.0	0.394	10.0	10,600	47.2	2,650	1,200
7/16	11.9	0.488	11.9	14,800	65.8	3,700	1,680
1/2	13.0	0.512	13.0	18,000	80.0	4,500	2,030
5/8	16.0	0.63	16.0	27,600	122.6	6,900	3,130
3/4	20.0	0.787	20.0	42,400	188.6	10,600	4,800
7/8	22.0	0.866	22.0	51,200	228.2	12,800	5,810
1	26.0	1.02	26.0	71,600	318.2	17,900	8,140

Grade 80

Nominal Chain Size		Material Diameter		Minimum Breaking Strength		Working Load Limit	
in	mm	in	mm	lb	kN	lb	kg
7/32	5.5	0.217	5.5	8,400	38.0	2,100	970
9/32	7.0	0.276	7.0	14,000	61.6	3,500	1,570
5/16	8.0	0.315	8.0	18,000	80.6	4,500	2,000
3/8	10.0	0.394	10.0	28,400	126.0	7,100	3,200
1/2	13.0	0.512	13.0	48,000	214.0	12,000	5,400
5/8	16.0	0.63	16.0	72,400	322.0	18,100	8,200
3/4	20.0	0.787	20.0	113,200	504.0	28,300	12,800
7/8	22.0	0.866	22.0	136,800	610.0	34,200	15,500
1	26.0	1.02	26.0	190,800	850.0	47,700	21,600
1-1/4	32.0	1.26	32.0	289,200	1,288.0	72,300	32,800

Alpha Chain

Nominal Chain Size		Material Diameter		Minimum Breaking Strength		Working Load Limit	
in	mm	in	mm	lb	kN	lb	kg
1/4	7.0	0.276	7.0	13,000	57.83	3,250	1,477.3
Meets ASTM B633 FE/ZN5 specifications.					DF = 4		

STAC Chain

Size	Inside Length	WLL (lb)
1/2"	3.74"	12,000

Forged Scaffolding Clamps (Cheeseboroughs)

Grade	Torque	Slippage Capacity	Tension Capacity
Industrial	50 ft/lb	4,000 lb	16,000 lb
Military	50 ft/lb		25,000 lb

Truss Data

Thomas Engineering

GP 12" x 12"   Maximum Center Point Load

Lbs Per Ft	10'	20'	30'	40'	50'	60'	70'	80'
5.5	4,497	1,550	865	428	-	-	-	-

ST 12" x 12"   Maximum Center Point Load

Lbs Per Ft	10'	20'	30'	40'	50'	60'	70'	80'
8.7	7,348	3,628	1,662	848	445	-	-	-

GP 15" x 15"   Maximum Center Point Load

Lbs Per Ft	10'	20'	30'	40'	50'	60'	70'	80'
6.2	4,600	2,250	1,450	1,000	650	-	-	-

ST 15" x 15"   Maximum Center Point Load

Lbs Per Ft	10'	20'	30'	40'	50'	60'	70'	80'
9.6	9,372	4,626	2,770	1,466	739	304	-	-

GP 20.5 x 20.5   Maximum Center Point Load

Lbs Per Ft	10'	20'	30'	40'	50'	60'	70'	80'
8.8	2,870	2,870	1,858	1,322	957	-	-	-

Tomcat

Super beam 13.7 x 10 spigoted   Maximum Center Point Load

Lbs Per Ft	10'	20'	30'	40'	50'	60'	70'	80'
7.7	3,831	1,863	1,184	827	-	-	-	-

Core truss 12 x 12 plated   Maximum Center Point Load

Lbs Per Ft	10'	20'	30'	40'	50'	60'	70'	80'
6.0	2,483	1,200	753	516	-	-	-	-

Core truss 12 x 18 plated   Maximum Center Point Load

Lbs Per Ft	10'	20'	30'	40'	50'	60'	70'	80'
6.2	2,481	1,195	746	506	-	-	-	-

Core truss 20.5 x 20.5 plated   Maximum Center Point Load

Lbs Per Ft	10'	20'	30'	40'	50'	60'	70'	80'
6.9	5,289	2,925	1,927	1,278	1,066	655	-	-

Light duty truss 12 x 12 plated   Maximum Center Point Load

Lbs Per Ft	10'	20'	30'	40'	50'	60'	70'	80'
6.1	1,673	1,063	650	426	-	-	-	-

Light duty truss 12 x 12 spigoted   Maximum Center Point Load

Lbs Per Ft	10'	20'	30'	40'	50'	60'	70'	80'
9.2	7,785	3,099	2,089	824	-	-	-	-

Light duty truss 12 x 18 plated   Maximum Center Point Load

Lbs Per Ft	10'	20'	30'	40'	50'	60'	70'	80'
6.7	2,229	1,058	643	6.7				

Ballroom truss 12 x 30 spigoted   Maximum Center Point Load

Lbs Per Ft	10'	20'	30'	40'	50'	60'	70'	80'
12.6	11,361	6,299	5,106	3,036	2,942	1,897	1,229	697

Medium duty truss 20.5 x 20.5 plated   Maximum Center Point Load

Lbs Per Ft	10'	20'	30'	40'	50'	60'	70'	80'
8.5	4,744	2,306	1,464	1,021	737	-	-	-

Medium duty truss 20.5 x 20.5 spigoted   Maximum Center Point Load

Lbs Per Ft	10'	20'	30'	40'	50'	60'	70'	80'
11.5	9,204	5,797	3,781	2,748	2,109	-	-	-

Heavy duty truss 30 x 20.5 spigoted   Maximum Center Point Load

Lbs Per Ft	10'	20'	30'	40'	50'	60'	70'	80'
13.2	17,780	8,775	5,725	4,163	3,195	2,359	-	-

Heavy duty 30 x 20.5 plated   Maximum Center Point Load

Lbs Per Ft	10'	20'	30'	40'	50'	60'	70'	80'
9.4	5,840	3,704	2,387	1,703	1,273	970	-	-

Extra heavy duty truss 36 x 24 spigoted   Maximum Center Point Load

Lbs Per Ft	10'	20'	30'	40'	50'	60'	70'	80'
24.9	20,683	20,220	17,077	10,264	9,877	6,458	4,649	2,733

Stacking truss 25 spigoted   Maximum Center Point Load

Lbs Per Ft	10'	20'	30'	40'	50'	60'	70'	80'
9.0	10,206	5,033	3,278	2,377	1,818	1,430	-	-

Tyler Truss Systems

Centerline 16" x 20"   Maximum Center Point Load

Lbs Per Ft	10'	20'	30'	40'	50'	60'	70'	80'
-	4,916	3,176	2,288	1,737	1,354	-	-	-

12" x 12"   Maximum Center Point Load

Lbs Per Ft	10'	20'	30'	40'	50'	60'	70'	80'
-	1,360	741	665	316	-	-	-	-

12" x 12" AV   Maximum Center Point Load

Lbs Per Ft	10'	20'	30'	40'	50'	60'	70'	80'
-	3,273	1,605	1,034	632	-	-	-	-

12" x 12" Custom Spigot Truss   Maximum Center Point Load

Lbs Per Ft	10'	20'	30'	40'	50'	60'	70'	80'
-	5,398	2,635	1,658	850	-	-	-	-

12" x 18"   Maximum Center Point Load

Lbs Per Ft	10'	20'	30'	40'	50'	60'	70'	80'
-	3,180	2,160	1,170	630	-	-	-	-

12" x 18" AV   Maximum Center Point Load

Lbs Per Ft	10'	20'	30'	40'	50'	60'	70'	80'
-	2,647	1,287	818	571	-	-	-	-

20" x 20" Bolt Plate   Maximum Center Point Load

Lbs Per Ft	10'	20'	30'	40'	50'	60'	70'	80'
-	6,060	2,975	1,924	1,380	1,039	-	-	-

20" x 20" Spigoted   Maximum Center Point Load

Lbs Per Ft	10'	20'	30'	40'	50'	60'	70'	80'
-	4,720	2,700	2,500	1,776	1,600	1,060	-	-

Turnbuckles

THE CROSBY GROUP
HG-226 EYE & EYE   DF 5:1
Recommended for Straight or in-line pull only.
Meets the performance requirements of Federal Specifications FF-T-791b, Type 1, Form 1 — CLASS 4
Except for those provisions required of the contractor

THREAD DIAMETER & TAKE UP	WWL (LBS)
1/4" x 4"	500
5/16" x 4-1/2"	800
3/8 x 6	1200
1/2" x 6"	2200
1/2" x 9"	2200
1/2" x 12"	2200
5/8" x 6"	3500
5/8" x 9"	3500
5/8" x 12"	3500

BREWER-TITCHENER
780 - G EYE TO EYE   DF 5:1
Recommended for Straight or in-line pull only.
Meets design requirements of federal specifications, FF-T791, Type 1, Class 4.
Drop forged carbon steel with galvanized finish.
Galvanizing meets ASTM A-153 specifications.
Weldless

THREAD DIAMETER & TAKE UP	WWL (LBS)
1/4" x 4"	500
5/16" x 4-1/2"	800
3/8" x 6"	1200
1/2" x 6"	2200
1/2" x 9"	2200
1/2" x 12"	2200
5/8" x 6"	3500
5/8" x 9"	3500
5/8 x 12"	3500
5/8" x 18"	3500

THE CROSBY GROUP
HG-227 JAW & EYE   DF 5:1
Recommended for Straight or in-line pull only.
Meets the performance requirements of Federal Specifications FF-T-791b, Type 1, Form 1 — CLASS 8,
Except for those provisions required of the contractor.

THREAD DIAMETER & TAKE UP	WWL (LBS)
1/4" x 4"	500
5/16" x 4-1/2"	800
3/8 x 6	1200
1/2" x 6"	2200
1/2" x 9"	2200
1/2" x 12"	2200
5/8" x 6"	3500
5/8" x 9"	3500
5/8" x 12"	3500

THE CROSBY GROUP
HG-228 JAW & JAW   DF 5:1
Recommended for Straight or in-line pull only.
Meets the performance requirements of Federal Specifications FF-T-791b, Type 1, Form 1 — CLASS 7,
Except for those provisions required of the contractor.

THREAD DIAMETER & TAKE UP	WWL (LBS)
1/4" x 4"	500
5/16" x 4-1/2"	800
3/8 x 6	1200
1/2" x 6"	2200
1/2" x 9"	2200
1/2" x 12"	2200
5/8" x 6"	3500
5/8" x 9"	3500
5/8" x 12"	3500

All rigging equipment and hardware should be inspected periodically
for wear, abuse and general adequacy.

Pear Rings

Crosby A-341 Alloy Pear Shaped Links

Size (in)	WLL (lb)
1/2	7,000
5/8	9,000
3/4	12,300
7/8	15,000
1	24,360

Design Factor = 5

Crosby G-341 Carbon Steel Pear Shaped Links

Size (in)	WLL (lb)
3/8	1,800
1/2	2,900
5/8	4,200
3/4	6,000
7/8	8,300
1	10,800

Design Factor = 6

Weight of Lighting Cable

Cable	Weight per Foot
19-pin 12/14 Multi	0.6
19-pin 12/19 Multi	0.8
12/3 SO	0.23
12/3 SJ0	0.15
14/1 SJO	0.11
7-pin Socapex 14/7	0.34
7-pin Socapex 16/7	0.19
12/3 SOOW	0.22
12/2 SJOOW	0.12
12/5 SOOW	0.13
10/5 SOOW	0.46

Threaded Rod and Bolts

Size	Stress Area (Sq. inches)	Grade 2 Tensile Strength (pounds)	Grade 5 Tensile Strength (pounds)	ASTM A193 B-7 Tensile Strength (pounds)	Grade 8 Tensile Strength (pounds)
1/4" - 20	0.0318	2,350	3,800	3,975	4,750
1/4" - 28	0.0364	2,700	3,800	4,550	5,450
5/16" - 18	0.0524	3,900	6,300	6,550	7,850
5/16" - 24	0.0580	4,300	6,300	7,250	8,700
3/8" - 16	0.0775	5,750	9,300	9,700	11,600
3/8" - 24	0.0878	6,500	9,300	11,000	13,200
7/16" - 14	0.1063	7,850	12,800	13,300	15,900
7/16" - 20	0.1187	8,800	12,800	14,850	17,800
1/2" - 13	0.1419	10,500	17,000	17,750	21,300
1/2" - 20	0.1599	11,800	17,000	20,000	24,000
9/16" - 12	0.1820	13,500	21,800	22,750	27,300
9/16" - 18	0.2030	15,000	21,800	25,400	30,400
5/8" - 11	0.2260	16,700	27,100	28,250	33,900
5/8" - 18	0.2560	18,900	30,700	32,000	38,400
3/4" - 10	0.3340	24,700	40,100	41,750	50,100
3/4" - 16	0.3730	27,600	44,800	46,650	56,000
7/8" - 9	0.4620	27,700	55,400	57,750	69,300
7/8" - 14	0.5090	30,500	61,100	63,650	76,400
1" - 8	0.6060	36,400	72,700	75,750	90,900
1" - 12 & 14	0.6630	39,800	7,900	84,900	99,400
1-1/8" - 7	0.7630	45,800	80,100	95,400	114,400
1-1/8" - 12	0.8560	51,400	89,900	107,000	128,400
1-1/4" - 7	0.9690	58,100	101,700	121,150	145,400
1-1/4" - 12	1.0730	64,400	112,700	134,150	161,000
1-3/8" - 6	1.1550	69,300	121,300	144,400	173,200
1-3/8" - 12	1.3150	78,900	138,100	164,400	197,200
1-1/2" - 6	1.4050	84,300	147,500	175,650	210,800
1-1/2" - 12	1.5810	94,900	166,000	197,650	237,200

Appendix 2:

Arena Rigging Quiz

Multiple Choice:
Chapter 1 – Arena Rigging Basics

1. Which of the following does NOT participate in the "Pre-Planning" meeting?
    a) House Head Rigger
    b) Up-riggers
    c) Production Rigger
    d) House Manager

2. What point must be established before the rigging points on the floor can be marked-out?
    a) Point 0-0
    b) Rigging point for Motor #1
    c) Center of the arena
    d) Center of the stage

3. What is the symbol for a 1-Ton chain hoist?

     a)   b)   c)

4. A stinger is a
    a) another name for a rigging rope
    b) a type of self-leveling laser
    c) a piece of steel that attaches to a basket or apex shackle of a bridle and used to lower the height of the chain hook
    d) none of the above

5. What color is used to indicate a 5'-piece of steel?
    a) RED
    b) WHITE
    c) BLUE
    d) GREEN

6. This chain is used to adjust the length of a bridle leg.
    a) Grade 30
    b) Grade 80
    c) Grade 100
    d) STAC

7. This device is used to run-out the chain of a chain hoist.
    a) Pickle
    b) Adjustable wrench
    c) Rigger's rope
    d) Prog wrench

8. This is used to pad the beam that the steel goes around.
    a) Neoprene
    b) Carpet padding
    c) Burlap
    d) None of the above

9. How many links of STAC chain are indicated on the bridle marking shown below?

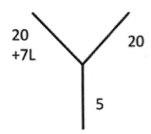

    a) 20
    b) 7
    c) 5
    d) none

10. This knot is used to attach the steel to the riggers' rope.
    a) Rigger's Hitch
    b) Bowline
    c) Clove Hitch
    d) Alpine Butterfly Loop

Chapter 2 – Tools for Riggers

1. Carabineers are marked with their breaking strength in
   a) pounds
   b) kilograms
   c) kiloNewtons
   d) tons

2. Climbing runners are marked with their breaking strength in
   a) pounds
   b) kilograms
   c) kiloNewtons
   d) tons

3. Single stitched daisy chains are
   a) not acceptable for use in most arena venues
   b) are acceptable for use in arena venues
   c) can become unstitched leaving the load clipped into nothing
   d) a and c

4. Grillions
   a) are acceptable as positioning devices
   b) have an adjustable ascender
   c) can be clipped into an anchor point
   d) all of the above

5. Riggers use recreational gear because it is lightweight.
   Name the only piece of recreational gear NOT acceptable for use by riggers.
   a) Climbing helmet
   b) Non-locking carabineer
   c) Metolius chain
   d) Grillion

Chapter 3 - Knots and Rope Handling

1. The knot shown below is an example of a bowline. What is the problem with the way this knot is tied?

a) There is no problem. The knot is tied correctly
b) The bowline tail is tied to the outside
c) The knot shown is an example of a slip knot
d) The bowline is tied backwards

2. The knot pictured below is an example of a

a) Sheep Shank
b) Alpine Butterfly Loop
c) Clove Hitch
d) Prussik

3. The knot pictured below is an example of a

a) Figure Eight
b) Prussik
c) Square Knot
d) Clove Hitch

4. The knot pictured below is an example of a

a) Bowline
b) Alpine Butterfly Loop
c) Figure Eight Loop
d) Trucker's Hitch

5. The knot pictured below is an example of a

a) Carrick Bend
b) Alpine Butterfly Loop
c) Figure Eight Loop
d) Double Sheet Bend

Chapter 4 – Fall Protection

1. It takes a person _____ to become aware that they are falling.
    a) 1 second
    b) 1/3 of a second
    c) 1.5 seconds
    d) 1/2 of a second

2. OSHA limits the forces on the body to no more than _____ pounds with an arresting harness.
    a) 3,600
    b) 800
    c) 1,800
    d) 900

3. *The Fall Arrest* system must be rigged so that an employee cannot free fall more than
_____ feet.
   a) 42 inches
   b) 3.5 feet
   c) 6 feet
   d) 10 feet

4. *The Fall Arrest* system must bring an employee to a complete stop and limit the employee's
maximum deceleration distance to _____ feet.
   a) 42 inches
   b) 3.5 feet
   c) 6 feet
   d) 10 feet

5. An Anchorage Point must be capable of supporting at least _____pounds per person
   attached.
   a) 3,600
   b) 900
   c) 1,800
   d) 5,000

6. Fall protection is required for vertical ladders without cages over _____ ft.
   a) 6 feet
   b) 12 feet
   c) 20 feet
   d) 24 feet

7. The maximum forces on a person wearing a Body Belt are _____ pounds.
   a) 3,600
   b) 800
   c) 1,800
   d) 900

8. Suspension trauma can begin in as little as _____ .
   a) 10 minutes
   b) 2 or 3 minutes
   c) 15 minutes
   d) 30 minutes

9. A personal fall arrest system (PFAS) is required whenever you are working
   a) in an Articulating and/or telescoping boom
   b) in a bucket truck.
   c) a scissor lift
   d) a and b only
   e) all of the above

10. The WLL of most SRLs is _____ pounds, (this includes all clothing, tools and gear). Check the label for WLL information.
    a) 310
    b) 1,800
    c) 3,600
    d) 5,000

Chapter 5 – Basic Bridle Math

1. Trim refers to
    a. the height of the truss measured from the upper chords to the floor of the stage or venue
    b. the height of the truss measured from the lower chords to the floor of the stage or venue
    c. the height of the truss measured from the equipment hung to the floor of the stage or venue
    d. a and c
    e. none of the above

2. It is important to avoid bridle angles exceeding
    a. 30 degrees
    b. 45 degrees
    c. 90 degrees
    d. 120 degrees

3. Drop is defined as
    a. the distance from the stage to the floor
    b. the distance from the bridle apex to the chain hoist hook in its final trim position
    c. the distance from the lower I-beam flange to the floor
    d. the distance from the lower I-beam flange to the deck of the stage.

4. Calculate the lengths of L1 and L2 where, V1 = 8', H1 = 11', V2 = 6, and H2 = 7'.

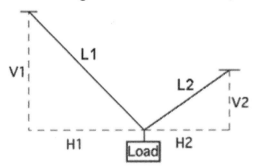

    a. L1 = 12.3, L2 = 10.4
    b. L1 = 15.6, L2 = 7.82
    c. L1 = 13.6, L2 = 9.22
    d. L1 = 14.15, L2 = 11.9

5. Calculate the bridle tension of L1 and L2 where, V1 = 8', H1 = 11', V2 = 6, and H2 = 7' and the load is 500 lb.

   a. L1 = 390.2 lb., L2 = 415.6 lb.
   b. L1 = 410.4 lb., L2 = 489.3 lb.
   c. L1 = 398.2 lb., L2 = 421.6 lb.
   d. L1 = 376.1 lb., L2 = 396.8 lb.

6. Calculate the bridle angle between L1 and L2 where, V1 = 8', H1 = 11', V2 = 6, and H2 = 7' and the load is 600 lb.
   a. 101.5 degrees
   b. 103.3 degrees
   c. 108.6 degrees
   d. 99.2 degrees

7. The photo below shows a quick way of checking bridle angles. The angle represented is approximately how many degrees?

   a. 30 degrees
   b. 45 degrees
   c. 60 degrees
   d. 90 degrees

8. Calculate the horizontal force on a breastline where V1 is 50', H1 is 7', and the Load = 1000 pounds.

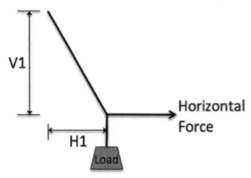

   a. 160 lb.
   b. 138 lb.
   c. 140 lb.
   d. 198 lb.

9. What is the tension on a flat bridle if the load is 500 lb, and the bridle angle is 165
    Degrees?
    a. 2,098.34 lb
    b. 1,773.99 lb
    c. 1,915.32 lb
    d. 3,782.56 lb

Chapter 6 – Two-Point Bridles in an Arena

1. H1 + H2 =
    a. SQRT of Leg 1 Length
    b. V1
    c. V2
    d. Span Distance

2. Leg 1 and Leg 2 meet at the
    a. Apex
    b. The plaster line
    c. The dasher
    d. Point 0-0

3. Steel that is only 2 ft or 2.5 ft is called
    a. dog bones
    b. shorts
    c. legs
    d. STAC

4. The distance from the CENTER of the beam (no matter the shape) to the shackle pin that connects
to the leg steel is called the
    a) Span Distance
    b) ELOH
    c) Apex
    d) None of the above

5. STAC chains are also refer to as
    a) Rigging Chains
    b) TRAC Chains
    c) Deck Chains
    d) b & c above

Chapter 7 – The Effective Length of a Hitch

1. A 5/8" screw-pin anchor shackle has an inside length of
   a) 2"
   b) 2.375"
   c) 2.5"
   d) 3.74"

2. The shape of the beams does NOT affect the ELOH
   a) True
   b) False

3. The Total Basket Length =
   a) Basket Steel Length + (1 x Inside Shackle Length)
   b) Basket Steel Length + (2 x Inside Shackle Length)
   c) Basket Steel Length + (3 x Inside Shackle Length)
   d) Basket Steel Length + (4 x Inside Shackle Length)

Chapter 8 – Calculating Bridle Lengths Using Little or No Math

1. The 80% and 90% rules are for beams
   a) that are the at the same height
   b) that are at different heights
   c) that are only I-beams
   d) that are under 50 feet in height

2. Bridle Charts are "cheat sheets" based on
   a) the Pythagorean Theorem
   b) the "give and take" method
   c) the 80% rule
   d) none of the above

3. The One-Eight Bridle Trick puts the apex 1/8 of the span distance from one beam and 7/8 of the span distance from other beam.
   a) True
   b) False

Chapter 9 – Calculating the Length of Long Bridle Legs

1. Which of the following are true?
    a) The longer the leg, the greater the sag
    b) The less tension on the leg, the greater the sag
    c) The closer the angle of the chord is to horizontal, the greater the sag
    d) All of the above

2. There is a simple way to calculate long bridle legs.
    a) True
    b) False

3. Most venues need to compensate for long bridle legs.
    a) True
    b) False

Chapter 10 – Bridle Apps

1. Most bridle apps will run on any mobile device.
    a) True
    b) False

2. Web apps will run on most mobile devices.
    a) True
    b) False

3. Most bridle apps will let you select the shape of the beam in the venue.
    a) True
    b) False

Chapter 11 – Aluminum Truss

1. Rigging hardware falls into one or two categories:
    a) industrial hardware and recreational hardware
    b) arena rigging hardware and theatrical rigging hardware
    c) aerial/ performance hardware and recreational hardware
    d) marine hardware and industrial hardware

2. Industrial hardware is stamped with a:
    a) working load limit (WLL)
    b) minimum breaking strength (MBS)
    c) safe working load limit (SWL)
    d) a. or c.

3. Recreational hardware is stamped with:
    a) working load limit (WLL)
    b) minimum breaking strength (MBS)
    c) safe working load limit (SWL)
    d) a. or c.

4. The top and bottom flanges of an I-beam correspond to
    a) the diagonal braces on a truss
    b) the panel points of a truss
    c) the top and bottom chords on the truss
    d) the web of the truss

5. The point where the diagonal, vertical and horizontal spreaders are welded to the chords is called the
    a) gusset plate
    b) panel point or node
    c) stretcher
    d) chord

6. According to OSHA, this person is capable of identifying existing and predictable hazards in the working environment and has the authorization to take prompt corrective measures to eliminate them.
    a) a job steward
    b) a qualified person
    c) a competent person
    d) a foreman

7. The degree or angle to which a structural element is displaced under a load is called:
    a) displacement
    b) deflection
    c) tension
    d) ductility

8. The markings shown on the bolt head indicate this as:

    a) Grade 5
    b) Grade 6
    c) Grade 7.5
    d) Grade 8

9. This action arises when a force is applied **perpendicularly** to the material cross section on which it acts.
   a) shear
   b) tension
   c) torque
   d) displacement
   e) a and d

10. A 20 ft. span of 20.5 x 20.5 plated box truss will allow a maximum of 6,120 pounds for a *Uniform Distributed Load*. What is the maximum allowable quarter point load on the same truss.

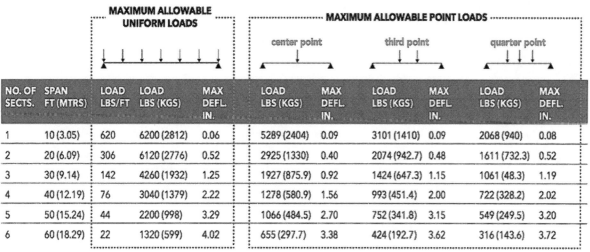

NO. OF SECTS.	SPAN FT (MTRS)	LOAD LBS/FT	LOAD LBS (KGS)	MAX DEFL. IN.	LOAD LBS (KGS)	MAX DEFL. IN.	LOAD LBS (KGS)	MAX DEFL. IN.	LOAD LBS (KGS)	MAX DEFL. IN.
			MAXIMUM ALLOWABLE UNIFORM LOADS		center point		third point		quarter point	
1	10 (3.05)	620	6200 (2812)	0.06	5289 (2404)	0.09	3101 (1410)	0.09	2068 (940)	0.08
2	20 (6.09)	306	6120 (2776)	0.52	2925 (1330)	0.40	2074 (942.7)	0.48	1611 (732.3)	0.52
3	30 (9.14)	142	4260 (1932)	1.25	1927 (875.9)	0.92	1424 (647.3)	1.15	1061 (48.3)	1.19
4	40 (12.19)	76	3040 (1379)	2.22	1278 (580.9)	1.56	993 (451.4)	2.00	722 (328.2)	2.02
5	50 (15.24)	44	2200 (998)	3.29	1066 (484.5)	2.70	752 (341.8)	3.15	549 (249.5)	3.20
6	60 (18.29)	22	1320 (599)	4.02	655 (297.7)	3.38	424 (192.7)	3.62	316 (143.6)	3.72

5/8" diameter Grade 8 Bolts with standard washers through 3/8" gusset plates

   a) 1,927 lb
   b) 1,611 lb
   c) 2,074 lb
   d) 1,061 lb

Chapter 12 – Rigging Hardware

1. Most industrial hardware is stamped
   a. with its dynamic load rating
   b. with its load rating in kiloNewtons (kN)
   c. with it a Working Load Limit (WLL) or Safe Working Load Limit (SWL)
   d. with its Breaking Strength (BS)

2. Manufacturers use a statistical method called "3 sigma" to determine the Material Breaking Strength (MBS) of their products. This process is best described as
    a. the minimum breaking strength is calculated by taking the mean or average breaking strength of 5 rope samples, and subtracting 3 standard deviations.
    b. the minimum breaking strength of the product is determined by a substantive electro-microscopic examination of the atomic structure of the material. This is compared to 5 samples of the same material.
    c. three separate structural analysis' of the product from 5 separate manufacturers.
    d. all of the above.

3. Synthetic core slings
    a. are made from 100% polyester strands
    b. are made from a continuous looped polyester core.
    c. have a synthetic fabric sleeve that protects the core.
    d. all of the above.

4. When bell shackles are used as collector rings, the angle cannot exceed

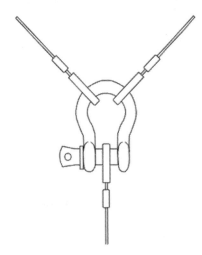

    a. 45 degrees
    b. 90 degrees
    c. 120 degrees
    d. 180 degrees

5. When attaching a bag to a chain hoist, the bag hooks
    a. must be placed facing down
    b. must be placed facing out
    c. must be place facing in
    d. must be taped with gaffer's tape to keep from snagging on the chain

6. Steel slings are generally color coded for easy identification. Blue is the color assigned for what length of steel?
    a.   2 ft or2.5 ft
    b.   5 ft
    c.   10 ft
    d.   20 ft

7. Wire rope core slings
    a.   are less flexible than polyester core slings
    b.   are made from an Independent Wire Rope Core (IWRC)
    c.   have a greater resistance to heat damage
    d.   all of the above
    e.   a and c only

8. A piece of rigging hardware has a Breaking Strength of 2,200 lb. The manufacturer gives the hardware a Working Load Limit of 440 lb. What is the Design Factor being used?
    a. 2
    b. 5
    c. 8
    d. 10

9. A shackle has a Working Load Limit of 4,500 lb. Using a Design Factor of 8, what is the shackle's breaking strength?
    a.   36,000 lb
    b.   22,500 lb
    c.   11,200 lb
    d.   48,000 lb

10. Generally, when flying people or objects over the heads of people, riggers use a Design Factor of
    1. 5
    2. 6
    3. 8
    4. 10

Chapter 13 – Chain Hoists

1. Load chain is made from grade 80 chain. Grade 80 (G80) refers to
    a.   the ultimate breaking strength (BS) of the chain
    b.   the working load limit (WLL) of the chain
    c.   the composite material of the chain.
    d.   the design factor (DF) of the chain

2. With CM hoists, the lift wheel
   a. connects to the brake
   b. connects directly to the drive shaft
   c. connects to the clutch pinion and to the clutch gear.
   d. connects to the motor

3. Mechanical Braking uses
   a. the motor to over-power the speed of the load being raised or lowered
   b. a magnetic field to *release* the clamps on the brake drum
   c. a magnetic field to *engage* the clamps on the brake drum
   d. the clutch to reduce the speed of the load being raised or lowered

4. The purpose of a limit switch is to
   a. limit the voltage running to the controller
   b. disengage the clutch should the hoist reach its over speed limits
   c. limit the extent of the run of chain in both the upper and lower direction
   d. shut down the hoist in the event of over heating

5. A rated load limit is
   a. the maximum rated amperage load
   b. the maximum load that a manufacturer recommends be applied to a piece of hardware
   c. the minimum breaking strength that a manufacturer recommends for a piece of hardware
   d. only as good as the maximum breaking strength of a piece of hardware

Chapter 14 - Electricity

1. Insulators are materials that do not allow electrons to flow at all. Check all the examples of insulators from the list below:
   a. Glass
   b. Rubber
   c. Plastic
   d. Copper

2. Electro-Motive Force (EMF)- is the force or pressure behind the flow of electrons. EMF It is measured in _____.
   a. Ohms
   b. Watts
   c. Volts
   d. Amps

3. A volt
   a. is a measurement of resistance
   b. is a measurement of the flow of electrons down a conductor
   c. is the force required to push 1 Amp though 1 Ohm of resistance
   d. occurs at a rate of 60 times per second

4. A model L chain hoist will draw 16A at full load. The Voltage is 120V. What is the Wattage or Power of the hoist?
    a.   1560 Watts
    b.   1920 Watts
    c.   7.5 Watts
    d.   136 Watts

5. A resistance of 10 Ω is placed across a 12 V battery. What is the current flow in Amps?
    a.   .83333 Amps
    b.   120 Amps
    c.   1.2 Amps
    d.   110 Amps

6. This illustration is an example of

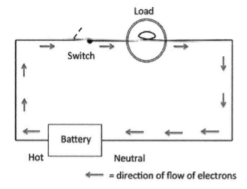

= direction of flow of electrons

    a.   direct current
    b.   alternating current
    c.   series circuit
    d.   a and c

7. Which of the following supply system generates rotating magnetic field with a specific direction and constant magnitude in electrical motors:
    a.   Single phase supply system
    b.   Two phase supply system
    c.   Three phase supply system
    d.   All of the above are correct

8. What is the best solution to fix a chain hoist that is running in reverse?
    a.   Reverse any two of the hot legs.
    b.   Swap any hot leg with a neutral.
    c.   Replace the hoist.
    d.   Swap out the wiring in the pickle.

9. Wires are color coded for identification. Green wires are identified as
    a. Hot
    b. Delta
    c. Neutral
    d. Ground

10. Three phase electrical motors run in what configuration?
    a. Series
    b. Delta
    c. Wye
    d. Parallel

Chapter 15 – Truss Math

Using the diagram below...

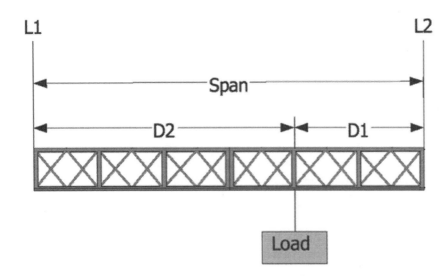

What is the tension on L1 and L2 if

1. the Span is 12', D1 is 5', D2 is 7' and the Load is 300 lb, what is the tension on L1 and L2?
    a. L1 = 182 lb, L2 = 118 lb
    b. L1 = 105 lb, L2 = 195 lb
    c. L1 = 125 lb, L2 = 175 lb
    d. L1 = 156 lb, L2 = 144 lb

2. the Span is 20', D1 is 11', D2 is 9' and the Load is 800 lb, what is the tension on L1 and L2?
    a. L1 = 652 lb, L2 = 148 lb
    b. L1 = 258 lb, L2 = 232 lb
    c. L1 = 548 lb, L2 = 252 lb
    d. L1 = 440 lb, L2 = 360 lb

3. the Span is 30', D1 is 8', D2 is 22' and the Load is 490 lb, what is the tension on L1
   and L2?
   a. L1 = 322.43 lb, L2 = 168.68 lb
   b. L1 = 440 lb, L2 = 360 lb
   c. L1 = 130.67 lb, L2 = 359.33lb
   d. L1 = 225 lb, L2 = 265 lb

Using the diagram below...

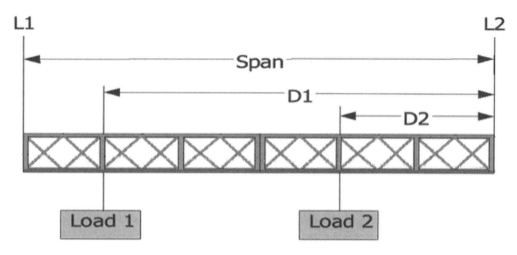

What is the tension on L1 and L2 if

4. If the Span is 20', D1 is 15', D2 is 5', Load 1 is 300 lb and Load 2 is 400 lb, what is the tension on
    L1 and L2?

    a. L1 = 300 lb, L2 = 400 lb
    b. L1 = 180 lb, L2 = 520 lb
    c. L1 = 225 lb, L2 = 475 lb
    d. L1 = 325 lb, L2 = 375 lb

5. If the Span is 25', D1 is 9', D2 is 16', Load 1 is 439 lb and Load 2 is 295 lb, what is the tension on L1
    and L2?

    a. L1 = 520 lb, L2 = 214 lb
    b. L1 = 532 lb, L2 = 202 lb
    c. L1 = 346.84 lb, L2 = 387.16 lb
    d. L1 = 625.3 lb, L2 = 109.7 lb

6. If the Span is 60', D1 is 20', D2 is 40', Load 1 is 840 lb and Load 2 is 732 lb, what is the tension on L1 and L2?

    a. L1 = 530 lb, L2 = 1042 lb
    b. L1 = 768 lb, L2 = 804 lb
    c. L1 = 652 lb, L2 = 920 lb
    d. L1 = 641 lb, L2 = 931 lb

Using the diagram below...

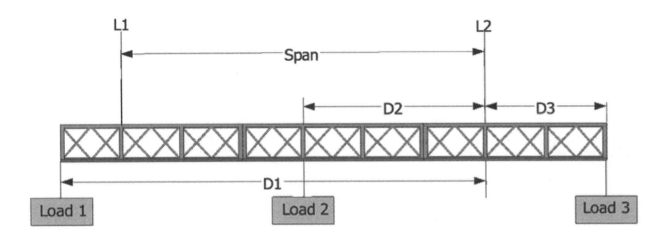

7. If the Span is 33.8', D1 is 44', D2 is 21', D3 is 4', Load 1 is 445 lb, Load 2 is 1,923 lb and Load 3 is 459 lb, what is the tension on L1 and L2?

    a. L1 = 1,719.73 lb, L2 = 1,107.27 lb
    b. L1 = 1,768.11 lb, L2 =1,804.43 lb
    c. L1 = 1,652.45 lb, L2 = 1,920.87 lb
    d. L1 = 1,641.23 lb, L2 = 1,931.65 lb

8. If the Span is 5', D1 is 8', D2 is 2.6', D3 is 4', Load 1 is 637 lb, Load 2 is 736 lb and Load 3 is 628 lb, what is the tension on L1 and L2?

    a. L1 = 720 lb, L2 = 1,107 lb
    b. L1 = 768 lb, L2 =1,804 lb
    c. L1 = 900 lb, L2 = 1,100 lb
    d. L1 = 41 lb, L2 = 1,739 lb

9. If the Span is 60', D1 is 45', D2 is 10', D3 is 0', Load 1 is 847 lb, Load 2 is 309 lb and Load 3 is 930 lb, what is the tension on L1 and L2?

a. L1 = 720.55 lb, L2 = 1,107.45 lb
b. L1 = 687.75 lb, L2 =1,399.25 lb
c. L1 = 556.11 lb, L2 = 1,104.88 lb
d. L1 = 414.56 lb, L2 = 1,739.34 lb

Chapter 16 – Truss Loading

1. A 20 ft. span of 20.5 x 20.5 plated box truss will allow a maximum of 6,120 pounds for a *Uniform Distributed Load*. What is the maximum allowable quarter point load on the same truss.

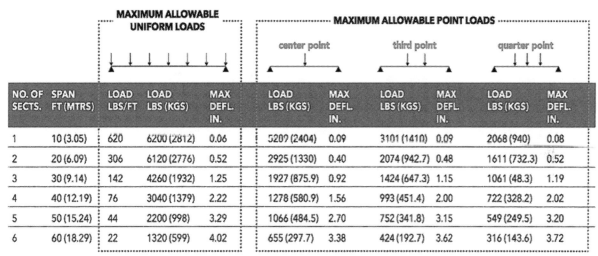

| | | MAXIMUM ALLOWABLE UNIFORM LOADS | | | MAXIMUM ALLOWABLE POINT LOADS | | | | | |
| | | | | | center point | | third point | | quarter point | |
NO. OF SECTS.	SPAN FT (MTRS)	LOAD LBS/FT	LOAD LBS (KGS)	MAX DEFL. IN.	LOAD LBS (KGS)	MAX DEFL. IN.	LOAD LBS (KGS)	MAX DEFL. IN.	LOAD LBS (KGS)	MAX DEFL. IN.
1	10 (3.05)	620	6200 (2812)	0.06	5209 (2404)	0.09	3101 (1410)	0.09	2068 (940)	0.08
2	20 (6.09)	306	6120 (2776)	0.52	2925 (1330)	0.40	2074 (942.7)	0.48	1611 (732.3)	0.52
3	30 (9.14)	142	4260 (1932)	1.25	1927 (875.9)	0.92	1424 (647.3)	1.15	1061 (48.3)	1.19
4	40 (12.19)	76	3040 (1379)	2.22	1278 (580.9)	1.56	993 (451.4)	2.00	722 (328.2)	2.02
5	50 (15.24)	44	2200 (998)	3.29	1066 (484.5)	2.70	752 (341.8)	3.15	549 (249.5)	3.20
6	60 (18.29)	22	1320 (599)	4.02	655 (297.7)	3.38	424 (192.7)	3.62	316 (143.6)	3.72

5/8" diameter Grade 8 Bolts with standard washers through 3/8" gusset plates

a) 1,927 lb
b) 1,611 lb
c) 2,074 lb
d) 1,061 lb

2. If the total load on the span is less than the Maximum UDL/2 for the specified span distance, then the span is
a) overloaded
b) not overloaded
c) a statically indeterminate structure
d) uniformly loaded

3. The total weight to be placed on the cantilevered truss must be less than the allowable CPL for a span that is
a) *2 times the length of the cantilever*
b) *3 times the length of the cantilever*
c) *4 times the length of the cantilever*
d) *5 times the length of the cantilever*

Appendix 3:

Arena Rigging Quiz - Answers

Multiple Choice:
Chapter 1 – Arena Rigging Basics

1. Answer: b) The up-riggers. The Venue Operator, House Head Rigger, House Manager, Production Head Rigger, and if necessary, a qualified engineer participate in this meeting.

2. Answer: a) All rigging points are based off the of point 0-0

3. Answer: b)

4. Answer: c) a piece of steel that attaches to a basket or apex shackle of a bridle and used to lower the height of the chain hook

5. Answer: a) RED

6. Answer: d) STAC chain

7. Answer: a) Pickle

8. Answer: c) Burlap

9. Answer: b) 7

10. Answer: b) Bowline

Chapter 2 – Tools for Riggers

1. Answer: c) kiloNewtons

2. Answer: c) kiloNewtons

3. Answer: a and c) Single stitched daisy chains are not acceptable for use in most arena venues. They can become unstitched leaving the load clipped into nothing.

4. Answer: d) Grillions are acceptable as positioning devices, have an adjustable ascender, and can be clipped into an anchor point

5. Answer: b) Non-locking carabiner

Chapter 3 – Knots and Rope Handling

1. Answer: b) The bowline tail is tied to the outside. Whereas the knot is tied correctly, if the bowline knot capsizes while being hauled over an I-beam, the knot could become loose or undone.

2. Answer: c) Clove Hitch

3. Answer: a) Figure Eight

4. Answer: b) The Alpine Butterfly Loop

5. Answer: d) Double Sheet Bend

Chapter 4 – Fall Protection

1. Answer: b) It takes a person about 1/3rd of a second for a person to become aware that they are falling and another 1/3rd of a second to react to the fall. In that 1/3rd of a second, the body has already free fallen 18 inches. In 2/3rd of a second approximately 7 feet of free fall has occurred. In 8/10th of a second, the brain is now able to respond to the fall, but the body has now travelled approximately 10 feet.

2. Answer: c) OSHA limits the forces on the body to no more than 1,800 pounds with an arresting harness.

3. Answer: c) *The Fall Arrest* system must be rigged so that an employee cannot free fall more than 6 feet.

4. Answer: b) *The Fall Arrest* system must bring an employee to a complete stop and limit the employee's maximum deceleration distance to 3.5 feet.

5. Answer: d) The Anchorage Point must be capable of supporting at least 5,000 pounds (22.2 kN) per person attached. It also must be independent of supporting any other structure or equipment.

6. Answer: d) Fall protection is required for vertical ladders without cages over 24 ft.

7. Answer: d) The maximum forces on a person wearing a Body Belt are 900 pounds (4 kN).

8. Answer: b) Suspension trauma or orthostatic hypotension (shock) is an effect, which occurs when the human body is held in vertical suspension due to the force of gravity and a lack of movement. The effects can begin in as little as 2 or 3 minutes. Venous pooling occurs in the legs due to gravity and can quickly lead to unconsciousness and even death. It is crucial that a rescue begin immediately! No one should ever use a PFAS without an Emergency Action Plan in place. If you do not have a plan, do not put yourself at risk.

9. Answer: d) A personal fall arrest system (PFAS) is required whenever you are working in an Articulating and/or telescoping boom and bucket truck. They are not required for scissor lifts as the bucket is enclosed and only moves in a vertical position.

10. Answer: a) The WLL of most SRLs is 310 pounds, (this includes all clothing, tools and gear). Check the label for WLL information.

Chapter 5 – Basic Rigging Math

1. Answer: c) the height of the truss measured from the equipment hung to the floor of the stage or venue

2. Answer: d) 120 degrees

3. Answer: b) the distance from the bridle apex to the chain hoist hook in its final trim position

4. Answer: c) L1 = 13.6, L2 = 9.22

5. Answer: a) L1 = 390.2 lb., L2 = 415.6 lb.

6. Answer: b) 103.4 degrees

7. Answer: c) 60 degrees

8. Answer: c) 140 lb.

9. Answer: c) 1,915.56 lb.

Chapter 6 – Two-Point Bridles in an Arena

1. Answer: d) Span Distance

2. Answer: a) Apex

3. Answer: a) dog bones

4. Answer: b) ELOH

5. Answer: c) Deck Chains

Chapter 7 – The Effective Length of a Hitch

1. Answer: b) 2.375"

2. Answer: b) False

3. Answer: c) Basket Steel Length + (3 x Inside Shackle Length)

Chapter 8 – Calculating Bridle Lengths Using Little or No Math

1. Answer: b) that are at different heights

2. Answer: a) the Pythagorean Theorem

3. Answer: c) True

Chapter 9 – Calculating the Length of Long Bridle Legs

1. Answer: d) All of the above

2. Answer: a) False. It is a very complicated task that requires a computer program.

3. Answer: c) False. The legs in most venues are short enough that the Pythagorean Theorem gets a close enough answer.

Chapter 10 – Bridle Apps

1. Answer: b) False

2. Answer: a) True

3. Answer: b) False

Chapter 11 – Aluminum Truss

1. Answer: a) industrial hardware and recreational hardware

2. Answer: d) a or c

3. Answer: b) minimum breaking strength (MBS)

4. Answer: c) the top and bottom chords on the truss

5. Answer: b) panel point or node

6. Answer: b) a qualified person

7. Answer: d) Grade 8

8. Answer: b) deflection

9. Answer: a) shear

10. Answer: b) 1,611 lb

Chapter 12 – Rigging Hardware

1. Answer: c) Most industrial hardware is stamped with a Working Load Limit (WLL) or Safe Working Load (SWL), whereas recreational hardware is mark with it Minimum Breaking Strength (MBS), usually expressed in kiloNewtons (kN).

2. Answer: a) The minimum breaking strength is calculated by taking the mean or average breaking strength of 5 samples, and subtracting 3 standard deviations. Statistically, this creates a confidence level of 99.87% that any sample of rope will actually be stronger than the quoted minimum breaking strength.

3. Answer: d) Synthetic core slings are made from 100% polyester strands. These strands are looped around forming a continuous core of strands. The core is then covered with a synthetic fabric sleeve that serves to hold the strands together and to protect them from wear.

4. Answer: c) The Crosby Group says…
SHACKLES, RINGS, LINKS AND MASTER LINKS CAN BE USED AS A COLLECTOR RING. DO NOT EXCEED AN INCLUDED ANGLE OF 120 DEGREES ON ANY COLLECTOR RING (60 DEGREES EITHER SIDE).

5. Answer: b) When attaching the bag hooks to the chain hoist, the hooks need to be placed facing out. This avoids the links of the chain from snagging the points of the hook.

6. Answer: d) Many rigging production companies in the United States color-code the ends of their wire rope slings for ease of *length* identification. This is not to be confused with load data charts, nor is this to be recognized as any industry standard. It is done simply to make it easy for the "down-rigger" to quickly identify the length of the steel when pulling slings from a road box. The ends of the steel are spray painted with a color to designate their length:

- Black for 2.5-foot long steel legs (called dog bones)
- Red for 5-foot long legs
- White for 10-foot long legs
- Blue for 20-foot long legs

7. Answer: d) Wire rope core slings, called GAC Flex or Steel-Flex, are made from steel Galvanized Aircraft Cable that is wound in an endless configuration forming an Independent Wire Rope Core (IWRC). They are then covered with a double-wall polyester jacket. A velcro tag may be opened allowing the inspection of the wire rope core. Wire rope core slings tend to be less flexible than polyester core slings, but have greater strength and are resistant to heat damage.

8. Answer: b) To calculate this, simply divide 2,200 by 440. Design Factor is 5.

9. Answer: a) 4,500 x 8 = 36,000 lb

10. Answer: d) General Rules of Thumb

- DF of 5:1 for Standing Rigging (i.e. rigging that does not move)
- DF of 8:1 for Running Rigging (rigging that moves)
- DF of 10:1 for rigging used in flying of people or moving over the heads of people

Chapter 13 - Chain Hoists

1. Answer: a) The *load chain* is what lifts the load. It is made up of high carbon, grade 80 (G80) chain. The number refers to the ultimate breaking strength of the chain. **G80** means that the maximum stress on the chain is 800 newtons per millimeter squared.

2. Answer: c) The *Lift Wheel* connects to the clutch pinion and the clutch gear connects to the drive shaft where it engages the chain links. The Classic Loadstar has a 4 sprocket Lift Wheel. The Next Generation Loadstars have 5 sprockets.

3. Answer: b) CM Hoists utilize two forms of braking:
   Mechanical Braking is mechanical device (seen right) that uses a magnetic field to release the clamps on the brake drum allowing the shaft to rotate freely. Normally, the clamps are engaged when there is no power to the hoist and released when the hoist is being raised or lowered. Regenerative braking occurs when a load is being lowered. The load on the hoist over-powers the rotors on the hoist and the motor serves as a speed reduction generator limiting the rate of decent.

4. Answer: c) The limit switch is found on all electric chain hoists except the Prostar. Its purpose is to limit the extent of the run of chain in both the upper and lower direction. As the hoist is raised and approaches the hook, it will automatically stop when its pre-set, upper limit is reached, thus preventing the hook from burying itself in the chain guide and damaging the hook, chain, and hoist. A similar limit is set for the opposite direction. As the hoist is lowered and reaches the end of its pre-set lower limit, the hoist automatically stops.

5. Answer: b) Most industrial hardware is rated with a Working Load Limit (WLL) or Safe Working Load (SWL). This rated load limit is the absolute maximum load that a manufacturer recommends be applied to a piece of hardware.

Chapter 14 – Basic Electricity

1. Answer: a. b. c.) Insulators are materials that do not allow electrons to flow at all. These are used to cover conductors to prevent the electrons from flowing into the earth (grounding). Some common insulators are:
   - Glass
   - Rubber
   - Plastic

2. Answer: c) Electro-Motive Force (EMF)- is the force or pressure behind the flow of electrons. It is measured in *Volts*.

3. Answer: c) A Volt is the force required to push 1 Amp through 1 Ohm of resistance. As the electrons flow down a conductor, it encounters resistance. This resistance is caused by a natural resistance in the copper wire and a resistance (effort) performing work.

4. Answer: b) 1,929 Watts

5. Answer: c) 1.2 Amps

6. Answer: d) a and c

7. Answer: c) Three phase supply system

8. Answer: a) There are times when a chain hoist motor WILL run backwards. This is an easy fix. Simply reverse any two of the "Hot" legs with each other. The hoist motor will now run in the correct direction.

9. Answer: d) Ground

10. Answer: b) Three-phase electrical motors run in a Wye configuration - so the power to the hoists will be at 208V.

Chapter 15 – Truss Math

1. Answer: c) L1 = 125 lb, L2 = 175 lb

2. Answer: d) L1 = 440 lb, L2 = 360 lb

3. Answer: c) L1 = 130.67 lb, L2 = 359.33lb

4. Answer: d) L1 = 325 lb, L2 = 375 lb

5. Answer: c) L1 = 346.84 lb, L2 = 387.16 lb

6. Answer: b) L1 = 768 lb, L2 = 804 lb

7. Answer: a) L1 = 1,719.73 lb, L2 = 1,107.27 lb

8. Answer: c) L1 = 900 lb, L2 = 1,100 lb

9. Answer: b) L1 = 684.604 lb, L2 = 1,186.39 lb

Chapter 16 – Truss Loading

1. Answer: b) 1,611 lb

2. Answer: b) Not overloaded

3. Answer: c) *4 times the length of the cantilever*

Appendix 4
Cheat Sheet of Formulas

Conversions

Meters to Feet: Meters x 3.28 = Feet   Feet to Meters: Feet / 3.28 = Meters

Centimeters to Inches: CM x .3937 = Inches   Inches to Centimeters: Inches / .3937 =

Millimeters to Inches: MM x .03937 =   Inches to Millimeters: Inches / .03937 =

kiloNewtons to Pounds: kN x 224.8 =   Pounds to Kilometers: Lb / 224.8 = kiloNewtons

Kilograms to Pounds: Kg x 2.2 = Pounds   Pounds to Kilograms: Lb / 2.2 = Kilograms

$$\underline{\text{Resultant Force}} = \text{Load} \times \frac{\text{sine of angle}}{\text{sine of (angle/2)}}$$

$$\underline{\text{Fleet Angles}} = \text{Maximum Allowable Offset} = \text{Distance} \times 0.026$$

$$\underline{\text{Bridle Angle}} = \text{Arctangent of} \left(\frac{\text{Offset}}{\text{Distance}}\right)$$

$$\underline{\text{Length of Bridle Leg}} = \sqrt{H^2 + V^2}$$

$$\underline{\text{Bridle Angle}} = \left(\text{Arctangent} \left(\frac{H1}{V1}\right)\right) + \left(\text{Arctangent} \left(\frac{H2}{V2}\right)\right)$$

Tension on Bridle Legs

$$\underline{\text{Tension on L1}} = \text{Load} \times \frac{L1 \times H2}{(V1 \times H2)+(V2 \times H2)}$$

$$\underline{\text{Tension on L2}} = \text{Load} \times \frac{L2 \times H1}{(V1 \times H2)+(V2 \times H2)}$$

$$\underline{\text{Horizontal Force on a Breastline}} = \text{Load} \times \frac{H1}{V1}$$

Center of Gravity for two loads on a beam

$$\underline{\text{Length of Side 1}} = \frac{\text{Load 2} \times \text{Span}}{\text{Load 1+Load 2}}$$

$$\underline{\text{Length of Side 2}} = \frac{\text{Load 1} \times \text{Span}}{\text{Load 1+Load 2}}$$

or

Length of Side 2 = Span – Length of Side 1

Dead-hang Tension (on one end of a truss)

$$\text{Tension on L1} = \text{Load} \times \frac{L1}{V1}$$

Simple load on a beam

$$\text{Tension on L1} = \frac{\text{Load} \times D1}{\text{Span}} \qquad\qquad \text{Tension on L2} = \frac{\text{Load} \times D2}{\text{Span}}$$

or

$$\text{Tension on L2} = \text{Load} - L1$$

Multiple loads on a beam

$$\text{Tension on L1} = \frac{(\text{Load 1} \times D1) + (\text{Load 2} \times D2)}{\text{Span}} \qquad \text{Tension on L2} = (\text{Load 1} + \text{Load 2}) - L1$$

Cantilevered (Complex) load on a beam

$$\text{Tension on L1} = \frac{(\text{Load 1} \times D1) + (\text{Load 2} \times D2) - (\text{Load 3} \times D3)}{\text{Span}}$$

Tension on L2 = (Load1 + Load 2 + Load3) – L1

Shock Load

$$\text{Force} = \text{Weight} \times \left(\frac{\text{Free Fall Distance}}{\text{Stopping Distance}} + 1\right)$$

Wind Force

Force = ((((Wind speed × Wind speed) × 0.00256) × Area) × Drag coefficient)
*Drag coefficient = 1.2 for curved surface and 2 for flat surface

Weight of Water

Weight = Square footage × inches of depth × 5.202 or Weight = Volume in cubic feet × 62.428

Horsepower

Adjusted weight = (Load / 32.2) × (32.2 + (Speed in fps / Acceleration time))
HP = Speed × Adjusted Weight / 550

Tension on a Deflecting Line (Resultant Force)

$$\textit{Deflected Angle} = \textit{Arctangent} \left(\frac{H1}{V1}\right)$$

$$\textbf{\textit{Resultant Force}} = \textit{Load} \times \frac{\textit{sine of angle}}{\textit{sine of (angle/2)}}$$

Appendix 5:
Bibliography

Breitfelder, Fred. <u>Bridle Dynamics for Production Riggers</u>. 1998.

Breitfelder, Fred. <u>Bridle Basics</u> (A Primer to *Bridle Dynamics*).

Box, Harry C. <u>Set Lighting Technician's Handbook</u>, Fourth Edition. Burlington: Focal Press, 2010.

Columbus McKinnon. <u>Lodestar, Operating, Maintenance & Parts Manual</u>, Manual No. E627. Amherst: Columbus McKinnon, 2006.

Donovan, Harry. <u>Entertainment Rigging - A Practical Guide for Riggers and Managers</u>. Seattle: Rigging Seminars, 2002, Revised 2008.

The Crosby Group. <u>The Crosby Group Product Application Seminar Workbook</u>, ASME/OSHA Version, Edition 7A, 2011.

Glerum, Jay O. <u>Stage Rigging Handbook</u>, Third Edition. Carbondale: Southern Illinois University Press, 2007.

Hall, Delbert L. <u>Rigging Math Made Simple</u>, Ninth Edition. Johnson City: Spring Knoll Press, 2023.

Hall, Delbert L., Sickels, Brian. <u>The Rigging Math Made Simple Workbook</u>, Johnson City: Spring Knoll Press, 2014.

Sapsis, Bill, editor. <u>Entertainment Rigging for the 21st Century</u>. Burlington: Focal Press, 2015.

Made in the USA
Monee, IL
04 December 2024

72456585R00149